— 4ᵀᴴ EDITION —

To make the most of your new life in Stardew Valley.

This book is based on Stardew Valley version 1.5.4.
Written March 2021.

— CREDITS —

KARI FRY
Concept, Illustration,
Shane's #1 Fan

RYAN NOVAK
Writing, Editing, Research,
Shane's #2 Fan

ERIC BARONE
ConcernedApe
himself!

LAURA VERDIN
Assistant Colorist,
Lead Sparklist

TOM KATKUS
Fact-checker, MVP,
Gunther's Apprentice

KENI SCHERBINSKI
Hand-lettering,
Best Baker

MITCH DONABERGER
Foreword Writer,
Strange Bun Provider

KRISTIN BOHATY
Proofreader,
Dust Sprite Collector

— ♥ SPECIAL THANKS ♥ —

Amber Hageman, Jared Behrend, Rosie Leick, Shane Waletzko,
Arthur Lee, Alex Erlandson, Tom Coxon, Stardew Valley Wiki,
Linda Fry, Glen Fry, Tony Kuchar, Amanda Johnson, Charlie Verdin,
Chihiro Sakaida, Jon Kay, Reid Young, Honey Bee Bakery.

This fourth edition copy was printed and bound in China, September 2021.

ISBN: 978-1-945908-92-7

THIS BOOK BELONGS TO:

YOUR NAME HERE

PROUD OWNER OF

FARM NAME HERE

FARM

Table of Contents

Foreword

Your adventure begins.

Your grandfather, on what may be his deathbed, surprises you with an envelope. Without a word, you take it and stash it away. Even now, years later, it sits in your desk at work. Hours at Joja feel like days, and days at Joja feel like an eternity. Frustrated, underpaid and overworked, you look at that envelope. Inside is a deed to your grandfather's farm, a farm where you spent many excruciatingly boring childhood summers far away from your friends, video games, and that embarrassingly delicious cheese that comes from a can. It was a prison for a busy mind then—but now, it's starting to look more and more like home.

Where do you even begin? "I couldn't even grow mold on leftovers," you whisper to yourself on the bus ride down into the valley. You haven't seen a car in an hour, maybe more. "Can you over-water plants?" This is all so new.

Contrary to your expectations, the valley teems with life—plants flower, trees creak, water rushes and the forest air fills your lungs with vitality and purpose. The feel of the axe handle clattering against wood gives you new life, and the crack of metal against stone connects you to people who lived long ago. The townsfolk are friendly and eager to involve you in their celebrations and their grief. The monsters are hideous, and are quick to chase you out of their slimy gullies.

This is Stardew Valley.

It's a familiar little refuge from the everyday stresses of life and a return to the kind of world we only daydream about when we're stuck in traffic or when we're waiting in line for the self-checkout machine in a grocery store that looks like every other grocery store.

What you do here—and the questions you answer—are up to you.

What will you do today?

Chapter 1
Getting Started

There is no wrong way to experience Stardew Valley.

As you set out to build this new life for yourself, you'll be presented with a seemingly endless stream of choices. You can customize your appearance as well as the type of land you'd like to settle on. You can choose whom you want to befriend and whom you want to romance, and how you'll go about garnering the attention and affection of each.

The farm belongs to you now, so you'll also choose how that farm is run.

You could live a typical farm life with Chickens, Cows and crops, or you could choose to be a professional spelunker and spend your days exploring and treasure hunting in the Mines. Or you could choose instead to live off the land, taking advantage of all that nature has to offer. No matter the choice, you'll develop skills that will shape you as a farmer, a citizen and a friend.

You've been given the opportunity for a fresh start. You can choose to carry on the family name and do your grandfather proud, but at the end of the day, it's your life to live.

WELCOME TO YOUR NEW HOME

You'll begin your new farm life with a spartan one-room cabin that you can choose to upgrade—as Robin is so kind to point out—to something much more spacious once you've got the money and resources. A table, bed and cozy little fireplace are about all you can fit in there at the start. But at least you have a TV that you can use to check tomorrow's weather, among other things. As your farm and social life begin to blossom, you'll be able to buy and even build furniture to spruce up your living space!

Hop into bed and get a good night's sleep to recover your energy, save your progress and prepare your body for a fresh start in the morning. Just be sure not to stay out too late; a farmer's day starts at 6am on the dot, so you won't be able to stay awake past 2am, no matter how hard you try!

REMEMBER:
You can't get everything done in one day.
PACE YOURSELF!

FARM OVERVIEW

Your humble Farmhouse sits on an equally humble plot of land. When you arrive, the fields are long unkempt and overgrown, littered with debris and a dilapidated old Greenhouse. But if you look just a bit harder, there's something else: limitless potential!

The soil is rich with nutrients and ready to be tilled, so you can get started planting crops right away. As your farm begins to grow, you'll be able to enlist Robin's help to build housing for Chickens, Cows and a host of other animals. Before you know it, you'll have enough to stock an entire grocery store!

At the end of the day, just fill your shipping box with fruits, vegetables and other goods, and Mayor Lewis will swing by in the wee hours of the morning to haul everything off to market. He's as quiet as a mouse, so the only proof you'll have that he was even there is a fatter wallet!

So, with nothing more than your newly acquired set of tools and a fistful of Parsnip seeds, you can begin to carve out your new life in Stardew Valley!

BASIC SKILLS

As you gain experience in the arts of farming and adventuring, you'll learn invaluable Skills to aid you in all facets of farm life. Each Skill increases in level as you use it—to a maximum level of 10—and offers the potential for specialization first at level 5, and again at level 10. Skill levels also affect how much energy goes into using related farm tools, or maximum health in the case of Combat Skill. If you have second thoughts about the specializations you choose, don't worry; you'll be able to change them later.

You'll unlock new cooking and crafting recipes with each new level as well.

FARMING

Increases in level as you harvest crops and care for animals. Crops that take longer to harvest will give more experience.

Each Farming level earned increases your efficiency with the Hoe and Watering Can.

Specialize as a Rancher for a profit bonus on animal products, or a Tiller for a crop bonus.

MINING

Increases in level as you break rocks with a Pickaxe.

Each Mining level earned increases your efficiency with the Pickaxe.

Specialize as a Miner to find more Ore, or a Geologist to find more Gems.

FORAGING

Increases in level as you pick up forageable items (including items grown from wild seeds) and chop down trees.

Each Foraging level earned increases your efficiency with the Axe.

Specialize as a Forester to collect more Wood, or a Gatherer to collect more foraged items.

COMBAT

Increases in level as you defeat monsters in the Mines and elsewhere.

Each Combat level earned increases your maximum health by 5 points.

Specialize as a Fighter for damage and HP bonuses, or a Scout for a crit rate boost.

FISHING

Increases in level as you catch fish (or trash). Tougher fish are generally worth more experience.

Each Fishing level earned increases your efficiency with fishing poles.

Specialize as a Fisher for a profit bonus on fish, or a Trapper to make Crab Pots using fewer materials.

TYPES OF FARMLAND

Before you arrive in the valley, you'll be given the option to choose what type of land best suits your interests. Each of these land types places importance on a different set of Skills, and supports the growth of a farm focused on the development of those Skills. Your choice will influence your home decor as well!

STANDARD FARM

This well-rounded field is perfect for the "traditional" farmer. It features plenty of soil for crops, as well as space for Coops, Barns and other structures, with plenty of wild grasses to feed livestock. Start an orchard, a ranch, a winery... the possibilities are endless!

HILL-TOP FARM

A craggy cliffside expanse, marked with Mineral veins and Coal beds. The rocky terrain here is rich with Ore Nodes and other natural deposits, making it a miner's delight!

FOREST FARM

The arable land has been compromised by the dense forest canopy, leaving little space for sowing crops. But the forest brings with it an ample supply of forageable fruits, nuts and other goodies; even some of the weeds can produce seeds! Those handy with an Axe are encouraged to take advantage of the renewable stumps.

WILDERNESS FARM

This wide-open space offers a beautiful view with its scenic cliffs and crystal blue lake. But beware when night falls, as dangerous creatures emerge from the darkness. And be especially careful when facing the Wilderness Golem; this fearsome beast grows more powerful as your Combat Skill evolves. Great for those who are looking to bring the adventure home!

RIVERLAND FARM

Dotted with ponds and rivers, this tranquil aquatic habitat is well suited to anglers and Ore panners. Freshwater fish are plentiful here, unlike on the Standard Farm, so you can catch to your heart's content without trekking all the way across town!

FOUR CORNERS FARM

A peculiar layout that separates the land into four quadrants; each quadrant offers its own unique challenges and benefits. The cliff walls keep farmhands comfortably separated, but still close enough to come to one another's aid should the need arise.

BEACH FARM

It's more difficult to grow crops in the sandy soil, as sprinklers don't work, but supply crates often wash up on shore full of useful items! A fun challenge for seasoned farmers.

FARMING with FRIENDS

As rewarding as it can be to turn that run-down old field into a beautiful farm all by yourself, there's nothing quite like sharing the experience with a few of your closest friends. Even if they live in other towns, other states or even on the other side of the world, you and your fellow farmer friends can come together and join in the fun!

Each farmhand gets their own Cabin, which they can decorate to reflect their tastes; and just like your Farmhouse, they can call on Robin to upgrade their Cabin to their liking at any time.

You and your friends can do just about everything together: work the land, explore the Mines, attend and participate in festivals... and if one of you crafts a Wedding Ring, even get married and have kids!

No matter where you are on the Farm or in town, you'll be able to communicate with your fellow farmers, even in the Mines! Plan your crop placements together, ask for help battling monsters or just let everyone know where you are and what you're doing.

And if you already have a thriving farm that you'd like to share, that's just as easy! All you have to do is have Robin build some Cabins, and you can start inviting your friends the very next day. And since the cost of Farmhand Cabins is subsidized by the Pelican Town Agricultural Fund, you won't have to break the bank to have them built!

Starting a brand new cooperative farm experience is simple; the process is the same as starting any farm, with just a couple of extra options:

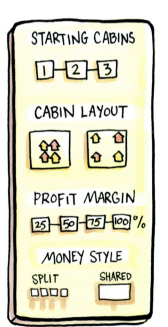

Starting Cabins: Start with up to three Farmhand Cabins pre-built, so your friends can join in and begin helping out on day one!

Cabin Spacing: Arrange the Cabins in a neat row near the Farmhouse to encourage community and cooperation, or space them out toward the corners of the farm to give everyone freedom and independence to create their own little landscapes.

Profit Margin: Increase the challenge by lowering the sale price on all items; the lower the profit margin, the harder everyone has to work (and work together) to make the farm profitable.

Money Style: Pool all of the farm's cash resources together for everyone's use, or allow each worker to handle their own income independently. This option can be changed at any time if you wish.

If you prefer to take on the workload by yourself, that's fine. No pressure!

TIPS AND GUIDELINES

It's OK to hoard!

Save at least one of each item. You never know when someone will want an item that's out of season or when you'll be jonesing for a Melon in the dead of winter.

Pick em as you're passin'

Forage as you move about the valley each day, even if you have to go a bit out of your way.

pick me!

It never hurts to be <u>friendly!</u>

Talk to everyone you come across. Even total grumps will eventually warm up to you... probably.

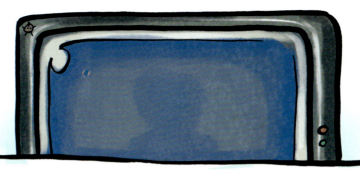

WATCH your TV DAILY!

· · · ·· ···· WEATHER REPORT · · · ·· ···· ·

Get the low-down on tomorrow's weather so you can plan your day. Every now and then, the forecast might be wrong, but Stardew Valley's meteorologists are the best in the business!

FORTUNE TELLER
· · ··· ·· ·· —Welwick's Oracle— · ···· ·· ·· ·

The clairvoyant Welwick will peer into her crystal ball and reveal the spirits' mood for the day. The spirits influence everything from how much Wood you collect from trees to frequency of lightning strikes, so heed the Oracle's words when venturing out to farm, forage or mine!

· ···· ·· ·· ·· LIVIN' off the LAND · · ··· ·· ·· ·

Handy tips for life out in the country, advice about foraging and fishing, information on getting the most out of your fancy farm machinery... this show has it all!

· ···· ·· ·· ·· Queen of Sauce · · ··· ·· ·· ·

This weekly cooking show will teach you lots of delicious recipes every Sunday. Remember, reruns air on Wednesdays, so be sure to watch to pick up recipes you may have missed!

· · ··· ···· ·· ·· F.I.B.S. · ··· ·· ·· ··

The Fishing Information Broadcasting Service provides detailed information on the season's best fishing opportunities. Tune in to learn which fish are biting, where and when they're biting, and more!

TIPS

BUILD A CHEST EARLY

If you can collect 50 pieces of Wood, you can craft yourself a handy Chest to keep items you'd like to save. Try to do it on day one!

BACKPACK UPGRADE ASAP (2,000g)

Inventory space is important, especially while mining and foraging, so save up for those spacious backpacks at Pierre's.

PACE YOURSELF, CONSERVE ENERGY

If your energy gets too low, you'll pass out! You'll wake up the next morning with less energy than usual.

CHECK THE CALENDAR AT PIERRE'S

The handy Calendar will keep you up to date on birthdays and the current season's events.

WATCH WHAT'S IN YOUR HANDS

If you're holding up an item, you'll give it to the person you're trying to talk to. Switch to a farm tool or weapon to prevent accidental gifts.

DON'T BE A NIGHT OWL

A farmer's day starts at 6am, and that means you'll pass out at 2am if you're not already in bed.

JOJA IS MORE EXPENSIVE THAN PIERRE'S

It pays to support the little guy! JojaMart isn't closed on Wednesdays and is open until 11pm daily, but you'll be paying more.

EXPENSIVE SEEDS MAKE VALUABLE CROPS

The greater the investment, the greater the reward! Those higher-priced seeds generally translate into more valuable fruits and vegetables.

PLANT EARLY IN THE SEASON

There are certain crops that will yield multiple harvests after the first. To maximize those benefits, plant on the first day of the season.

CHOP TREES AWAY FROM WATER

If you chop down a tree in the direction of a body of water, the tree will fall in the water. Bye-bye, precious Wood!

SHAKE THOSE BERRY BUSHES

Many forageables can be found on the ground, but some berries have to be rustled out of their bushes.

FORAGE ON THE BEACH

While waiting for your crops to grow, stroll down to the beach to look for Mussels, Clams, Rainbow Shells and other sea goodies.

DIG THESE UP WITH THE HOE

Uncover forageables, artifacts for the Museum, resources and more by digging with the Hoe where you see these protrusions.

DON'T CLEAR ALL OF YOUR GRASS

Grass will spread and grow over time, so if you cut it all down, you'll have to buy Grass Starter if you want it to grow again.

SILO BEFORE COOP

Before buying farm animals, have a plan on how to feed them. Hay is expensive, but grass can be cut and stored in the Silo.

SWINGING A SCYTHE OR WEAPON USES NO ENERGY

Unlike other tools which will deplete your energy, you can swing your Scythe or weapon all day and not get tired.

MAKE SURE TO EQUIP WEARABLES

Rings, Boots and Hats are great, but they'll do you no good just sitting in your backpack. You've got to wear them!

UPGRADE WATERING CAN IN WINTER OR IF IT'S GOING TO RAIN

Crops need daily watering, so try to time your upgrades to coincide with future rainy days or wait for winter. Sprinklers are helpful, too!

FISHING GETS EASIER

Fishing might be tough at first, but with some practice, a higher Skill level and better rods, you'll turn the tide in your favor.

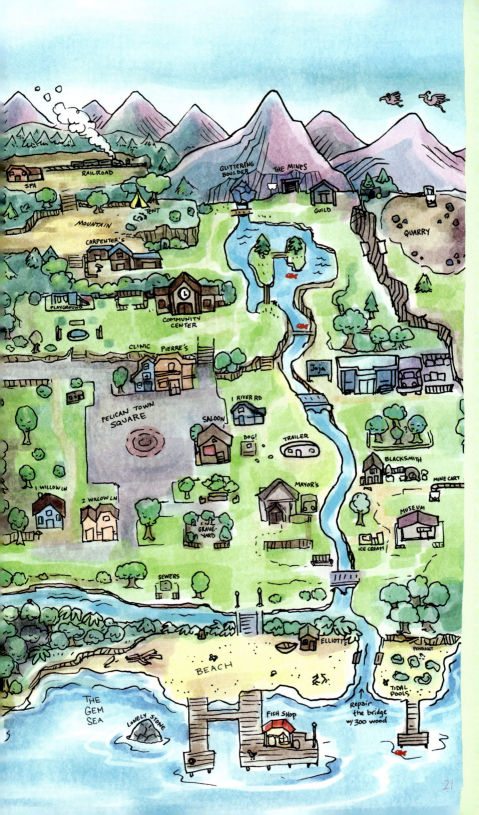

the MOUNTAIN

PELICAN TOWN

CINDERSAP
FOREST

the BEACH

CALICO DESERT

Chapter 2
People & Places

Stardew Valley is home to a wide range of colorful characters, each with distinct personalities and tastes. You'll meet people young and old, and maybe even a couple of otherworldly beings! Some folks will be friendly from the start, while others might need some time to warm up to you. A nice gift every now and then wouldn't hurt, either!

Some of your fellow villagers run shops and other businesses out of their homes in town where you can have a friendly chat while stocking up on supplies. You'll also find many of them out and about throughout the day, as each villager has a unique schedule that changes from day to day and season to season.

As your farm and friendships grow, your adventure will lead you to new places and new faces beyond your first season, and even your first year!

Pierre's
GENERAL STORE

 Home of Pierre, Caroline and Abigail. The building also holds certain events on Tuesday and Sunday mornings. Located in central Pelican Town.

Open from 9am to 5pm, closed on Wednesday. In the event that JojaMart shuts down, Pierre's will remain open 7 days a week.

In addition to the store's everyday stock, Pierre's also sells seeds for the current growing season. It's a good idea to save up gold in preparation for the coming season.

Grass Starter (Recipe for 1,000g)	100g	Quality Fertilizer	150g	Cherry Sapling	3,400g
Sugar	100g	Basic Retaining Soil	100g	Apricot Sapling	2,000g
Wheat Flour	100g	Quality Ret. Soil	150g	Orange Sapling	4,000g
Rice	200g	Speed-Gro	100g	Peach Sapling	6,000g
Oil	200g	Deluxe Speed-Gro	150g	Pomegranate Sapling	6,000g
Vinegar	200g	Wallpaper of the Day	100g	Apple Sapling	4,000g
Basic Fertilizer	100g	Flooring of the Day	100g	Bouquet	200g

Backpack upgrade - 24 slots   2,000g   Backpack upgrade - 36 slots   10,000g

SPRING		SUMMER		FALL	
Parsnip Seeds	20g	Melon Seeds	80g	Eggplant Seeds	20g
Bean Starter	60g	Tomato Seeds	50g	Corn Seeds	150g
Cauliflower Seeds	80g	Blueberry Seeds	80g	Pumpkin Seeds	100g
Rice Shoot	40g	Hot Pepper Seeds	40g	Bok Choy Seeds	50g
Potato Seeds	50g	Wheat Seeds	10g	Yam Seeds	60g
Tulip Bulb	20g	Radish Seeds	40g	Cranberry Seeds	240g
Kale Seeds	70g	Poppy Seeds	100g	Sunflower Seeds	200g
Jazz Seeds	30g	Spangle Seeds	50g	Fairy Seeds	200g
Garlic Seeds (year 2)	40g	Hops Starter	60g	Amaranth Seeds	70g
		Corn Seeds	150g	Grape Starter	60g
		Sunflower Seeds	200g	Wheat Seeds	10g
		Red Cabbage Seeds (year 2)	100g	Artichoke Seeds (year 2)	200g

CATALOGUE OF ALL FLOORING AND WALLPAPERS
30,000g

CARPENTER'S SHOP

Home of Robin, Demetrius, Sebastian and Maru. Also houses Demetrius's science lab. Located at the foot of the Mountains in the northeast.

Open from 9am to 5pm, closed on Tuesday.

Wood	10g YR1 50g YR 2+	Basic Log	250g	Carved Brazier Recipe	2,000g
Stone	20g YR1 100g YR 2+	Log Section	350g	Skull Brazier Recipe	3,000g
Basic Window	300g	Brick Fireplace	1,000g	Marble Brazier Recipe	5,000g
Small Window	300g	Stone Fireplace	1,500g	Wood Lamp-post Recipe	500g
Calendar	2,000g	Stove Fireplace	3,000g	Iron Lamp-post Recipe	1,000g
Workbench	2,000g	Deluxe Red Double Bed	6,000g	Wood Floor Recipe	100g
Wood Chipper	1,000g	Bed	500g	Stone Floor Recipe	100g
Mini-Fridge	3,000g	Double Bed	2,000g	Brick Floor Recipe	500g
Telephone	2,000g	Child Bed	2,000g	Rustic Plank Recipe	200g
Floor TV	700g	Wooden Brazier Recipe	250g	Stone Walkway Recipe	200g
Budget TV	750g	Stone Brazier Recipe	400g	Stepping Stone Path Recipe	100g
Plasma TV	4,500g	Barrel Brazier Recipe	800g	Straw Floor Recipe	200g
Furniture Catalogue	200,000g	Stump Brazier Recipe	800g	Crystal Path Recipe	200g
Seasonal Plant	400g	Gold Brazier Recipe	1,000g		

 Farmhand Cabin 10 Stone, 100g
Build up to 3 Cabins to
farm with friends!   10 Wood, 100g
Their appearances and
material costs vary.   5 Wood, 10 Fiber, 100g

House Upgrade 1 10,000g, 450 Wood
Increases the size of the house and adds a kitchen,
allowing you to cook.

House Upgrade 2 50,000g, 150 Hardwood
Allows you to have children. Adds two new rooms,
one empty, and one with a crib and two single beds.
The size of the kitchen is increased.

House Upgrade 3 100,000g
Adds a cellar underneath your house. The cellar houses
Casks, which allow you to age Cheeses and alcohols.

House Renovations Free of charge
Customization options for your house.

Community Upgrade: Trailer
500,000g, 950 Wood
Provides a permanent house for Pam and Penny, and
helps to bring the community a bit closer together!

Community Upgrade: Town Shortcuts
300,000g
Creates shortcuts throughout Stardew Valley.

Barn	6,000g , 350 Wood, 150 Stone
Big Barn	12,000g, 450 Wood, 200 Stone
Deluxe Barn	25,000g, 550 Wood, 300 Stone
Coop	4,000g, 300 Wood, 100 Stone
Big Coop	10,000g, 400 Wood, 150 Stone
Deluxe Coop	20,000g, 500 Wood, 200 Stone
Silo	100g, 100 Stone, 10 Clay, 5 Copper Bar
Slime Hutch	10,000g, 500 Stone, 10 Refined Quartz, 1 Iridium Bar
Stable	10,000g, 100 Hardwood, 5 Iron Bar
Well	1,000g, 75 Stone
Shed	15,000g, 300 Wood
Big Shed	20,000g, 550 Wood, 300 Stone
Fish Pond	5,000g, 200 Stone, 5 Seaweed, 5 Green Algae
Mill	2,500g, 150 Wood, 50 Stone, 4 Cloth
Shipping Bin	250g, 150 Wood

BUILDING RELOCATION SERVICES
AVAILABLE ON ANY
PREVIOUS CONSTRUCTION

Painting services available for fully
upgraded building, free of charge.

BLACKSMITH

Home and workshop of Clint, Pelican Town's blacksmith. Located just north of the Museum in east Pelican Town.

Open from 9am to 4pm. Closed on Friday after the Community Center is renovated.

ORE FOR SALE:

	Copper Ore	75g$^{YR 1}$	150g$^{YR 2+}$
	Iron Ore	150g$^{YR 1}$	250g$^{YR 2+}$
	Coal	150g$^{YR 1}$	250g$^{YR 2+}$
	Gold Ore	400g$^{YR 1}$	750g$^{YR 2+}$

TOOL UPGRADES AVAILABLE:

	Copper Tool Upgrade	2,000g, 5 Copper Bar
	Steel Tool Upgrade	5,000g, 5 Iron Bar
	Gold Tool Upgrade	10,000g, 5 Gold Bar
	Iridium Tool Upgrade	25,000g, 5 Iridium Bar

For upgrades, Clint will need to borrow your tool for two days—or three if one of those days is a day off for Clint—so plan carefully!

GEODE PROCESSING

25g EACH.

ANY TYPE OF GEODE

Marnie's Ranch

Marnie, Shane and Jas live on this ranch located just south of your farm in Cindersap Forest.

Open from 9am to 4pm,
closed on Monday and Tuesday.

FARM ANIMALS:

			Price	Building required
	Chicken	Well cared-for adult Chickens lay Eggs every day.	800g	Coop, Big Coop or Deluxe Coop
	Cow	Adults can be milked daily with the Milk Pail.	1,500g	Barn, Big Barn or Deluxe Barn
	Goat	Happy adults provide Goat Milk every other day with the Milk Pail.	4,000g	Big Barn or Deluxe Barn
	Duck	Happy adults lay Duck Eggs every other day.	1,200g	Big Coop or Deluxe Coop
	Sheep	Adults can be shorn for Wool by using Shears.	8,000g	Deluxe Barn
	Rabbit	They shed precious Wool every few days.	8,000g	Deluxe Coop
	Pig	These Pigs are trained to find Truffles!	16,000g	Deluxe Barn

SHOP:

			Price	
	Hay	Dried grass used as animal food.	50g	
	Ornamental Hay Bale	A decorative bale of hay.	250g	
	Heater	Keeps your animals warmer and happier during the winter.	2,000g	
	Milk Pail	Gather Milk from your animals.	1,000g	
	Shears	Use this to collect Wool from Sheep.	1,000g	
	Auto Grabber	Automatically collects Milk, Eggs and other Animal Products from your Barns and Coops.	25,000g	

MUSEUM

The Museum exhibits old artifacts, Minerals and books. It is run by Gunther, the new Museum curator. On Tuesday, Wednesday and Friday, Penny tutors Vincent and Jas here.

Open every day from 8am to 6pm.

Rewards for Donation Milestones:

9 Cauliflower Seeds	5 items donated	5 Warp Totem: Farm	80 items donated
9 Melon Seeds	10 items donated	Magic Rock Candy	90 items donated
1 Starfruit Seed	15 items donated	Stardrop	All 95 items donated
A Night on Eco Hill Painting	20 items donated		
Jade Hills Painting	25 items donated		
Large Futan Bear	30 items donated	Rewards for Number of Minerals Donated:	
9 Pumpkin Seeds	35 items donated	Standing Geode	11
Rarecrow #8	40 items donated	Singing Stone	21
Bear Statue	50 items donated	Obsidian Vase	31
Rusty Key	60 items donated	Crystal Chair	41
3 Triple Shot Espresso	70 items donated	Crystalarium	50

Rewards for Specific Donated Artifacts

Reward given:	Item(s) donated:
Drum Block	Ancient Drum
Ancient Seed & Crafting Recipe	Ancient Seed
Flute Block	Bone Flute
Chicken Statue Furniture	Chicken Statue
Dwarvish Translation Guide	Dwarf Scrolls I, II, III and IV
Sloth Skeleton Left	Prehistoric Skull, Scapula & Skeletal Hand
Sloth Skeleton Middle	Prehistoric Rib & Vertebra
Sloth Skeleton Rear	Prehistoric Tibia & Skeletal Tail
Burnt Offering	11 Artifacts Donated
Skeleton	15 Artifacts Donated
Rarecrow #7	20 Artifacts Donated

Adventurer's GUILD

The Guild is managed by Marlon, who sells equipment. The Monster Eradication Goals are posted here, which Gil manages.

Open every day from 2pm to 10pm.   Unlocked after Mine level:

Item	Price	Unlocked after Mine level
Wooden Blade	250g	
Iron Dirk	500g	15
Silver Saber	750g	20
Pirate's Sword	850g	30
Cutlass	1,500g	25
Wood Mallet	2,000g	40
Claymore	2,000g	45
Templar's Blade	4,000g	55
Bone Sword	6,000g	75
Steel Falchion	9,000g	90
Lava Katana	25,000g	120
Galaxy Sword	50,000g	after finding Galaxy Sword
Galaxy Dagger	35,000g	after finding Galaxy Sword
Galaxy Hammer	75,000g	after finding Galaxy Sword
Sneakers	500g	after "Initiation"
Leather Boots	500g	10
Tundra Boots	750g	50
Combat Boots	1,250g	40
Firewalker Boots	2,000g	80
Dark Boots	2,500g	80
Space Boots	5,000g	110
Amethyst Ring	1,000g	after "Initiation"
Topaz Ring	1,000g	after "Initiation"
Aquamarine Ring	2,500g	40
Jade Ring	2,500g	40
Emerald Ring	5,000g	40
Ruby Ring	5,000g	80
Slingshot	500g	40
Master Slingshot	1,000g	70
Explosive Ammo	300g	after unlocking recipe

Lost an item after passing out?

ITEM RECOVERY SERVICE
NOW AVAILABLE

THE STARDROP SALOON

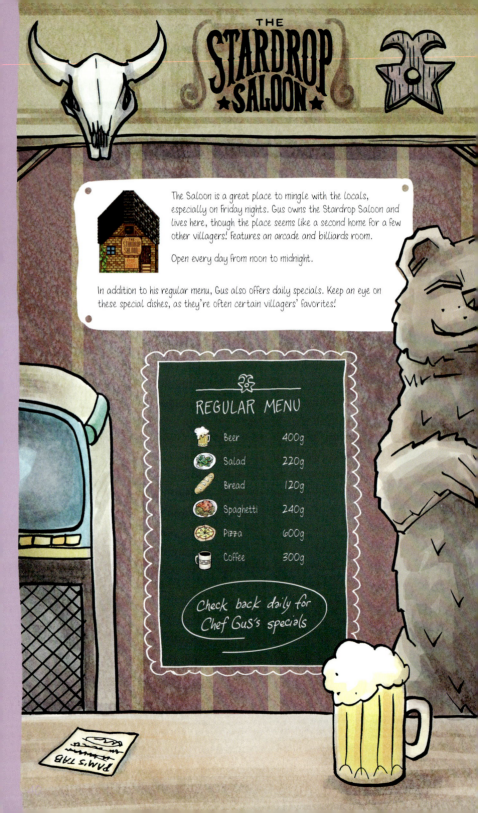

The Saloon is a great place to mingle with the locals, especially on Friday nights. Gus owns the Stardrop Saloon and lives here, though the place seems like a second home for a few other villagers! Features an arcade and billiards room.

Open every day from noon to midnight.

In addition to his regular menu, Gus also offers daily specials. Keep an eye on these special dishes, as they're often certain villagers' favorites!

REGULAR MENU

Beer	400g
Salad	220g
Bread	120g
Spaghetti	240g
Pizza	600g
Coffee	300g

Check back daily for Chef Gus's specials

WILLY'S FISH SHOP

The Fish Shop sells a variety of fishing goods and will also buy any fish or shells.
Willy lives on the second floor.

Open from 9am to 4pm, closed on Saturday, unless it is raining.

	Item	Price	Description	Unlock
	Bait	5g	Causes fish to bite faster. Attach to fishing pole.	Fishing lvl 2
	Crab Pot	1,500g	Passive catches in streams, lakes and the ocean.	Fishing lvl 3
	Spinner	500g	Slightly increases the bite-rate.	Fishing lvl 6
	Trap Bobber	500g	Causes fish to escape slower.	Fishing lvl 6
	Lead Bobber	200g	Adds weight and stability to your fishing bar.	Fishing lvl 6
	Treasure Hunter	750g	Assists in collecting treasure when fishing.	Fishing lvl 7
	Cork Bobber	750g	Slightly increases the size of your fishing bar.	Fishing lvl 7
	Barbed Hook	1,000g	Causes the fishing bar to cling to your catch.	Fishing lvl 8
	Dressed Spinner	1,000g	Increases the bite-rate when fishing.	Fishing lvl 8
	Magnet	1,000g	Increases the chance of finding treasures.	Fishing lvl 9
	Bamboo Pole	500g	A basic no-frills pole.	
	Training Rod	1,000g	An easier-to-use rod. Can only catch basic fish.	
	Fiberglass Rod	1,800g	A intermediate pole which can use bait.	Fishing lvl 2
	Iridium Rod	7,500g	An expert's pole which can use bait and tackle.	Fishing lvl 6
	Copper Pan	2,500g	Allows you to pan for Ore in rivers.	After obtaining a Copper Pan
	Trout Soup	250g	+100 Energy, +40 Health, temp +1 Fishing Skill Boost	-
	Small Fish Tank	500g	Display your favorite live fish!	-
	Large Fish Tank	2,000g	Holds more fish than the Small Fish Tank.	-
	Fisher Double Bed	25,000g	A fishing-themed double bed for your home.	-

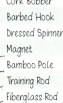

WANTED

IF IT SMELLS,
IT SELLS!
*NO TRASH, PLEASE.

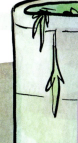

PELICAN TOWN

COMMUNITY CENTER

The old Community Center has certainly seen better days: this once-bustling center of activity is now a dilapidated pile of wood and stone, overrun with weeds and vines. Perhaps someday someone will come along to breathe new life into its halls... or maybe a certain megamart will turn it into a warehouse.

ᗡᕆ ᏯᕲᏕ ᏗᖶᏔᏔᕲᏢᏐ ᏯᏯᏢᏐᏔ ᏖᏖᏕᏕ ᏯᏯ ᏯᏕᏖᏖ ᏖᏯᏖᏔᏯᏕᏖ ᏖᏕᏖᏔᏯᏒᏔ ᏯᏯᏍᏯᏕ

JOJA MART

The big-box retailer that's been stirring things up in Pelican Town. They offer a special membership which allows you to help in cleaning and revitalizing the area via the Joja Community Development Project, but at what cost?

1 RIVER ROAD

Home of George, Evelyn and Alex. It always smells like home cooking.

MAYOR'S MANOR

Home of Lewis, the mayor of Pelican Town. He keeps a lovely garden!

1 WILLOW LANE

Home of Jodi, Sam, Vincent and—after some time has passed—Kent.

TRAILER

Home of Pam and her daughter, Penny.

2 WILLOW LANE

Home of the curiously dissimilar sisters Emily and Haley.

BUS STOP

You have the power to get this bus running to the Calico Desert again! Just complete the Vault bundles in the Community Center (or invest in the Joja bus project).

BEACH

ELLIOTT'S CABIN

Elliott resides in this humble beach cabin and draws inspiration from the sea.

TIDAL POOLS

You'll need to repair the bridge with 300 Wood to access this prime beach foraging spot.

MOUNTAIN

TENT

Linus lives in this cozy tent, which suits his solitary lifestyle just fine.

QUARRY

You'll need to repair the bridge in the Mountains (by completing the Crafts Room or investing through Joja) to access this Ore-rich area. Mine carts can service the area as well, making it easy to check back often for newly-unearthed stones and Nodes. A golden prize sleeps in the depths of a treacherous cavern nearby.

CINDERSAP FOREST

LEAH'S COTTAGE

Leah lives in this serene artist's studio down by the river.

WIZARD'S TOWER

Wizard spends his days in the Tower communing with the elementals and researching the arcane.
Once Wizard has accepted you as a friend, he will grant you access to his Shrine of Illusions, which allows you to alter your appearance for a 500g offering.

SECRET WOODS

What lies beyond that huge log in the forest? It's a secret, and you'll need a Steel Axe to find out!
Slimes dwell here, so use caution. The forest's Hardwood stumps and Mushrooms make it a great place to find uncommon resources.

ABANDONED HOUSE

This is the world's cutest li'l hat shop. Any hat, 1,000g.

MEDICAL CLINIC

Dr. Harvey's medical practice. Maru works here part-time. All residents have a yearly physical here.

Open every day from 9am to 3pm.

Energy Tonic	1,000g	+500 Energy, +200 Health
Muscle Remedy	1,000g	+50 Energy, +20 Health, removes exhaustion

If you pass out from exhaustion or stay up past 2am, Dr. Harvey will take care of you and charge you a fee. If you pass out in the Mines, Dr. Harvey may have to perform emergency surgery!

TRAVELLING CART

Open from 6am to 8pm, on Friday and Sunday only.

The Travelling Cart sells a random assortment of items each day, from seeds, crops and other food products to furniture and even Mineral Ores.

Pricing may vary based on a number of complicated market factors. This is the only place where you'll find the elusive Rare Seed, Coffee Beans and the Snowman Rarecrow, so be sure to stop by every chance you get!

SPA & RAILROAD

This area will become accessible in early summer after an earthquake clears the path north of the Mountain.

Open all day, every day; using the Spa is free!

Relax and soak in the Spa's rejuvenating waters to fully restore your energy.

Occasionally a train will pass through Stardew Valley. As the train cars go by, there's a small chance they could drop materials, Ore and other goodies!

There's some kind of creepy statue back by the rock wall. Best not to worry about it.

THE MINES

Venture forth in search of Ore, Minerals and monsters! ...And maybe after you get the Steel Pickaxe, friendship? You'll need the Dwarvish Translation Guide in order to communicate with the shopkeeper.

Open all day, every day.

Life Elixir	2,000g	Mega Bomb	1,000g
Oil of Garlic	3,000g	Miner's Treat	1,000g
Cherry Bomb	300g	Rarecrow #6	2,500g
Bomb	600g	Weathered Floor Recipe	500g
Stone Cairn	200g		

SEWERS

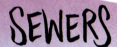

The Sewers have two entrances: one in Pelican Town, just south of Town Square, and the other in south Cindersap Forest. You'll need the Rusty Key from Gunther to enter.

Open all day, every day.

Stardrop (one-time buy)	20,000g	(Tues) Omni Geode	300g
Void Egg	5,000g	(Wed) Fish-related item	Varies
Void Essence (up to 10)	100g	(Fri) Iridium Sprinkler	10,000g
Solar Essence (up to 10)	80g	(Sat) Random Food	Varies
Crystal Floor recipe	500g	Monster Fireplace	20,000g
Wicked Statue recipe	1,000g	Return Scepter	2,000,000g
Sign of the Vessel	350g		

Skull Cavern

The cavern is a dangerous place. Take care to stock up on supplies and the best equipment, or you'll end up on Dr. Harvey's operating table.

Iridium Ore is found in higher concentrations the deeper you descend. Bringing Bombs to help clear rocks quickly will make your mining experience easier.

Heed the warning call of the frighteningly fast Serpent and ready your sword. Big Slimes will often burst into a gaggle of smaller Slimes upon defeat. Mummies are slow and easily felled, but will keep coming back for more unless you finish them off with a Bomb.

To this day, no one has ever reached the cavern's bottom.

Oasis

Sandy runs this shop in the Calico Desert which you'll be unable to access until bus service resumes.

Open from 9am to 11:50pm. Bus service to Calico Desert begins at 10am and the last departure is at 5pm. Once in the desert, the driver will stay until you're ready to return to the valley.

Everyday stock:			
Rhubarb Seeds	100g	(Mon) Coconut	200g
		(Mon) Large Cottage Rug	2,000g
Starfruit Seeds	400g	(Tues) Cactus Fruit	150g
		(Tues) Wall Sconce	500g
Beet Seeds	20g	(Wed) Omni Geode	1,000g
		(Wed) Jade Hills Extended	5,000g
Cactus Seeds	150g	(Thur) Deluxe Speed-Gro	80g
		(Thur) Old World Rug	2,500g
Seasonal Plant	100g	(Fri) Honey	200g
		(Fri) Large Green Rug	2,500g
Shirt (Random)	1,000g	(Sat) Quality Retaining Soil	200g
		(Sat) Wall Sconce	500g
Wall Cactus	700g	(Sun) Ice Cream	240g
		(Sun) Large Brown Couch	3,000g

Casino

Tucked away in the back of the Oasis and protected by a diligent Bouncer, the Casino is the only place where you can obtain certain exclusive items.

The owner, Mr. Qi, vets prospective members through a rigorous process, so gaining access to this club will not be a simple task.

		Top Hat	8,000 Qi Coins
Artwork:		Rarecrow #3	10,000 Qi Coins
Primal Motion	5,000 Qi Coins	Hardwood Fence	100 Qi Coins
Burnt Offering	4,000 Qi Coins	Magnet	1,000 Qi Coins
Highway 89	4,000 Qi Coins	Warp Totem: Farm	500 Qi Coins
Spires	3,000 Qi Coins	Modern Double Bed	8,000 Qi Coins

DESERT TRADER

The Desert Trader offers a wide variety of rare and exotic goods, trading for other items of value instead of selling them outright.

Open all day, every day... except for Winter 15-17, when the Desert Trader provides piping hot Coffee for free at the Winter Night Market.

Everyday stock:		(Mon) Hay (x3)	Omni Geode
Artifact Trove	5 Omni Geode	(Tues) Fiber	5 Stone
Warp Totem: Desert	3 Omni Geode	(Wed) Cloth	3 Aquamarine
Triple Shot Espresso	Diamond	(Thur) Magic Rock Candy	3 Prismatic Shard
Spicy Eel	Ruby	(Fri) Cheese	Emerald
Mega Bomb	5 Iridium Ore	(Sat) Spring Seeds	2 Summer Seeds
Bomb	5 Quartz	(Sat) Summer Seeds	2 Fall Seeds
Warp Totem: Desert Recipe	10 Iridium Bar	(Sat) Fall Seeds	2 Winter Seeds
Butterfly Hutch	200 Bat Wing	(Sat) Winter Seeds	2 Spring Seeds
Green Turban	50 Omni Geode	(Sun) Staircase	Jade
Birch Double Bed	Pearl	(Even Days) Magic Turban	333 Omni Geode
		(Odd Days) Magic Cowboy Hat	333 Omni Geode
		(???) Void Ghost Pendant	200 Void Essence

GIFTS

Universally Loved Gifts +80 pts

Pearl   Prismatic Shard   Magic Rock Candy   Rabbit's Foot   Golden Pumpkin

UNIVERSALLY DISLIKED GIFTS -20 pts

As a general rule, most villagers dislike all fish, Minerals (see p154), Geodes, crafting items, building materials, fertilizers, monster loot, tackle and seeds.

UNIVERSALLY HATED GIFTS: -40 pts

If you're really looking to ruin someone's day, trash, bait and furniture are effective choices. ...But why would you?

EVERYONE BUT PENNY HATES POPPY

Universally Liked Gifts

+45 pts

Villagers tend to like Gems, home-cooked meals, artisan goods, tree fruits, vegetables and flowers. However, different people have different tastes, so there are exceptions for nearly every item. This is a quick, handy list of things that *most people will like*; refer to page 244 to 247 for specific Likes and Loves for all villagers.

MOST FLOWERS

Sweet Pea, Crocus, Tulip, Blue Jazz, Summer Spangle, Sunflower, Fairy Rose
(Excludes Daffodil, Dandelion and Poppy)

GEMS

Earth Crystal, Frozen Tear, Fire Quartz, Emerald, Aquamarine, Ruby, Amethyst, Topaz, Jade, Diamond

TREE FRUIT

Apricot, Cherry, Peach, Orange, Apple, Pomegranate

COOKING

All Cooking, including Life Elixir, except for Fried Egg, Bread, Strange Bun, Seafoam Pudding

VEGETABLE CROPS

Amaranth, Artichoke, Beet, Bok Choy, Cauliflower, Corn, Eggplant, Fiddlehead Fern (Forageable), Garlic, Green Bean, Kale, Parsnip, Potato, Pumpkin, Radish, Red Cabbage, Yam
(Excludes Hops, Wheat, Tea Leaves and Unmilled Rice)

ARTISAN GOODS

MADE FROM ANIMAL-RELATED PRODUCTS

KEG PRODUCTS

ANY KIND OF JELLY, PICKLES, AGED ROE, CAVIAR, OR HONEY

X NO PINE TAR! X NO OAK RESIN!

Cheese, Goat Cheese, Cloth, Mayo, Duck Mayo, Dino Mayo, Truffle Oil

Pale Ale, Beer, Green Tea, Coffee, Juice, Mead, Wine

Jelly, Pickles, Caviar, Aged Roe, Honey, Maple Syrup

The Residents of Stardew Valley

Each of the dozens of citizens of Stardew Valley is a unique individual, with their own personalities, stories, likes, dislikes, hopes and dreams. Some have families, while others live alone; others still are single and open to courtship and eventually marriage. You'll learn more about each character as you get to know them, building lifelong friendships and maybe even a family of your own!

INFO KEY

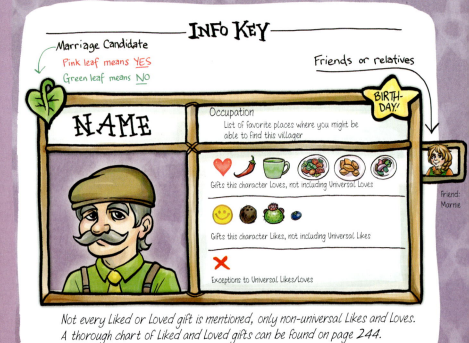

Marriage Candidate
Pink leaf means YES
Green leaf means NO

Friends or relatives

BIRTH-DAY!

NAME

Occupation
List of favorite places where you might be able to find this villager

Gifts this character Loves, not including Universal Loves

Gifts this character Likes, not including Universal Likes

✖

Exceptions to Universal Likes/Loves

Friend: Marnie

Not every Liked or Loved gift is mentioned, only non-universal Likes and Loves. A thorough chart of Liked and Loved gifts can be found on page 244.

Universal Likes: Most flowers, Gems, tree fruit, cooking, vegetable crops, artisan goods

PIERRE

Owner of the General Store
Pierre's General Store, Stardrop Saloon

SPRING 26

❤ Fried Calamari

🙂 Daffodil, Dandelion, all Milk, Egg, Duck Egg

❌ Gems other than Diamonds, Corn, Garlic, Parsnip Soup, Tortilla

Wife: Caroline

Daughter: Abigail

CAROLINE

Tea Enthusiast
Pierre's, fountain near Community Center,
Town Square, Museum

WINTER 7

❤ Fish Taco, Summer Spangle, Green Tea, Tropical Curry

🙂 Daffodil, Tea Leaves

❌ Amaranth, all Mayonnaise

Family: Pierre, Abigail

Friends: Jodi, Kent

ABIGAIL

Champion of the Egg Hunt
Pierre's, East bridge, Saloon arcade, Museum,
Mountain Lake, near Tower, ocean pier

FALL 13

❤ Amethyst, Pumpkin, Pufferfish, Chocolate Cake,
Blackberry Cobbler, Spicy Eel, Banana Pudding

🙂 Quartz

❌ Vegetables

Family: Pierre, Caroline

Friends: Sebastian, Sam

MARNIE

Owner of The Ranch
Ranch, Saloon

FALL 18

❤️ Farmer's Lunch, Pink Cake, Pumpkin Pie, Diamond

🙂 All Milk, Egg, Duck Egg, Quartz

❌ No exceptions to Universal Likes

Nephew: Shane
Niece: Jas
Friend: Lewis

SHANE

Joja Stockboy, Chicken Whisperer
Ranch, JojaMart, Saloon

SPRING 20

❤️ Hot Pepper, Beer, Pizza, Pepper Poppers

🙂 All fruit crops, all foraged fruits, Egg, Duck Egg

❌ Pickles

Aunt: Marnie
Goddaughter: Jas
Friend: Emily

JAS

A kid who doesn't like Juice
Ranch, Museum

SUMMER 4

❤️ Fairy Rose, Pink Cake, Plum Pudding

🙂 Daffodil, Coconut

❌ Vegetables, Juice, Coffees, Tea, Alcoholic Drinks, Piña Colada, Artisan Goods

Aunt: Marnie
Godfather: Shane
Friend: Vincent

Universal Likes: Most flowers, Gems, tree fruit, cooking, vegetable crops, artisan goods

LEWIS

Mayor of Pelican Town
Mayor's Manor, Saloon, various businesses

★ SPRING 7

Hot Pepper, Green Tea, Veg Medley, Glazed Yams, Autumn's Bounty

Coconut, Cactus Fruit, Blueberry

No exceptions to Universal Likes

Friend: Marnie

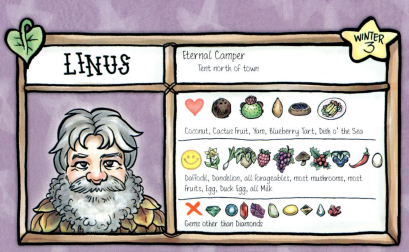

LINUS

Eternal Camper
Tent north of town

★ WINTER 3

Coconut, Cactus Fruit, Yam, Blueberry Tart, Dish o' the Sea

Daffodil, Dandelion, all forageables, most mushrooms, most fruits, Egg, Duck Egg, all Milk

Gems other than Diamonds

WIZARD

Denizen of Mysterious Tower
Tower west of Cindersap Forest

★ WINTER 17

Purple Mushroom, Super Cucumber, Solar Essence, Void Essence

All Minerals

No exceptions to Universal Likes

52

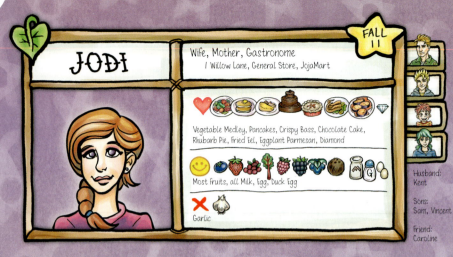

JODI

FALL 11

Wife, Mother, Gastronome
1 Willow Lane, General Store, JojaMart

❤️ Vegetable Medley, Pancakes, Crispy Bass, Chocolate Cake, Rhubarb Pie, Fried Eel, Eggplant Parmesan, Diamond

🙂 Most fruits, all Milk, Egg, Duck Egg

❌ Garlic

Husband: Kent

Sons: Sam, Vincent

Friend: Caroline

SAM

SUMMER 17

Rock Star in Training
1 Willow Lane, JojaMart, Saloon Arcade

❤️ Cactus Fruit, Maple Bar, Pizza, Tigerseye

🙂 Joja Cola, Egg, Duck Egg

❌ Vegetables, all Mayonnaise, Pickles

Family: Kent, Jodi, Vincent

Friends: Penny, Sebastian, Abigail

VINCENT

SPRING 10

Another kid who doesn't like Juice
1 Willow Lane, Museum

❤️ Grape, Cranberry Candy, Ginger Ale, Pink Cake, Snail

🙂 Daffodil, Coconut

❌ Vegetables, Juice, Coffees, Tea, Alcoholic Drinks, Piña Colada, most Artisan Goods

Family: Kent, Jodi, Sam

Friend: Jas

Universal Likes: Most flowers, Gems, tree fruit, cooking, vegetable crops, artisan goods

ELLIOTT

FALL 5

Aspiring Author
Cabin on the beach, Museum, Saloon

❤️ Pomegranate, Lobster, Duck Feather, Crab Cakes, Tom Kha Soup, Squid Ink

🙂 All fruit crops, all foraged fruits (except Salmonberry), Octopus, Squid

❌ Amaranth, Pizza

Friends:
Leah, Willy

LEAH

WINTER 23

Aspiring Artist
Cottage south of the ranch, Saloon,
Cindersap Forest, the beach

❤️ Truffle, Goat Cheese, Wine, Poppyseed Muffin, Salad, Stir Fry, Vegetable Medley

🙂 Daffodil, Dandelion, all forageables, all fruits, most mushrooms, all Milk, Egg, Duck Egg, Driftwood

❌ Gems other than Diamonds, Pancakes, Hashbrowns, Carp Surprise, Pizza, Cookie, Ice Cream, Pink Cake, Rice Pudding, Survival Burger, Tortilla

Friend:
Elliott

WILLY

SUMMER 24

Owner of the Fish Shop
Fish Shop, Saloon

❤️ Pumpkin, Catfish, Octopus, Sea Cucumber, Sturgeon, Mead, Diamond, Iridium Bar

🙂 Tiger Trout, Lingcod, Gold Bar, Quartz, Seafoam Pudding

❌ Life Elixir, Sashimi, Maki Roll, Dish O' The Sea, Escargot, Spicy Eel, Tom Kha Soup, cooked foods that don't contain fish

friend:
Elliott

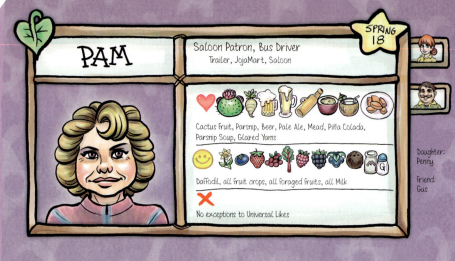

PAM

Saloon Patron, Bus Driver
Trailer, JojaMart, Saloon

♥ Cactus Fruit, Parsnip, Beer, Pale Ale, Mead, Piña Colada, Parsnip Soup, Glazed Yams

🙂 Daffodil, all fruit crops, all foraged fruits, all Milk

❌ No exceptions to Universal Likes

Daughter:
Penny

Friend:
Gus

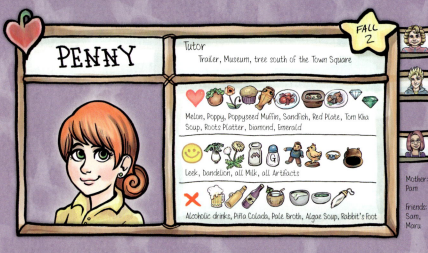

PENNY

Tutor
Trailer, Museum, tree south of the Town Square

♥ Melon, Poppy, Poppyseed Muffin, Sandfish, Red Plate, Tom Kha Soup, Roots Platter, Diamond, Emerald

🙂 Leek, Dandelion, all Milk, all Artifacts

❌ Alcoholic drinks, Piña Colada, Pale Broth, Algae Soup, Rabbit's Foot

Mother:
Pam

Friends:
Sam,
Maru

GUS

Proprietor of the Stardrop Saloon
Saloon

♥ Orange, Fish Taco, Escargot, Tropical Curry, Diamond

🙂 Daffodil

❌ Coleslaw

Friends:
Pam,
Emily

Universal Likes: Most flowers, Gems, tree fruit, cooking, vegetable crops, artisan goods

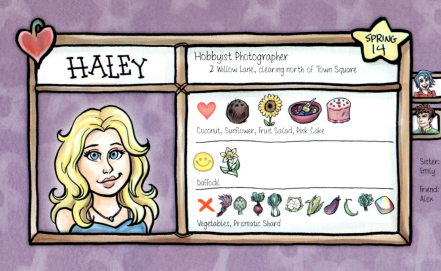

HALEY

Hobbyist Photographer
2 Willow Lane, clearing north of Town Square

SPRING 14

❤️ Coconut, Sunflower, Fruit Salad, Pink Cake

🙂 Daffodil

❌ Vegetables, Prismatic Shard

Sister: Emily

Friend: Alex

EMILY

Waitress, Tailor, Dancing Queen
2 Willow Lane, Saloon

SPRING 27

❤️ Wool, Cloth, Survival Burger, Emerald, Aquamarine, Ruby, Amethyst, Topaz, Jade

🙂 Daffodil, Quartz

❌ Ice Cream, Sashimi, Fried Eel, Spicy Eel, Rice Pudding, Salmon Dinner, Fish Taco, Maki Roll

Sister: Haley

Friends: Sandy, Shane, Clint, Gus

CLINT

Blacksmith
Blacksmith's shop, Saloon

WINTER 26

❤️ Artichoke Dip, Fiddlehead Risotto, Emerald, Aquamarine, Ruby, Amethyst, Jade, Gold Bar, Iridium Bar, Omni Geode, Topaz

🙂 Copper Bar, Iron Bar

❌ Flowers

Friend: Emily

ALEX

Pro Gridball Hopeful
1 River Road

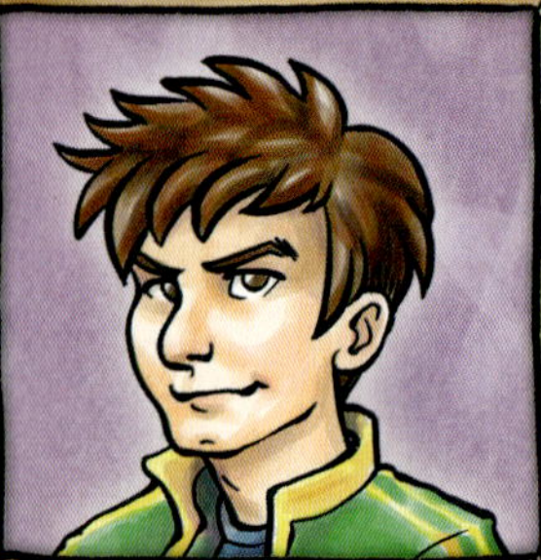

❤️ Complete Breakfast, Salmon Dinner

🙂 Egg, Duck Egg

❌ No exceptions to Universal Likes

Grandparents
George,
Evelyn

Friend:
Haley

GEORGE

Retired Grandfather
1 River Road

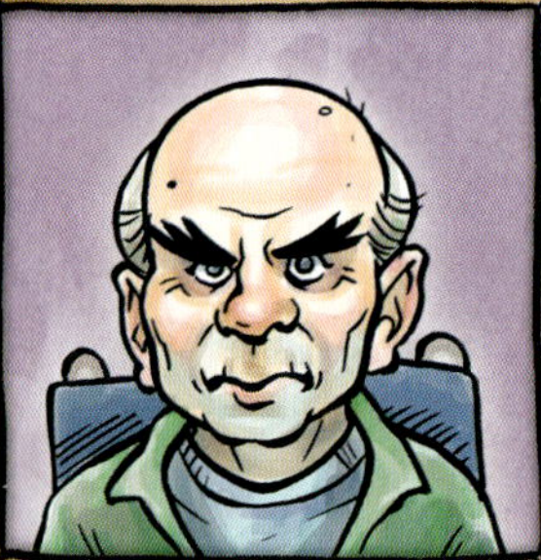

❤️ Leek, Fried Mushroom

🙂 Daffodil

❌ Flowers

Wife:
Evelyn

Grandson:
Alex

EVELYN

Proud Grandmother
1 River Road, gardens near the Town Square

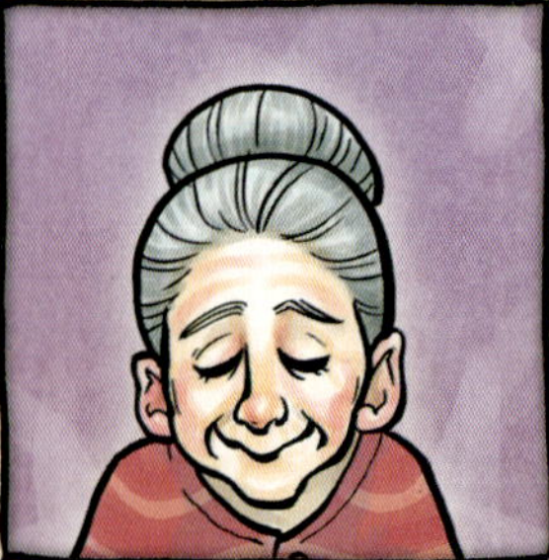

❤️ Tulip, Beet, Fairy Rose, Chocolate Cake, Stuffing, Diamond

🙂 Daffodil, all Milk

❌ Garlic, Sashimi, Spicy Eel, Fried Eel, Maki Roll, Trout Soup

Husband:
George

Grandson:
Alex

Universal Likes: Most flowers, Gems, tree fruit, cooking, vegetable crops, artisan goods

ROBIN

FALL 21

Owner of the Carpenter's Shop
Carpenter's Shop, cliffside east of the shop

❤️ Peach, Goat Cheese, Spaghetti

🙂 All fruit crops, all foraged fruits, all Milk, Hardwood, Quartz

❌ No exceptions to Universal Likes

Husband: Demetrius

Son: Sebastian

Daughter: Maru

DEMETRIUS

SUMMER 19

All-Around Science Man
Carpenter's Shop, riverside near the shop

❤️ Strawberry, Bean Hotpot, Rice Pudding, Ice Cream

🙂 All fruit crops, all foraged fruits, Purple Mushroom, Egg, Duck Egg

❌ No exceptions to Universal Likes

Wife: Robin

Daughter: Maru

Step-son: Sebastian

SEBASTIAN

WINTER 10

Computer Enthusiast
Carpenter's Shop

❤️ Void Egg, Sashimi, Pumpkin Soup, Frozen Tear, Obsidian

🙂 Quartz, Flounder

❌ Omelet, Complete Breakfast, Farmer's Lunch, alcoholic drinks, Juice, artisan goods (except Coffee and Green Tea), flowers

Mother: Robin

Step-father: Demetrius

Half-sister: Maru

Friends: Abigail, Sam

MARU

Nurse, Master Roboticist
Carpenter's Shop, Clinic

SUMMER 10

♥ Cauliflower, Strawberry, Cheese Cauliflower, Miner's Treat, Pepper Poppers, Rhubarb Pie, Diamond, Gold Bar, Iridium Bar, Radioactive Bar, Battery Pack

🙂 Copper Bar, Iron Bar, Quartz, Oak Resin, Pine Tar, Radioactive Ore

❌ Maple Syrup, Honey, Pickles

Parents:
Robin,
Demetrius

Half-brother
Sebastian

Friends:
Harvey, Penn

HARVEY

Town Doctor
Clinic, Saloon

WINTER 14

♥ Coffee, Pickles, Truffle Oil, Wine, Super Meal

🙂 Daffodil, Dandelion, all fruit crops, all foraged fruits (except Salmonberry and Spice Berry), most forageables, most mushrooms, Duck Egg, Duck Feather, Goat Milk, Quartz

❌ All Cheese, Fried Mushroom, Hashbrowns, Pizza, most sugary foods

Friend:
Maru

SANDY

Owner of The Oasis
The Oasis

FALL 15

♥ Daffodil, Sweet Pea, Crocus, Mango Sticky Rice

🙂 All fruit crops, all foraged fruits, Goat Milk, Wool, Quartz

❌ No exceptions to Universal Likes

Friend:
Emily

Universal Likes: Most flowers, Gems, tree fruit, cooking, vegetable crops, artisan goods

KENT

Soldier, Family Man
1 Willow Lane, riverbank south of the Town Square

SPRING 4

❤️ Fiddlehead Risotto, Roasted Hazelnuts

🙂 Daffodil, all fruit crops, all foraged fruits, Egg, Duck Egg

❌ Algae Soup, Sashimi, Tortilla, Piña Colada

Wife: Jodi

Sons: Vincent, Sam

Friend: Caroline

KROBUS

Friendly Shadow Brute
The Sewer

WINTER 1

❤️ Wild Horseradish, Pumpkin, Void Mayonnaise, Void Egg, Diamond, Iridium Bar

🙂 Gold Bar, Quartz, Seafoam Pudding

❌ Life Elixir, cooked foods

DWARF

Smoluanu
The Mines

SUMMER 22

❤️ Emerald, Aquamarine, Ruby, Amethyst, Topaz, Jade, Lemon Stone, Omni Geode

🙂 Quartz, all Artifacts, Cave Carrot

❌ No exceptions to Universal Likes

Some folks in and around the valley just want to keep it professional. Each of them plays an important role in the community, but they're not interested in friendship or gifts. Still, it doesn't hurt to pay them each a visit whenever you get the chance!

GUNTHER This kind archaeology buff has inherited the unfortunate task of rebuilding the entire Museum from scratch, since the collection disappeared with the previous curator! The only gift he wants is to see the Museum returned to its former glory.

MORRIS The smug, bespectacled manager of the local JojaMart, a big-box store that's putting pressure on Pelican Town's local economy. He's more concerned with profits than friendship, and would love nothing more than to sell you a JojaMart membership (which would surely earn him a nice bonus)!

MARLON This battle-hardened warrior runs the Adventurer's Guild; the monsters in the Mines may have taken his eye, but they could never quell his fighting spirit! He'll provide you with the best equipment money can buy.

GIL This wizened old man distributes awards for completing Monster Eradication Goals. He's had his fill of combat for one lifetime, so now he spends his days and nights enjoying a crackling fire and his favorite rocking chair.

BOUNCER This stoic bouncer guards the front door to the Casino; he'll only let you in if you have the proper credentials. He takes his job VERY seriously, so it would not be advisable to try to sneak past him!

MR. QI The mysterious owner of the Casino in the Calico Desert. His eyes and ears are everywhere, monitoring your every move; he'll present you with a number of increasingly bizarre tasks if you can prove you're up to the challenge.

JUNIMO!

Nature spirits of Stardew Valley

♥

ᔑᓭ╎↸ᒷ ᒲᔭᒷᔑᓭ ⨀ᒷ╎⨀ᒷ ᔭᒷᔑ╎ᓭ

✖ Joja

ᔑᓭ╎↸ᒷ ᒲᔭᒷᔑᓭ ⨀ᒷ╎⨀ᒷ ᔭᒷᔑ╎ᓭ

Who are they?
How long have they been living in Stardew Valley?

These mysterious little nature spirits only want to clean up the valley and make it a peaceful, happy place, but they can't do it without your help. They've requested a number of different sets of items, called Bundles, that only someone with a kind heart can complete. For each Bundle you finish for the Junimos, you'll be given rare and valuable gifts.

You'll also breathe new life into the Community Center; each room contains a number of related Bundle requests. When all Bundles for a room have been fulfilled, the Junimos will use their powers to instantly renovate that room! And what's more, they'll band together and restore part of the local environment during the night!

By working alongside the Junimos, you'll achieve things not even money can buy, deepening friendships and recovering the pristine beauty of the valley!

Friendship

FOR ME? WOW!

As you embark on your new rural life journey, you'll forge lasting relationships with all of your neighbors, young and old. You might even find love waiting out there!

Strengthening relationships with your fellow villagers is as easy as talking to them each day, but there are many ways in which you can win their affection more quickly.

TALKING TO A VILLAGER: +20pts/day   IGNORING A VILLAGER: −2 pts/day

Your relationship status with each villager is indicated by 10 heart icons, with 2 initially inaccessible for the bachelors & bachelorettes. These hearts start out empty, and fill as your relationships grow stronger. Each heart actually represents 250 friendship points, with a total of 2,500 required to fill all 10 hearts and become someone's best friend... or more!

1 × ♥ = 250 pts

At certain points in the development of friendships, you'll share tender moments and learn more about the people of Stardew Valley and their personal stories.

♥ HEART EVENTS ♥

Each villager can be given 1 gift each day, and up to 2 per week. Everyone has their own likes and dislikes, loves and hates, so be careful; giving someone something they don't care for can cost you!

STAR BONUS APPLY to Loved and LIKED Gifts					
IRIDIUM ★STAR	GOLD ★STAR	SILVER ★STAR	NORMAL		
+120pts	+100pts	+88pts	+ 80pts	Loved gift	
+68pts	+57pts	+50pts	+ 45pts	Liked gift	
			+ 20pts	Neutral gift	
			− 20pts	Disliked gift	
			− 40pts	Hated gift	

GIFT VALUE MULTIPLIERS:		
1x	NORMAL DAY
5x	WINTER STAR
8x	BIRTHDAY

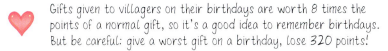

Gifts given to villagers on their birthdays are worth 8 times the points of a normal gift, so it's a good idea to remember birthdays. But be careful: give a worst gift on a birthday, lose 320 points!

During the Feast of the Winter Star, you'll be able to give a gift to your secret gift exchange friend (Lewis will let you know who your secret friend is a week in advance). This gift is worth 5 times the points of a normal gift, good or bad!

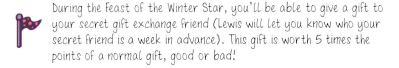

Personal requests and help wanted requests will help along your friendships as well, awarding you 150 points per request.

Pelting people with rocks is a bad way to make friends, and will cost you friendship points with your target. Put that slingshot away!

Once you've completely filled all available hearts for a villager, you'll no longer lose relationship points by not talking to them every day. Best friends forever!!!

A Guide to Wooing and Marriage

Once your relationship reaches 8 hearts with a bachelor or bachelorette, you can start considering taking it to the next level. That's when Pierre's General Store will begin carrying the Bouquet, a universal token of affection, for just 200g!

Giving a Bouquet to a prospective 8-heart romantic interest will unlock the final 2 hearts, and things can start getting more serious. In no time at all, you'll have all 10 hearts filled, and you can start getting ready to propose if you'd like. You won't need a bouquet to start courting a fellow farmer.

Exploring your romantic options

While it may not be your style, you can absolutely give a Bouquet to every single eligible bachelor and bachelorette in Stardew Valley. It's the only way to get to a full 10 hearts with everyone. Just be careful when playing the field; if you can't commit to a single long-term relationship, you might find yourself totally alone! If you've decided you want to end a relationship, try wilting a Bouquet in a Furnace to send the message loud and clear.

12 BOUQUETS..?
CERTAINLY.

THAT'LL BE 2,400g.

UM, THANKS!

SALE: 2400g
PIERRE'S

HOW TO PROPOSE

Once you've finally reached that 10-heart milestone, it's time to pop the question. Tradition around these parts dictates you present your beloved with the rare and beautiful Mermaid's Pendant, the legendary symbol of eternal devotion.

WHAT YOU'LL NEED:

♥ 5,000 g

♥ 10 HEARTS w/ YOUR BOYFRIEND OR GIRLFRIEND

♥ FIRST HOUSE UPGRADE

♥ ACCESS TO TIDAL POOLS ON A RAINY DAY (SPRING — FALL)
   YOU CAN'T BUY THE PENDANT IN WINTER, SO PLAN AHEAD!

Your wedding will take place three days after you propose, and your spouse will move into your house right away. They'll have a small room in your house similar to their bedroom back home. Make sure you're completely ready to say goodbye to the single life before proposing!

As long as you keep them happy, your husband or wife will eagerly help out with the daily chores, including watering crops, feeding animals and repairing broken fences. You might even wake up to a delicious, nutritious meal to help start your day!

Marriage is a much deeper kind of relationship, and so you'll be able to shower your sweetheart with gifts—still one per day, but with no weekly limit—to reach as many as 14 hearts.

Jealousy's an ugly beast, so consider the consequences before giving other bachelors & bachelorettes gifts if you're more than just friends. And don't even think about giving someone else a Bouquet after getting married!

If the object of your affection is a fellow farmer, you'll want to craft a Wedding Ring before you pop the question. A certain travelling merchant can probably help track down the recipe.

For those of you who just want a friendly shadow housemate, you're in luck; the rare Void Ghost Pendant is what you're looking for. The Desert Trader and Skull Cavern are your best bets there.

Kids and Married Life

Once you've enjoyed the bliss of married life for a while, that spacious Farmhouse might start feeling a bit empty. After all, Robin's second house upgrade added a nursery, and she even included two beds and a crib. It would be a shame not to put them to use.

The decision to have children is a delicate subject, so it's best to wait for your spouse to bring it up. Of course, if you're not ready, you shouldn't feel pressured to give in right away. When the time is right, you'll know, and then you can start building your nuclear family.

Time flies in the valley, so in what will seem like just a couple of weeks, you'll welcome your new son or daughter into the world! If natural childbirth isn't an option, you can instead choose to adopt: your spouse will gladly handle all the necessary paperwork, and in no time at all, your new child will be brought to you by the adoption agency.

You can play with your child every day, forging a strong parental bond as you watch them grow from a tiny, sleepy newborn to a rambunctious toddler. And when your first child is old enough to sleep in a big kid bed, you and your spouse can start thinking about having or adopting another!

If you have children with a fellow farmer, they'll live with one parent or the other depending on a few factors. Regardless of where they live, though, you'll be able to play and develop bonds with your children every day.

⊰ IRRECONCILABLE DIFFERENCES ⊱

Not every marriage is a perfect, happy paradise. Even after many joyful years, cherished memories and loving children, some couples find that they just can't keep going. The spark they once had is gone, and they don't have the desire to try and rekindle it.

Divorce proceedings must be initiated through Mayor Lewis by signing the appropriate form in the town ledger, available in the Mayor's Manor during his normal business hours of 8:30am to 10pm. After you sign the divorce papers, place them in the ledger and pay a 50,000g fee, you'll have until the end of the day to think it over, or at least until 10pm when the Mayor's Manor closes. If you change your mind, you can simply remove the paperwork from the ledger to cancel.

But once the divorce proceedings have been finalized, that's it. Your ex-spouse will move out of the Farmhouse during the night and return to their normal life, understandably embittered by the experience; you'll retain custody of any children the two of you had together.

With your return to the single life, you'll be free to begin romancing any of the other eligible bachelors and bachelorettes if you so choose; if you can obtain a second Mermaid's Pendant, you'll also be able to remarry.

If your spouse was a fellow farmer, any children you had together will continue to live with the parent they've always lived with; the process remains the same, and both of you are free to romance and remarry.

HELP WANTED!

Take up quests posted in front of Pierre's shop (a ! will appear). Each job appears for one day and you have two days to complete each quest.

The quest's complexity will affect the value of the reward. The tougher the quest, the greater the gold.

You gain 150 friendship points with the person who started the request.

personal requests

As you earn the trust and respect of the townspeople, they'll begin to see you as someone they can rely on. In time, they may even start coming directly to you for help, by mail or in person. Don't be surprised if you wake up one morning to find a neighbor on your doorstep, gathering the courage to ask a special favor of you.

Personal requests don't have deadlines, so if you're in no position to procure the item someone is looking for at that moment, don't worry! You've got all the time in the world.

SPECIAL ORDERS

Once you've established yourself as a regular member of Pelican Town society and your fellow villagers have learned to depend on your generosity, a new Special Orders board will be constructed outside the Mayor's manor.

The extra special requests posted here are more complex with extended deadlines, and the rewards include crafting recipes, special events and maybe even a new TV channel!

starting FALL 2 year one

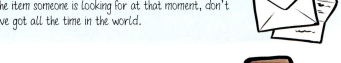

CHOOSE ONE: GREAT REWARDS

TRASH CAN DIVING

A bit of digging in the trash never hurt anyone! However, if someone catches you in the act, they'll think a little less highly of you, except for Master Scavenger Linus.

Different trash cans yield different treasures. Clint's trash will sometimes have Ore, Gus's will have leftovers and the Museum's may have Geodes! Each season provides its own bounty of fish and forageable trash treasures as well.

Somehow, spelunking in an old mine is very similar to spelunking in a trash can, so your depth in the Mines affects trash-digging results. After reaching the bottom of the Mines, you could find precious gems in someone's trash!

COMMON:

SEASONAL:
SPRING   SUMMER   FALL   WINTER

STARDROP SALOON:

AFTER REACHING BOTTOM OF THE MINES:

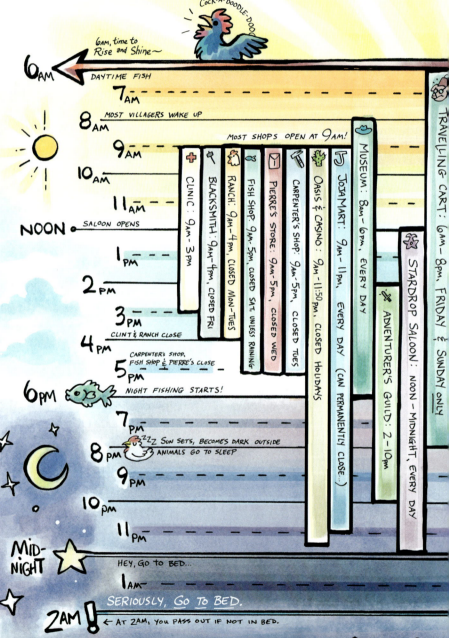

DAY CYCLE

COCK-A-DOODLE-DOO

6AM, time to Rise and Shine~

6AM

DAYTIME FISH

7AM

8AM — MOST VILLAGERS WAKE UP

MOST SHOPS OPEN AT 9AM!

9AM

10AM

11AM

NOON — SALOON OPENS

1PM

2PM

3PM

CLINT & RANCH CLOSE

4PM

CARPENTER'S SHOP, FISH SHOP & PIERRE'S CLOSE

5PM

6PM — NIGHT FISHING STARTS!

7PM

8PM — ZZZ SUN SETS, BECOMES DARK OUTSIDE — ANIMALS GO TO SLEEP

9PM

10PM

11PM

MID-NIGHT — HEY, GO TO BED...

1AM

SERIOUSLY, GO TO BED.

2AM ← AT 2AM, YOU PASS OUT IF NOT IN BED.

CLINIC : 9AM – 3PM

BLACKSMITH : 9AM – 4PM, CLOSED FRI

RANCH : 9AM – 4PM, CLOSED MON–TUES

FISH SHOP : 9AM – 5PM, CLOSED SAT UNLESS RAINING

PIERRE'S STORE : 9AM – 5PM, CLOSED WED

CARPENTER'S SHOP : 9AM – 5PM, CLOSED TUES

OASIS & CASINO : 9AM – 11:50PM, CLOSED HOLIDAYS

JOJAMART : 9AM – 11PM, EVERY DAY (CAN PERMANENTLY CLOSE...)

MUSEUM : 8AM – 6PM, EVERY DAY

ADVENTURER'S GUILD : 2 – 10PM

STARDROP SALOON : NOON – MIDNIGHT, EVERY DAY

TRAVELING CART : 6AM – 8PM, FRIDAY & SUNDAY ONLY

72

WEATHER

Weather can affect everyone's daily schedules, including yours, so plan accordingly. Though the valley is sheltered from the most extreme weather phenomena—tornadoes, hurricanes, blizzards and the like—every season still has its own elements to brave:

SUN There's abundant sunshine in Stardew Valley, granting plenty of opportunities for outdoor activities like gardening, sports and even festivals.

RAIN There's no need to water crops when it's raining, so you can take care of other matters. Many villagers choose to stay indoors, so they'll follow different schedules on these days. In addition, certain types of fish will only surface when it rains, so cast a line every now and then and see what bites!

STORM Take care when the weather gets ugly, as lightning can damage crops and fruit trees. If you have the materials, you can craft Lightning Rods to intercept lightning strikes and charge Battery Packs.

SNOW Stardew Valley sees a bit more snow than neighboring areas, making it something of a winter wonderland. Snowfall doesn't affect anything, so just enjoy the crisp winter air and gentle tinkling of the snowflakes as they pile up around you.

You'll always be one step ahead of the weather as long as you keep an eye on the Weather Forecast each day.

Occasionally, the valley will experience an unusual meteorological or geological event; fortune favors the brave, so if you're awakened in the middle of the night by a mighty rumbling or booming sound, get out there and investigate in the morning!

Chapter 3
Farm Life

Farming is more than just planting seeds and picking things out of the ground; it's quite literally a way of life.

As a farmer, you'll spend your days managing your crops and trees, and maintaining your fields. You'll devise innovative ways to keep your crops watered, healthy and thriving throughout each season. And as your farm begins to flourish, you'll be able to construct new buildings to raise animals for Milk, Eggs and a range of other products. With the aid of modern technology, those products can be made into fine artisan goods, which will fetch top dollar at market.

With a little planning and perseverance, your farm can grow into a booming multifaceted business!

FARMHOUSE

ORIGINAL FARMHOUSE

Just the way your grandfather left it. It's not much, but it's cozy.

ROBIN'S 1ST UPGRADE

10,000g
450 wood

Adds a kitchen, allowing you to prepare home-cooked meals.

Robin's 2ND Upgrade

50,000g
150 HARDWOOD

Larger, with a nursery; spacious enough for a family. Allows for additional rooms and other free interior renovations.

Robin's 3RD Upgrade

100,000g

Adds a basement with Casks, allowing you to age Wines and other beverages, as well as Cheeses.

UPGRADABLE FARM TOOLS

The tools of the trade; each can be upgraded by providing Clint with the proper materials and covering the fee. Upgraded tools are stronger and more effective, covering larger areas or breaking larger and tougher obstacles.

PICKAXE

Pickaxes are used to break rocks; each upgrade allows you to break them in fewer swings, and some stronger rocks require certain upgrades to break.

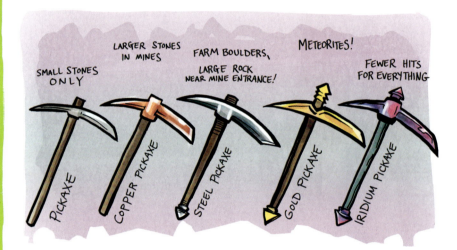

SMALL STONES ONLY — PICKAXE

LARGER STONES IN MINES — COPPER PICKAXE

FARM BOULDERS, LARGE ROCK NEAR MINE ENTRANCE! — STEEL PICKAXE

METEORITES! — GOLD PICKAXE

FEWER HITS FOR EVERYTHING — IRIDIUM PICKAXE

HOE

Hoes are an essential farmer's tool, used to till the land for planting. Each upgrade allows you to charge up and till a larger area in a single swing!

1 x 1 tile — HOE

1 x 3 tiles — COPPER HOE

1 x 5 tiles — STEEL HOE

3 x 3 tiles — GOLD HOE

3 x 6 tiles — IRIDIUM HOE

AXE

Axes are used to fell trees and break wood obstacles. Each upgrade allows you to finish in fewer swings, and some stumps and logs require certain upgrades to break.

FELLS A TREE IN 10 HITS	FELLS A TREE IN 8 HITS	FELLS A TREE IN 6 HITS	FELLS A TREE IN 4 HITS	FELLS A TREE IN 2 HITS
CHOPS STUMPS IN 5 HITS	CHOPS STUMPS IN 4 HITS	CHOPS STUMPS IN 3 HITS	CHOPS STUMPS IN 2 HITS	CHOPS STUMPS IN 1 HIT
NO LARGE STUMPS OR LOGS	NO LOGS ✓LARGE STUMPS	✓LOGS LARGE STUMPS (SECRET WOODS!)	✓LOGS ✓LARGE STUMPS	✓LOGS ✓LARGE STUMPS
AXE	COPPER AXE	STEEL AXE	GOLD AXE	IRIDIUM AXE

WATERING CAN

Watering Cans are (obviously) used to water crops and flowers; each upgrade lets you water a larger area at once.

- WATERING CAN — 1 x 1 tile — 40
- COPPER WATERING CAN — 1 x 3 tiles — 55
- STEEL WATERING CAN — 1 x 5 tiles — 70
- GOLD WATERING CAN — 3 x 3 tiles — 85
- IRIDIUM WATERING CAN — 3 x 6 tiles — 100

TRASH CAN

Upgrading your personal Trash Can allows you to recoup a portion of an item's value when throwing it away. Each upgrade increases the amount of money you receive.

STANDARD	COPPER	STEEL	GOLD	IRIDIUM
0%	15%	30%	45%	60%

GROWING CROPS

CROPS CHANGE APPEARANCE AS THEY PROGRESS THROUGH THEIR GROWTH PHASES

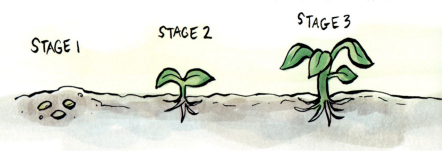

STAGE 1

STAGE 2

STAGE 3

The soil in Stardew Valley supports a wide variety of fruit and vegetable crops, as well as flowers. The crops available differ by season, and can only withstand the climates of their growing seasons; plants will wither as a new season begins. The only exceptions are Corn, Coffee and Sunflowers, which can each grow during two seasons.

Each type of crop requires a different amount of time to grow and ripen, progressing through several stages of growth until they reach maturity and can be harvested; the length of each growth stage can be shortened using Speed-Gro. Some crops will continue producing fruit after the initial harvest.

High-quality crops are more nutritious and more valuable; you can increase your chance of producing high-quality crops using Fertilizers.

STAGE 4

READY TO HARVEST

Every crop must be watered daily in order to continue growing. Retaining Soils can be used to save a day of watering here and there, and Sprinklers can be installed to automatically water surrounding crops. For the rest, you'll need your trusty Watering Can.

While many crops can simply be pulled from the ground by hand, tools are required to harvest a few and return the soil to a usable state.

Seeds for the current season's crops are always available from Pierre's and JojaMart, and the Travelling Cart has been known to offer different seeds at different times (though for very different prices). Once your farming skills have truly matured, you'll even be able to produce your own seeds from harvested fruits and vegetables using the Seed Maker!

CROP GRADING

QUALITIES

GOOD   BETTER   BEST!

BASE QUALITY   SILVER STAR   GOLD STAR
(NO STAR)

Every crop has a star rating based on its quality.
This rating determines the item's sale price, and even its nutritional yield! Refer to the chart below to determine the values for each.

SALE PRICES

 No STAR
base price
x 1
100g

 SILVER STAR
base price
x 1.25
125g

GOLD STAR
base price
x 1.5
150g

HEALTH BENEFITS

 No STAR
base value
x 1

ENERGY: 50
HEALTH: 22

 SILVER STAR
base value
x 1.4

ENERGY: 70
HEALTH: 31

 GOLD STAR
base value
x 1.8

ENERGY: 90
HEALTH: 40

Wine, Beer, Pale Ale, Mead, Cheese, tree fruit, animal products and other items can potentially carry an Iridium star rating. This doubles the base price!

Special Crops

SWEET GEM BERRY   **COFFEE BEAN**   **ANCIENT FRUIT**

WILD SEEDS   **RICE SHOOT**   **MIXED SEEDS**

Sweet Gem Berry seeds are called "Rare Seeds" and can be purchased from the Travelling Cart, usually for 1,000g. They grow in fall and take 24 days to harvest.

Ancient Seeds are found in the Mines as a rare drop from various bugs. If you donate an Ancient Seed to the Museum, Gunther will teach you the secrets to planting these seeds to grow your very own Ancient Fruit plants. They grow from spring to fall and take 28 days to initially harvest, and then will continue to produce every 7 days.

Coffee Beans can be purchased from the Travelling Cart for 2,500g and are sometimes dropped in the Mines by Dust Sprites. Their growing season lasts from spring to summer. They take 10 days to initially harvest, and then will produce at least 4 beans every 2 days. Put 5 beans in your Keg for fresh Coffee!

Wild Seeds grow into seasonal forageables in a week's time.

Rice Shoots produce Unmilled Rice. Plant them within 3 spaces of a body of water and they'll be naturally irrigated, saving you the hassle of watering. Rice Shoots that are irrigated will fully grow in 6 days, while conventionally-watered Rice Shoots require 8 days to grow. They're a nice low-maintenance crop for Riverland Farms!

Mixed Seeds are found while clearing out your farm with the Scythe; occasionally your Seed Maker will produce them as well. If you plant Mixed Seeds outdoors, they will grow into one of the crops for the current growing season. If you plant them in the Greenhouse, they can grow into any normal crop.

SPRING

SPRING 13 : EGG FESTIVAL
SPRING 24 : FLOWER DANCE

1	2	3	4	5	6	7
8	9	10	11	12	13	14
15 *Salmonberry season 15-18*	16	17	18	19	20	21
22	23	24	25	26	27	28

Spring is a time for new beginnings, when color returns to the land. Race to find the most eggs at the Egg Festival, and maybe even charm a lucky lady or gent at the Flower Dance.

FISH

Anchovy	Halibut	Sardine
Bream	Herring	Scorpion Carp
Bullhead	Ice Pip	Shad
Carp	L.mouth Bass	S.mouth Bass
Catfish	Lava Eel	Stonefish
Chub	Legend*	Sunfish
Eel	Mutant Carp*	Void Salmon
Flounder	Sandfish	Woodskip
Ghostfish		

CAULIFLOWER
12 days
80g 175g

COFFEE
10 days;
2 days
15g
SUMMER,
TOO!

GARLIC
4 days
yr 2
40g 60g

KALE
6 days
70g 110g

PARSNIP
4 days
20g 35g

RHUBARB
13 days
OASIS 100g 220g

POTATO
6 days
50g 80g

UNMILLED
RICE
6-8 days
30g

GREEN BEAN
10 days; 3 days
60g 40g

STRAWBERRY
8 days; 4 days
EGG FEST 100g 120g

APRICOT
Tree fruit
50g

CHERRY
80g

TULIP
6 days
20g 30g

BLUE JAZZ
7 days
30g 50g

WILD HORSERADISH
50g

MOREL
Secret woods
150g

COMMON
MUSHROOM
Secret woods
40g

DANDELION
40g

LEEK
60g

DAFFODIL
30g

SALMON BERRY
in bushes
Spring 15-18
5g

SPRING ONION
Cindersap forest
8g

85

SUMMER

SUMMER 11: the LUAU
SUMMER 28: DANCE OF THE MOONLIGHT JELLIES

1	2	3	4	5	6	7
8	9	10	11	12	13	14
15	16	17	18	19	20	21
22	23	24	25	26	27	28

Summer is an important season for farmers, but watch out for thunderstorms. Impress the Governor with the best soup ever at the Luau, and witness the mysterious spectacle that is the Dance of the Moonlight Jellies.

— F I S H —

Bream	Ghostfish	Pufferfish	Sturgeon
Bullhead	Halibut	Rainbow Trout	Sunfish
Carp	Ice Pip	Red Mullet	Super Cucumber
Catfish *Secret Woods	L..mouth Bass	Red Snapper	Tilapia
Chub	Lava Eel	Sandfish	Tuna
Crimsonfish*	Mutant Carp*	Scorpion Carp	Void Salmon
Dorado	Octopus	Shad	Woodskip
Flounder	Pike	Stonefish	

BLUEBERRY 80g 50g
13 days; 4 days

CORN 150g 50g
14 days; 4 days
and into FALL

RADISH 40g 90g
6 days

HOPS 60g 25g
11 days; every day

MELON 80g 250g
12 days

HOT PEPPER 40 40g
5 days; 3 days

STARFRUIT OASIS #400g 750g
NOT A STAR-DROP!
13 days

RED CABBAGE →Year 2 100 260g
9 days

TOMATO 50g 60g
11 days; 4 days

WHEAT 10g 25g
4 days

COFFEE 15g
10 days; 2 days

ORANGE 100g

PEACH 140g

POPPY 100g 140g
7 days

SUNFLOWER 200g 80g
8 days

SUMMER SPANGLE 50g 90g
8 days

SPICE BERRY 80g

RED MUSHROOM 75g
Secret woods,
The Mines

SWEET PEA 50g

GRAPE 80g

FIDDLEHEAD FERN 90g
Secret woods

87

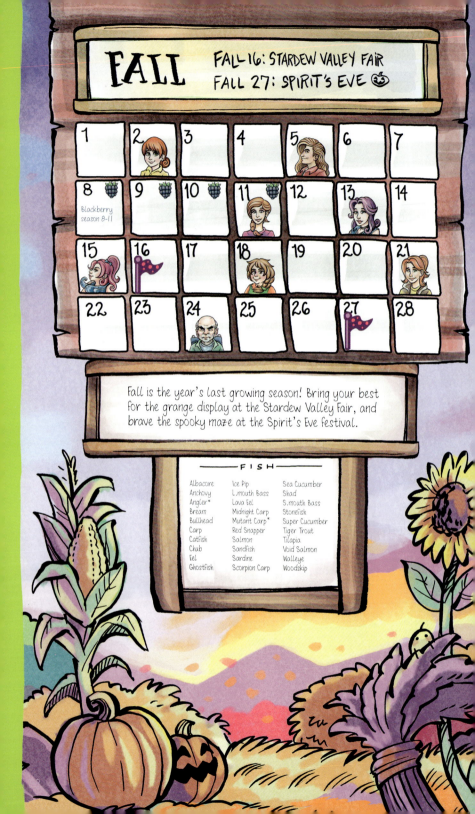

AMARANTH
7 days

ARTICHOKE
8 days

BEET
6 days

BOK CHOY
4 days

GRAPE
10 days; 3 days

EGGPLANT
5 days; 5 days

PUMPKIN
13 days

CORN
14 days; 4 days

YAM
10 days

CRANBERRIES
7 days; 5 days

FAIRY ROSE
12 days

SUNFLOWER
8 days

POMEGRANATE

CHANTERELLE
Secret woods

HAZELNUT
look near the bus stop!

BLACKBERRY
Shake their bushes!

APPLE

COMMON MUSHROOM

WILD PLUM

89

There are actually no crops that can grow outside on your farm during the winter, other than the normal forageable Winter Seeds. You can use this time to prepare for spring!

 Keep the Hoe with you and till the ground where you see worm activity!
...Or are those things stems?
You'll unearth a lot of artifacts for the Museum this way.
...Hmm, maybe they're actually roots?

 Hit the Mines hard! It's best to go on days when your luck is good, so be sure to watch the Fortune Teller on TV.

 Socialize! Winter's a great season for gift-giving.

 Visit Clint and get those tools upgraded!
The Watering Can is an especially good choice to upgrade since you won't need to water any crops.

CROCUS 60g

SNOW YAM 100g

HOLLY 80g

WINTER ROOT 70g

CRYSTAL FRUIT 150g

Trees

Maple, oak and pine trees grow in abundance in the valley. Each produces a valuable substance that can be harvested using a Tapper; these substances are important ingredients in the crafting of artisan goods-producing equipment and other items.

Some trees outside your farm can be cut down and harvested for their materials. They will start regrowing the next day if you cut them down completely—stump and all.

MAPLE

Its leaves are larger than oak tree leaves. Turns a lovely shade of magenta in the fall. Loses its leaves in winter.

When tapped, maple trees produce Maple Syrup every 7 to 8 days.

OAK

Its leaves are smaller and more dense than maple tree leaves. Turns a lovely shade of orange in the fall. Loses its leaves in winter.

When tapped, oak trees produce Oak Resin every 6 to 7 days.

PINE

This coniferous tree looks the same year-round, though it's covered with snow in the winter.

When tapped, pine trees produce Pine Tar every 4 to 5 days.

MAHOGANY TREE

Mahogany Seeds can be found by chopping large stumps or logs, and from Slimes in the Secret Woods. Mahogany Seeds grow into Mahogany Trees, a renewable source of Hardwood!

When tapped, Mahogany Trees provide sap daily.

BIG MUSHROOM TREE

These rare trees grow from the elusive Mushroom Tree Seed, though they can occur randomly. They spread naturally like other trees.

When tapped, Big Mushroom Trees will produce Common, Purple and Red Mushrooms over time.

FRUIT TREES

After a sapling is planted, it will grow into a fully developed fruit tree in 28 days. Once matured, it will produce one fruit per day during its growing season.

Fruit tree saplings only grow in the center of a 3×3 square, planted in untilled soil, and require no water. Fruit trees produce higher quality fruit as they age— once star rank per year—up to Iridium-star quality.

Trees require a little more room to grow, but you can crowd them with crops once they reach maturity and start fruiting. Since they don't require watering, you can plant saplings and simply ignore them until they're fully grown.

Like crops, fruit trees will grow and produce fruit year-round in the Greenhouse.

SPRING

SUMMER

FALL

FARM BUILDINGS

Farm buildings allow you to raise Chickens, Cows and other animals. Larger buildings can comfortably house more animals and make new types available.

Just remember, your animals need to eat if you want to keep them happy and productive, so make sure you have lots of Hay, especially during the winter!

COOP

Houses 4 Coop-dwelling animals.
Allows you to raise Chickens.

4,000g, 300 Wood, 100 Stone

BIG COOP

Upgrade for Coop.
Houses 8 Coop-dwelling animals.
Comes with an Incubator. Unlocks Ducks.

10,000g, 400 Wood, 150 Stone

DELUXE COOP

Upgrade for Big Coop.
Houses 12 Coop-dwelling animals.
Comes with an auto-feed system.
Unlocks Rabbits.

20,000g, 500 Wood, 200 Stone

SILO

A good first choice for a farm building!
Allows you to cut and store grass for feed.
Holds up to 240 pieces of Hay.

100g, 100 Stone,
10 Clay, 5 Copper Bar

BARN

Houses 4 Barn-dwelling animals.
Allows you to raise Cows.

6,000g , 350 Wood, 150 Stone

BIG BARN

Upgrade for Barn.
Houses 8 Barn-dwelling animals.
Allows animals to give birth.
Unlocks Goats.

12,000g, 450 Wood, 200 Stone

DELUXE BARN

Upgrade for Big Barn.
Houses 12 Barn-dwelling animals.
Comes with an auto-feed system.
Unlocks Sheep and Pigs.

25,000g, 550 Wood, 300 Stone

SLIME HUTCH

Raise up to 20 Slimes.
Fill water troughs and
Slimes will create Slime Balls.

10,000g, 500 Stone, 10 Refined Quartz, 1 Iridium Bar

THEY CAN STILL HURT YOU!
BE CAREFUL!

STABLE

Horses run twice as fast as you, saving time
everywhere you go! Your horse will find its way
back to its Stable should you choose to ditch it.
And it won't even guilt trip you about it.

10,000g, 100 Hardwood, 5 Iron Bar

HORSES LOOK GREAT IN HATS♡

WELL

Provides a convenient place for you to refill your Watering Can.

1,000g, 75 Stone

MILL

Processes Wheat into Wheat Flour, Beets into Sugar and Unmilled Rice into Rice overnight.
One harvested Wheat yields one Wheat Flour.
One Beet yields three Sugars.
One Unmilled Rice yields one bag of Rice.

2,500g, 150 Wood, 50 Stone, 4 Cloth

FEWER TRIPS TO PIERRE'S FOR GROCERIES!

SHED

An empty room that can be filled with whatever you like. It can also be decorated in the same way as your home.

15,000g, 300 Wood

BIG SHED

An upgraded Shed with double the space of a normal Shed. This extra large room can be filled with whatever you like and decorated to your heart's content. Twice the space means twice the possibilities!

20,000g, 550 Wood, 300 Stone

FISH POND

Allows you to raise fish and harvest their products. Fish multiply over time, and will occasionally ask for different items to make them more comfortable in their new home. Most fish produce Roe along with other items.

5,000g, 200 Stone, 5 Seaweed, 5 Green Algae

CABIN

| 100g, 5 Wood, 10 Fiber | 100g, 10 Wood | 100g, 10 Stone |

Your farm can comfortably accommodate up to three additional cabins, allowing you to invite friends to help revitalize the land! Cabins require no build time, so your friends can move in right away!

SHIPPING BIN

Additional Shipping Bins for your (and your friends') convenience! Requires no build time, so it's ready to use immediately.

250g, 150 Wood

FARM BUILDINGS
of Arcane Origin

Once Wizard catches wind of your deeds throughout the community, he may see fit to charge you with a most dangerous task: retrieving a bottle of Magic Ink. Succeed in this task, and he'll gladly summon magical structures for you.

Unlike Robin, who has to sweat and labor for days, Wizard can simply materialize an arcane building with a flick of the pen. The structures summoned by Wizard all have strange connections to other planes of existence, with unique powers and benefits unlike anything found in a "normal" farm building.

JUNIMO HUT

An enchanted hut that makes Junimos feel right at home on your farm! Each hut houses three Junimos, giving them a comfortable place to live once the Community Center is rebuilt.

Each morning, the Junimos will repay your kindness by wandering the fields, harvesting any nearby crops that are ready. The items they harvest will be placed in a bag beside the hut for you to grab at your leisure. Place a gem in the bag to change the Junimos' color!

20,000g, 200 Stone, 9 Starfruit, 100 Fiber

GOLD CLOCK

Grants fences immunity from the ravages of time, meaning they'll never need replaced. Pesky weeds, twigs and stones will no longer appear on your farm.

10,000,000g

EARTH OBELISK

An interdimensional tether to the statue in the Mountains enabling instant travel. Similar to the Mountain Warp Totem, but a permanent structure.

500,000g, 10 Iridium Bar, 10 Earth Crystal

WATER OBELISK

An interdimensional tether to the statue on the beach enabling instant travel. Similar to the Beach Warp Totem, but a permanent structure.

500,000g, 5 Iridium Bar, 10 Clam, 10 Coral

DESERT OBELISK

An interdimensional tether to the statue in the Calico Desert enabling instant travel. Similar to the Desert Warp Totem, but a permanent structure.

1,000,000g, 20 Iridium Bar, 10 Coconut, 10 Cactus Fruit

FARM ANIMALS

Happy animals produce larger, higher-quality products! Make your animals happy by petting them every day, letting them outside to graze in nice weather, keeping them warm in the winter and putting out Hay to keep them well-fed.

Happy Cows and Goats produce more Milk, which translates to Gold-star quality Cheeses. Happy Chickens lay larger Eggs, which can be made into higher-quality Mayonnaise.

BUK-BUK!

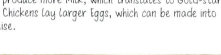

CHICKEN

BUY FOR 800g

Brown Chickens lay brown Eggs, while white Chickens lay white Eggs. When purchasing a Chicken from Marnie, its color will be revealed before you place it in its Coop, allowing you to effectively choose your Chicken color.

BAWK!

SMALL: 50g → 190g

LARGE: 95g

→ 285g

CLUCK!

VOID CHICKEN

NOT FOR SALE

A stark black Chicken with red eyes that lays mysterious spotted Void Eggs.

It has been said that Void Chickens and their Eggs are the product of an angry witch's curse.

HOW TO GET ONE: IF YOU FIND A VOID EGG, INCUBATE IT!
Krobus sells them!

VOID EGGS ARE TREASURED IN SOME CULTURES!

65g →

VOID MAYONNAISE!

275g

BUH...

BLUE CHICKEN

BUY FOR 800g
AFTER 8 HEARTS W/ SHANE

Like white Chickens, blue Chickens lay white Eggs. Once you've become close enough with Shane, each Egg placed in an Incubator has a 25% chance of hatching a Blue Chicken.

SMALL: 50g → 190g   LARGE: 95g → 285g

QUACK!!

DUCK

BUY FOR 1,200g

Lays Duck Eggs every other day, and will occasionally drop a beautiful feather.

← Seems to fit in the chest in the back room of the Saloon...

250g   95g →   375g

RABBIT

BUY FOR 8,000g

Rabbits can shed Wool daily, and sometimes extra feet. It's probably best not to ask.

WOOL BECOMES CLOTH IN LOOM

UNIVERSAL LOVE
565g   340g   470g

DINOSAUR

NOT FOR SALE

If you dig up a Dinosaur Egg, place it in an Incubator to hatch your very own Dinosaur! Produces another fresh Dinosaur Egg once a week.

TIP:
Don't donate your first dinosaur egg to the museum!

DINOSAUR MAYONNAISE!

350g   800g

IT IS RUMORED THAT FARMERS WHO ACHIEVE "PERFECTION" CAN OBTAIN A SPECIAL CHICKEN EGG

COW
BUY FOR 1,950g

Both brown and white Cows produce the same kind of Milk. Each cow can produce a bottle's worth of milk per day, and will sometimes produce enough to fill a large bottle when happy and well cared for.

125 g → 230 g   190 g → 345 g

GOAT
BUY FOR 4,000g

Produces a bottle's worth of fresh, tangy, delicious Goat Milk every two days. Sometimes, if they're especially happy, they'll produce a large bottle!

225 g → 400 g   345 g → 600 g

SHEEP
BUY FOR 8,000g

Their Wool is harvested with the Shears. It grows back within a few days, if not sooner.

WOOL BECOMES CLOTH IN LOOM

340 g → 470 g

PIG
BUY FOR 16,000g

If full-grown Pigs are let outdoors, they'll sniff around and dig up Truffles (but not in winter; they can't smell through the snow).

TRUFFLES CAN BE TURNED INTO TRUFFLE OIL WITH THE OIL MAKER

625 g → 1,065g

FISH

STOCK IN YOUR FISH POND

Fish multiply over time when placed in a Fish Pond, periodically producing Roe. Roe can be aged in Preserves Jars to create Aged Roe and Caviar. Fish occasionally produce other items besides Roe as well.

SQUID INK!
GOOD FOR DYEING

SLIME

HATCH A SLIME EGG IN AN INCUBATOR

With the right equipment and a little know-how, wild Slimes can be raised right on your farm! By hatching Slime Eggs in a Slime Incubator, up to 20 Slimes can be raised in a Slime Hutch (or even more outdoors).

Just be careful: they're still wild, and they can still hurt you if you're not properly equipped.

SLIMES MATE AND PRODUCE ... SLIME BALLS!

THESE BURST INTO MANY GLOBS OF SLIME (SAME AS MONSTER LOOT)

PUT 100 GLOBS INTO A SLIME EGG PRESS

1 SLIME EGG, RANDOM COLOR

SELL OR HATCH!

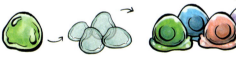

Slimes of all colors produce Slime Balls when given water in a Slime Hutch. The globs of slime contained within can be pressed into Slime Eggs using a Slime Egg-Press.

SLIME BALL

SLIME GLOBS

SLIME EGGS

CAN'T SELL

5g

1,000g

1,750g

2,500g

5,000g

103

RAISING ANIMALS

If you want to keep your animals happy and productive in the winter, make sure they're well fed and warm. Marnie can provide you with a Heater for each of your buildings for 2,000g; one Heater per building is all you need.

You can also purchase Hay from Marnie to feed your animals, but it's more economically sound to make your own by cutting grass with your Scythe and storing it in a Silo.

It certainly can't hurt to have a fully-stocked Silo ready to go before constructing any other buildings.

If you've taken in a dog or a cat, you won't need to do much to take care of it. Pets are self-sufficient, so all you'll have to do is just pay it a little attention each day and it'll be perfectly happy.

Likewise, once you've arranged for Robin to build a Stable, your new horse will be able to fend for itself with no problem. It'll even find its way back home at night if you accidentally leave it behind while exploring, as long as it has a Stable to return to!

OTHER TOOLS

SCYTHE

Used to clear fields,
cut grass and bushes,
and harvest some crops

SHEARS

Harvest Wool from Sheep
(not needed for Rabbits)

MILK PAIL

Collects Milk
from Cows and
Goats

HEATER

Keeps your farm
animals happy
during the winter

INCUBATOR

Found in Big or Deluxe Coops,
used to hatch Eggs

AUTOGRABBER

Automatically harvests milk
and other products from
Barn & Coop animals

Deluxe Coops and Barns feature an automatic feeding system which distributes Hay from Silos; it's still up to you to keep them stocked, though! Remember, grass doesn't grow in winter, so make sure your Silos are full by the end of fall.

And when there's plenty of grass growing, you can place fences around your buildings to keep the animals contained in areas where they can get their fill without wandering off.

All animals will return to their Coops and Barns to roost at 5pm, and will start drifting off to sleep around 8pm. Just be careful not to close the doors before they've all come in for the night; there are hungry wolves and other creatures out there that would love a fresh meal!

ARTISAN GOODS

Artisan goods are an excellent way to take your farming and earnings one step further. By using the skills and crafting recipes you've learned—and maybe a Bundle reward or two—you can create a number of exquisite products that fetch a nice price and make excellent gifts.

Brew some humble Hops into a refreshing batch of Pale Ale, or a bundle of Wheat into a stout Beer. Eggs and Milk are transformed into Mayonnaise and Cheese with just a bit of patience and the right equipment.

Since the quality of the crops used doesn't affect the quality of the end product, base-quality crops are ideal for artisan goods.

TAPPER FORAGING LVL 3

TAP A PINE TREE
PINE TAR
4-5 DAYS
100g

TAP AN OAK TREE
OAK RESIN
6-7 DAYS
150g

TAP A MAPLE TREE
MAPLE SYRUP
7-8 DAYS
200g

PUT YOUR TREES TO WORK!

LOOM FARMING LVL 7

SHEEP OR RABBIT WOOL 340g
4 HOURS

CLOTH 470g

OIL MAKER FARMING LVL 8

OIL
80g 50g
2 DAYS
100g

TRUFFLE OIL
625g
5-6 HOURS
1,065g

PRESERVES JAR FARMING LVL 4

JELLY

ANY FRUIT   NO SWEET GEM BERRY

~2 DAYS

FRUIT'S BASE VALUE ×2 +50g   60-1,550g

GREAT FOR BASE-QUALITY (NO STAR) CROPS AND FRUIT FORAGEABLES

PICKLES

ANY VEGETABLE   +TEA LEAVES   NO FORAGEABLES

~2 DAYS

VEGETABLE'S BASE VALUE ×2 +50g   100-570g

AGED FISH ROE

ANY FISH ROE

FISH'S BASE VALUE +60g

~3 DAYS   90-760g

ADD FISH ROE FROM FISH PONDS TO YOUR PRESERVES JARS

CAVIAR

STURGEON ROE

~4 DAYS   500g

MAYONNAISE MACHINE   FARMING LVL 2

ALL MAYONNAISE TAKES ~3 HOURS

MAYONNAISE	GOLD STAR MAYONNAISE LARGE EGGS	DUCK MAYONNAISE	VOID MAYONNAISE	DINOSAUR MAYONNAISE
50g	95g	95g	65g	350g
190g	285g	375g	275g	800g

BEE HOUSE   FARMING LVL 3

Bees won't produce honey in the Greenhouse

ALL HONEY TAKES 3~4 DAYS

When placed near a blooming flower, the bees will make unique, more valuable honey.

BASIC WILD HONEY	TULIP HONEY	BLUE JAZZ HONEY	SUNFLOWER HONEY	SUMMER SPANGLE HONEY	POPPY HONEY	FAIRY ROSE HONEY
NO NEARBY FLOWERS						
100g	160g	200g	260g	280g	380g	680g

BEE HOUSE

FLOWER

RANGE

CLOSEST FLOWER TAKES PRIORITY. AT EQUAL DISTANCE, MOST EXPENSIVE FLOWER TAKES PRIORITY.

CHEESE PRESS — FARMING LVL 8

Cheese takes ~3 HOURS

LARGE MILK WILL PRODUCE CHEESE of GOLD STAR quality

125g → 230g

190g → 345g ⭐

225g → 400g

345g → 600g ⭐

KEG — FARMING LVL 8

BEER

25g
1~2 DAYS
200g

PALE ALE

25g
1~2 DAYS
300g

GREEN TEA

50g
3hrs
100g

COFFEE!

Keg-brewed for that extra KICK!

15g EACH BEAN — FIVE BEANS EQUAL ONE CUP

2 hrs
150g

WINE

FRUIT of CHOICE
~7 DAYS
3x FRUIT's BASE VALUE

JUICE

VEGETABLE of CHOICE
~4 DAYS
2.25 x VEGETABLE's BASE VALUE

MEAD

HONEY
< 1 DAY
200g

AGING IN CASKS

 CASKS CAN ELEVATE PRODUCTS TO IRIDIUM STAR QUALITY!

CHEESE and GOAT CHEESE

3 DAYS   4 DAYS   7 DAYS

PALE ALE

7 DAYS   7 DAYS   14 DAYS

BEER

7 DAYS   7 DAYS   14 DAYS

MEAD

7 DAYS   7 DAYS   14 DAYS

WINE

14 DAYS   14 DAYS   28 DAYS

BASE VALUE | BASE VALUE x1.25 | BASE VALUE x1.5 | BASE VALUE x2

GIANT CROPS

According to rumors, if you plant a lot of certain types of crops close together, say in a 3x3 grid, there's a chance that those crops will grow together into a monstrous Giant Crop, yielding double the produce. No one can say for sure what causes this phenomenon, which has so far been reported with Cauliflower, Melons and Pumpkins.

If one of these enormous crops turns up in your fields, you'd better have an Axe handy; the only way you're going to be able to harvest something of this size is in pieces!

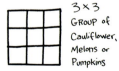

3 x 3
GROUP of
Cauliflower,
Melons or
Pumpkins

GREENHOUSE

As thanks for completing all of the Bundles in the Community Center's Pantry, the Junimos will repair the run-down Greenhouse on your farm. Once the Greenhouse is fully operational, crops and trees will grow inside year-round, unaffected by the changing of the seasons.

Crows don't know how to open doors (yet), so Scarecrows aren't necessary in the Greenhouse.

It doesn't look like it would be possible, but fruit trees can actually grow around the edge of the Greenhouse!

Crops will still need to be watered daily, but clever placement of Sprinklers can alleviate that problem, making the Greenhouse a veritable treasure trove of fruits and veggies.

IRIDIUM SPRINKLER PLACEMENT

FARM TIPS

PROCESS IT!

SHIP IT!

Producing artisan goods from crops is a great way to maximize your farm's income, but the quality of the product isn't dependent on the quality of the crop. So in general, it's best to only process normal-quality crops while simply shipping high-quality ones.

Keg products are worth more than Jellies and Pickles, but take longer to produce. And Cask-aged products require more time still. If you can keep your Kegs and Preserves Jars working all the time, though, you'll be practically sitting on a gold mine!

Any crop or tree will grow and bear fruit any time of year in the Greenhouse, and crops that produce multiple harvests will continue to do so year-round. So you'll have a steady supply of Hot Peppers, Corn, Tomatoes and even Ancient Fruit! Pickles, Jellies, Juices and Wines from these crops turn a handsome profit, and they also make wonderful gifts.

Amazingly, farm buildings are larger on the inside, so they can be a useful way to pack more equipment into a smaller space. Crops and trees certainly won't grow inside, but Kegs, Looms, Preserves Jars, Cheese Presses and all other manners of artisan goods-producing equipment work beautifully.

If you find yourself short on equipment with an overabundance of items that need processing, you can craft a storage Chest near the relevant tools or devices. For example, a Chest full of the trash you find could be placed next to the Recycler for quick access.

You can even place Chests outside your farm; just be sure not to potentially put a Chest in a villager's path, or you may find its contents spilled out everywhere!

One point that's easy to forget: you can pick up and move a Chest after you initially place it, but the Chest must be emptied first.

Once you become well acquainted with Caroline, she'll be happy to share her passion for Green Tea with you. Tea Saplings can be crafted from common materials: just 2 Wild Seeds (any season), 5 Fiber and 5 Wood. They take 20 days to grow, and can grow outside any time of year, with no need to water.

Tea Bushes are rigid and woody, so you can't walk through them the way you can with other crops. Plant them in rows for a beautiful natural barrier, as an alternative to fences.

Try planting Tea Saplings at the very start of Spring, and enjoy three weeks of harvests—21 Tea Leaves in total—from Spring through Fall. Alternatively, you can plant Tea Saplings in the Greenhouse or in Garden Pots for a bounty of Tea Leaves in all four seasons. And if you don't want to plant your own Tea Bushes but still have a need for some Tea Leaves, you're free to visit Caroline's sunroom to take one each day when they're in season.

Put one Tea Leaves in a Keg to produce one cup of Green Tea. It makes a fine gift for most villagers; kids might be too young to appreciate the subtle taste, but every grown-up likes or loves Green Tea!

Chapter 4
Crafting & Cooking

As your farm begins to thrive, you'll likely find yourself in the market for machinery to process raw animal products and fertilizer to improve the quality of your produce. Though some supplies and equipment are available from Pierre's General Store and elsewhere, there are some things you'll just have to build yourself. A number of crafting recipes, especially for decorative items, must be purchased from Robin. Others are learned as you gain levels in related Skills.

In addition, once your house has been upgraded with a kitchen, you'll be able to prepare home-cooked meals using recipes received from friends or learned from episodes of the Queen of Sauce television show. Gus is willing to sell you a few of his tried and true recipes as well.

The Wonders of Crafting

Throughout your farming career, you'll learn how to craft an enormous variety of furniture pieces, machinery and other objects. Some items are purely decorative and used to spruce up your home, but others are crucial to the continued success of your farm.

Machines like the Loom, Cheese Press and Keg can transform ordinary farm products into fancier and more valuable artisan goods for healthy profits, while Braziers and Lamp-posts provide light to your fields into the night.

And don't forget about the supremely handy Chest: for a mere 50 pieces of Wood, it will safely store 36 types of item, and up to 999 units of each type. And you can make as many as you want or need!

For those who can't get enough crafting, a Workbench is an absolute must. Available from Robin for just 2,000g, a Workbench allows you to use materials stored in adjacent Chests in your crafting projects. Never again will you be caught walking around with a backpack stuffed full of odds and ends: you can store everything you need nearby and have all of your crafting materials within arm's reach!

CRAFTING

You'll likely make a lot of these!

Tip: Chests can be picked up ONLY when empty

20 color variations!

CHEST
50 WOOD

Fencing keeps grass and animals contained! They wear out over time.

OK

WOOD FENCE
2 WOOD

LASTS 44-66 DAYS

GOOD

STONE FENCE
2 STONE

FARMING LVL 2

LASTS 110-132 DAYS

BETTER

IRON FENCE x10
1 IRON BAR

FARMING LVL 4

LASTS 240-264 DAYS

BEST!

HARDWOOD FENCE
1 HARDWOOD

FARMING LVL 6

LASTS 520-600 DAYS

Lets you pass through a fence

GATE
10 WOOD

LASTS 100 DAYS

SPOOOOKY

WICKED STATUE
25 STONE, 5 COAL

PURCHASE the RECIPE FROM A FRIENDLY SEWER-DWELLER

JACK-O-LANTERN
1 PUMPKIN, 1 TORCH

BUY the RECIPE on SPIRIT'S EVE

TUB O' FLOWERS
15 WOOD, TULIP SEED, BLUE JAZZ SEED, POPPY SEED, SUMMER SPANGLE SEED

BUY the RECIPE at the FLOWER DANCE

PLAYS A DRUM SOUND AS YOU PASS

DRUM BLOCK
10 STONE, 2 COPPER ORE, 20 FIBER

ROBIN'S 6-HEART EVENT

FLUTE BLOCK
10 WOOD, 2 COPPER ORE, 20 FIBER

ROBIN'S 6-HEART EVENT

PLAYS A FLUTE WHISTLE AS YOU PASS ♪

WOOD PATH

1 WOOD

COBBLESTONE PATH

1 STONE

GRAVEL PATH

1 STONE

WOOD FLOOR

1 WOOD

CARPENTER'S SHOP

STEPPING STONE PATH

1 STONE

CARPENTER'S SHOP

CRYSTAL PATH

1 REFINED QUARTZ

CARPENTER'S SHOP

BRICK FLOOR

5 STONE, 2 CLAY

CARPENTER'S SHOP

STRAW FLOOR

1 WOOD, 1 FIBER

CARPENTER'S SHOP

STONE FLOOR

1 STONE

CARPENTER'S SHOP

STONE WALKWAY FLOOR

1 STONE

CARPENTER'S SHOP

RUSTIC PLANK FLOOR

1 WOOD

CARPENTER'S SHOP

WEATHERED FLOOR

1 WOOD

BUY FROM DWARF

CRYSTAL FLOOR

1 REFINED QUARTZ

BUY FROM KROBUS

WOOD SIGN

25 WOOD

CAN DISPLAY ANY
ITEM ON SIGN

STONE SIGN

25 STONE

CAN DISPLAY ANY
ITEM ON SIGN

DARK SIGN

5 BONE FRAGMENT
5 BAT WING

CAN DISPLAY ANY
ITEM ON SIGN

RECIPE FROM KROBUS, 3 HEARTS

TORCH

1 WOOD, 2 SAP

CAMPFIRE

10 STONE, 10 WOOD, 10 FIBER

WOODEN BRAZIER

10 WOOD, 1 COAL, 5 FIBER

CARPENTER'S SHOP

STONE BRAZIER

10 STONE, 1 COAL, 5 FIBER

CARPENTER'S SHOP

STUMP BRAZIER

5 HARDWOOD, 1 COAL

CARPENTER'S SHOP

BARREL BRAZIER

50 WOOD, 1 COAL
1 SOLAR ESSENCE

CARPENTER'S SHOP

GOLD BRAZIER

1 GOLD BAR, 1 COAL, 5 FIBER

CARPENTER'S SHOP

CARVED BRAZIER

10 HARDWOOD, 1 COAL

CARPENTER'S SHOP

SKULL BRAZIER

10 BONE FRAGMENT

CARPENTER'S SHOP

MARBLE BRAZIER

1 MARBLE, 100 STONE
1 AQUAMARINE

CARPENTER'S SHOP

WOOD LAMP-POST

50 WOOD,
1 BATTERY PACK

CARPENTER'S SHOP

IRON LAMP-POST

1 IRON BAR,
1 BATTERY PACK

CARPENTER'S SHOP

119

ARTISAN GOODS

MAYONNAISE MACHINE

15 WOOD, 15 STONE,
1 EARTH CRYSTAL,
1 COPPER BAR

FARMING LEVEL 2

TURN AN EGG INTO
- MAYONNAISE -
(TRY USING A VOID EGG!)

BEE HOUSE

40 WOOD, 8 COAL,
1 IRON BAR,
1 MAPLE SYRUP

FARMING LEVEL 3

↑ Outdoor only

BEES WILL MAKE HONEY!
(EXCEPT IN THE WINTER)

TAPPER

40 WOOD,
2 COPPER BAR

FORAGING LEVEL 3

TAP NON-FRUIT TREES
AND WAIT SEVERAL DAYS

PRESERVES JAR

50 WOOD,
40 STONE,
8 COAL

FARMING LEVEL 4

TURNS VEGGIES INTO PICKLES
TURNS FRUIT INTO JELLY
GREAT FOR BASE-QUALITY CROPS!

CHEESE PRESS

45 WOOD, 45 STONE,
10 HARDWOOD,
1 COPPER BAR

FARMING LEVEL 6

TURNS MILK INTO CHEESE AND
GOAT MILK INTO GOAT CHEESE

LOOM

60 WOOD
30 FIBER
1 PINE TAR

FARMING LEVEL 7

TURNS WOOL INTO CLOTH

OIL MAKER

50 SLIME,
20 HARDWOOD,
1 GOLD BAR

FARMING LEVEL 8

TURNS TRUFFLES INTO TRUFFLE OIL,
TURNS CORN, SUNFLOWERS AND
SUNFLOWER SEEDS INTO OIL.

KEG

30 WOOD,
1 COPPER BAR,
1 IRON BAR,
1 OAK RESIN

FARMING LEVEL 8

WHEAT INTO BEER
HOPS INTO PALE ALE
FRUIT INTO WINE
VEGGIES INTO JUICE

CASK

20 WOOD,
1 HARDWOOD

FINAL HOUSE UPGRADE

ONLY WORKS IN THE CELLAR

AGES WINE, BEER, PALE ALE,
MEAD and CHEESE, INCREASING
THEIR QUALITY and VALUE

MAKERS

SEED MAKER

25 WOOD,
10 COAL,
1 GOLD BAR

FARMING LEVEL 9

PLACE A CROP INSIDE AND IT
WILL PRODUCE 1 to 3 SEEDS.
(WON'T WORK ON TREE FRUIT
OR MOST FORAGEABLES)

CHARCOAL KILN

20 WOOD,
2 COPPER BAR

FORAGING LEVEL 4

TURNS 10 WOOD INTO 1 COAL.
COAL IS THE KEY TO SMELTING
METALS INTO USABLE BARS!

FURNACE

20 COPPER ORE
25 STONE

LEARNED FROM CLINT

TURNS 5 ORE INTO A METAL BAR.
EACH BAR REQUIRES 1 COAL.
QUARTZ CAN ALSO BE REFINED.

WORM BIN

25 HARDWOOD,
1 GOLD BAR,
1 IRON BAR,
50 FIBER

FISHING LEVEL 8

IT JUST MAKES WORMS HAPPEN!
PRODUCES BAIT REGULARLY.

RECYCLING MACHINE

25 WOOD,
25 STONE,
1 IRON BAR

FISHING LEVEL 4

TURNS TRASH INTO VALUABLE RESOURCES!
THROW IN TRASH, DRIFTWOOD, SOGGY NEWSPAPER,
BROKEN CDs OR BROKEN GLASSES.

CRYSTALARIUM

99 STONE,
5 GOLD BAR,
2 IRIDIUM BAR,
1 BATTERY PACK

MINING LEVEL 9

Feed me diamonds!

INSERT A GEM AND IT
WILL PRODUCE COPIES!

SLIME EGG-PRESS

25 COAL,
1 FIRE QUARTZ,
1 BATTERY PACK

COMBAT LEVEL 6

SOMEHOW COMPRESSES 100 SLIMES
INTO A SLIME EGG. WOW!

SLIME INCUBATOR

2 IRIDIUM BAR,
100 SLIME

COMBAT LEVEL 8

HATCHES SLIME EGGS INTO SLIMES!
LETS YOU RAISE SLIMES OUTDOORS

SCARECROW

50 WOOD
1 COAL
20 FIBER

FARMING LEVEL 1

PROTECTS 8 TILES
IN EACH DIRECTION
(6 DIAGONAL)
FROM CROWS

DELUXE SCARECROW

50 WOOD
40 FIBER
1 IRIDIUM ORE

COLLECT ALL 8
RARECROWS

PROTECTS 16 TILES
IN EACH DIRECTION!

RAIN TOTEM

1 HARDWOOD
1 TRUFFLE OIL
5 PINE TAR

FORAGING LVL 9

INCREASES CHANCE OF
RAIN NEXT DAY

WARP TOTEM: BEACH

1 HARDWOOD
2 CORAL
10 FIBER

FORAGING LVL 6

WARP TOTEM: MOUNTAINS

1 HARDWOOD
1 IRON BAR
25 STONE

FORAGING LVL 7

WARP TOTEM: FARM

1 HARDWOOD
1 HONEY
20 FIBER

FORAGING LVL 8

WARP TOTEM: DESERT

2 HARDWOOD
1 COCONUT
4 IRIDIUM ORE

DESERT TRADER

SPRINKLER

1 COPPER BAR
1 IRON BAR

FARMING LVL 2

WATERS 4 TILES

QUALITY SPRINKLER

1 IRON BAR
1 GOLD BAR
1 REFINED QUARTZ

FARMING LVL 6

WATERS 8 TILES

IRIDIUM SPRINKLER

1 GOLD BAR
1 IRIDIUM BAR
1 BATTERY PACK

FARMING LVL 9

WATERS 24 TILES

LIGHTNING ROD

1 IRON BAR
1 REFINED QUARTZ
5 BAT WING

FORAGING LVL 6

CREATES A BATTERY PACK
1 DAY AFTER STRUCK
BY LIGHTNING

TRANSMUTE Fe

3 COPPER BAR

MINING LVL 4

TURN COPPER
INTO IRON

TRANSMUTE Au

2 IRON BAR

MINING LVL 7

TURN IRON
INTO GOLD

BASIC FERTILIZER

2 SAP

FARMING LVL 1

~33% NORMAL, ~33% SILVER, ~33% GOLD

QUALITY FERTILIZER

2 SAP
ANY FISH

FARMING LVL 9

~10% NORMAL, ~30% SILVER, ~60% GOLD

TREE FERTILIZER

5 FIBER
5 STONE

FORAGING LVL 7

DOESN'T WORK ON FRUIT TREES

GRASS STARTER

10 FIBER

RECIPE AT PIERRE'S

SPEED-GRO

1 PINE TAR
1 CLAM

FARMING LVL 3

INCREASES GROWTH RATE BY >10%

DELUXE SPEED-GRO

1 OAK RESIN
1 CORAL

FARMING LVL 8

INCREASES GROWTH RATE BY >25%

BASIC RETAINING SOIL

2 STONE

FARMING LVL 4

CHANCE OF STAYING WATERED OVERNIGHT

QUALITY RETAINING SOIL

3 STONE
1 CLAY

FARMING LVL 7

HIGHER CHANCE OF STAYING WATERED OVERNIGHT

 x10   x10   x10   x10

WILD SEEDS
— SPRING —

WILD HORSERADISH
DAFFODIL
LEEK
DANDELION

FORAGING LVL 1

SPRING FORAGEABLES

WILD SEEDS
— SUMMER —

SPICE BERRY
GRAPE
SWEET PEA

FORAGING LVL 4

SUMMER FORAGEABLES

WILD SEEDS
— FALL —

COMMON MUSHROOM
WILD PLUM
HAZELNUT
BLACKBERRY

FORAGING LVL 6

FALL FORAGEABLES

WILD SEEDS
— WINTER —

WINTER ROOT
CRYSTAL FRUIT
SNOW YAM
CROCUS

FORAGING LVL 7

WINTER FORAGEABLES

GARDEN POT

1 CLAY
10 STONE
1 REFINED QUARTZ

RECIPE GIVEN BY EVELYN
AFTER GREENHOUSE REPAIR

 x1

ANCIENT SEED

ANCIENT SEED

DONATE ANCIENT SEED TO MUSEUM

TEA SAPLING

2 WILD SEEDS
5 FIBER
5 WOOD

RECIPE FROM CAROLINE

FIELD SNACK

1 ACORN
1 MAPLE SEED
1 PINE CONE

FORAGING LVl 1

+45 +18

LIFE ELIXIR

1 RED MUSHROOM
1 PURPLE MUSHROOM
1 MOREL
1 CHANTERELLE

COMBAT LVL 2

+200 +80

OIL of GARLIC

10 GARLIC
1 OIL

COMBAT LVL 6

MONSTERS AVOID YOU

STAIRCASE

99 STONE

MINING LVL 2

MOVE TO NEXT FLOOR

COOKOUT KIT

15 WOOD
10 FIBER
3 COAL

FORAGING LVL 9

COOK ON-THE-GO!

BUG STEAK

10 BUG MEAT

COMBAT LVL 1

+45 +20

CHERRY BOMB

4 COPPER ORE
1 COAL

MINING LVL 1

RADIUS OF 3 TILES

BOMB

4 IRON ORE
1 COAL

MINING LVL 6

RADIUS OF 5 TILES

EXPLOSIVE AMMO

1 IRON BAR
2 COAL

COMBAT LVL 8

SLINGSHOT ITEM
RADIUS OF 3 TILES

MEGA BOMB

4 GOLD ORE
1 SOLAR ESSENCE
1 VOID ESSENCE

MINING LVL 8

RADIUS OF 6-8 TILE

STURDY RING

2 COPPER BAR
25 BUG MEAT
25 SLIME

COMBAT LVL 1

WARRIOR RING

10 IRON BAR
25 COAL
10 FROZEN TEAR

COMBAT LVL 4

RING of YOBA

5 GOLD BAR
5 IRON BAR
1 DIAMOND

COMBAT LVL 7

IRIDIUM BAND

5 IRIDIUM BAR
50 SOLAR ESSENCE
50 VOID ESSENCE

COMBAT LVL 9

WEDDING RING

5 IRIDIUM BAR
1 PRISMATIC SHARD

TRAVELLING CART

GLOWSTONE RING

5 SOLAR ESSENCE
5 IRON BAR

MINING LVL 4

THORNS RING

50 BONE FRAGMENT
50 STONE
1 GOLD BAR

COMBAT LVL 7

CRAB POT
40 WOOD
3 IRON BAR

FISHING LVL 3

(WITH **TRAPPER** PROFESSION:
25 WOOD, 2 COPPER BAR)

BARBED HOOK
1 COPPER BAR
1 IRON BAR
1 GOLD BAR

FISHING LVL 8

x5

BAIT
1 BUG MEAT

FISHING LVL 2

x5

WILD BAIT
10 FIBER
5 BUG MEAT
5 SLIME

LINUS FRIENDSHIP EVENT

x3

MAGNET
1 IRON BAR

FISHING LVL 9

CORK BOBBER
10 WOOD
5 HARDWOOD
10 SLIME

FISHING LVL 7

TRAP BOBBER
1 COPPER BAR
10 SAP

FISHING LVL 6

TREASURE HUNTER
2 GOLD BAR

FISHING LVL 7

SPINNER
2 IRON BAR

FISHING LVL 6

DRESSED SPINNER
2 IRON BAR
1 CLOTH

FISHING LVL 8

SOLAR PANEL
10 REFINED QUARTZ
5 IRON BAR
5 GOLD BAR

CAROLINE SP. ORDER

FARM COMPUTER
1 DWARF GADGET
1 BATTERY PACK
10 REFINED QUARTZ

DEMETRIUS SP. ORDER

BONE MILL
10 BONE FRAGMENT
3 CLAY
20 STONE

GUNTHER SP. ORDER

GEODE CRUSHER
2 GOLD BAR
50 STONE
1 DIAMOND

CLINT SP. ORDER

STONE CHEST
50 STONE

ROBIN SP. ORDER

MINI OBELISK
30 HARDWOOD
20 SOLAR ESSENCE
3 GOLD BAR

WIZARD SP. ORDER

QUALITY BOBBER
1 COPPER BAR
20 SAP
5 SOLAR ESSENCE

WILLY SP. ORDER

FIBER SEEDS
1 MIXED SEEDS
5 SAP
1 CLAY

LINUS SP. ORDER

MONSTER MUSK
30 SLIME
30 BAT WING

WIZARD SP. ORDER

Good Old-Fashioned Home Cookin'

Once Robin has renovated your house and added a kitchen, you'll be able to create wonderful, delicious meals at home. Prepared meals are packed with nutrition, making them invaluable for hard-working farmers, miners and monster slayers alike. Some dishes even grant a temporary boost to skills!

Most villagers have at least one favorite dish, so cooking for your friends is a great way to build relationships. Imagine presenting a friend with their favorite food on their birthday!

Although you can ship prepared food to market, few dishes fetch as much gold as their raw ingredients, so mail order chef probably isn't the best career choice.

Many of the ingredients you'll need will come straight from your farm or from foraging, though others must be bought or made using specialized equipment (such as Cheese, Sugar or Oil). Ingredients stored in your refrigerator will be used automatically, saving precious time.

The more ambitious chef will find the Mini-Fridge a wise investment. Available from Robin for just 3,000g, you can place it anywhere in your Farmhouse (well, anywhere except for the basement) and you'll have access to its contents as well when cooking!

RECIPES

KEY

NAME of FOOD $\rightarrow$
INGREDIENTS $\rightarrow$
+ ENERGY and HEALTH $\rightarrow$
RECIPE SOURCE $\rightarrow$
EXTRA INFO $\rightarrow$

ALGAE SOUP

 ×4

+75   +33

RECIPE FROM CLINT

Kent hates it!

ARTICHOKE DIP

+100   +44

RECIPE FROM TV

Clint loves this!

AUTUMN'S BOUNTY

 YAM

+220   +98

RECIPE FROM DEMETRIUS

+2 FORAGING +2 DEFENSE

BAKED FISH

SUNFISH
BREAM
FLOUR

+75   +33

RECIPE FROM TV

BEAN HOTPOT

 ×2

+125   +56

RECIPE FROM CLINT

Demetrius loves this!
+32 MAGNETISM +30 MAX ENERGY

BLACKBERRY COBBLER

 ×2

+175   +78

RECIPE FROM TV

♡ Abigail loves this ♡

BLUEBERRY TART

+135   +56

RECIPE FROM PIERRE

Linus loves this!

BREAD

+50   +22

RECIPE FROM TV or GUS

Leah hates bread!

127

BRUSCHETTA

+113 +50

RECIPE FROM TV

CARP SURPRISE

 x 4 CARP

+90 +40

RECIPE FROM TV

Everyone likes it except for Leah and Krobus.

CHEESE CAULIFLOWER

+138 +62

RECIPE FROM PAM

♡MARU LOVES THIS!

CHOCOLATE CAKE

+150 +67

RECIPE FROM TV

♡ Abigail, Evelyn & Jodi love IT!

CHOWDER

+225 +101

RECIPE FROM WILLY

+1 FISHING BOOST

COLESLAW

+213 +95

RECIPE FROM TV

Gus hates this.

COMPLETE BREAKFAST

+200 +89

RECIPE FROM TV

ALEX loves this!
+2 FARMING, +50 MAX ENERGY

COOKIES

+90 +40

RECIPE FROM EVELYN

Sometimes found in the garbage can outside Alex's! Evelyn must make too many...

CRAB CAKES

+225 +101

RECIPE FROM TV

+1 SPEED, +1 DEFENSE
Elliott loves them ♡

CRANBERRY CANDY

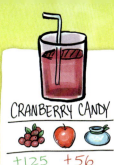

+125 +56

RECIPE FROM TV

CRANBERRY SAUCE

+125 +56

RECIPE FROM GUS

CRISPY BASS

+90 +40

RECIPE FROM KENT

Jodi loves it! +64 MAGNETISM

DISH O' the SEA

 x2

+150 +67

LEARNED AT FISHING LVL 3

Linus loves this dish!
+ 3 FISHING

EGGPLANT PARMESAN

+175 +78

RECIPE FROM LEWIS

+1 MINING, +1 DEFENSE
Jodi loves this!

ESCARGOT

+225 +101

RECIPE FROM WILLY

Gus loves this! +2 FISHING

FARMER'S LUNCH

+200 +89

LEARNED AT FARMING LVL 3

+3 FARMING BOOST
Marnie loves this!

FIDDLEHEAD RISOTTO

+225 +101

RECIPE FROM TV

Clint & Kent love it!

FISH STEW

+225 +101

RECIPE FROM WILLY

+3 FISHING BOOST

FISH TACO

+165 +74

RECIPE FROM LINUS

+ 2 FISHING BOOST
Gus & Caroline love it!

FRIED CALAMARI

+80 +35

RECIPE FROM JODI

PIERRE'S FAVORITE!

FRIED EEL

+75 +33

RECIPE FROM GEORGE

+ 1 LUCK BOOST
Jodi loves this!

FRIED EGG

+50 +20

Used in the Chef's Bundle

A universally neutral dish

FRIED MUSHROOM

+135 +54

RECIPE FROM DEMETRIUS

+2 COMBAT
George loves this!

FRUIT SALAD

+263 +105

RECIPE FROM TV

Haley loves fruit salad ♡

GLAZED YAMS

+200 +80

RECIPE FROM TV

Lewis & Pam love these!

HASHBROWNS

+90 +36

RECIPE FROM TV

+1 FARMING BOOST
PART OF a COMPLETE BREAKFAST!

ICE CREAM

+100 +40

RECIPE FROM JODI

Demetrius loves ice cream!

LOBSTER BISQUE

+225 +90

RECIPE FROM TV + WILLY

+3 FISHING BOOST, +50 MAX ENERGY

LUCKY LUNCH

+100 +40

RECIPE FROM TV

+3 LUCK!

MAKI ROLL

 ANY FISH

+100 +40

RECIPE FROM TV OR GUS

EMILY & EVELYN HATE IT

MAPLE BAR

+225 +90

RECIPE FROM TV

+1 BOOST FARMING+
FOR FISHING+
SAM loves it! MINING+

MINER'S TREAT

×2

+125 +50

MINING LVL 3 RECIPE

+3 MINING +64 MAGNETISM
MARU LOVES THIS!

OMELET

+100 +40

RECIPE FROM TV

Sebastian hates this.

PALE BROTH

×2

+125 +50

RECIPE FROM MARNIE

PANCAKES

+90 +36

RECIPE FROM TV

+2 FORAGING   Jodi loves
BOOST   pancakes

PARSNIP SOUP

+85 +34

RECIPE FROM CAROLINE

PAM loves it! Goes well with beer?

PEPPER POPPERS

+130 +52

RECIPE FROM SHANE

MARU & SHANE LOVE 'EM!
+2 FARMING, +1 SPEED

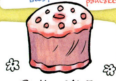

PINK CAKE

+250 +100

RECIPE FROM TV

JAS ♡ VINCENT ♡ HALEY ♡ MARNIE
~ALL LOVE THIS CUTE CAKE~

PIZZA

+150 +60

RECIPE FROM TV

SAM & SHANE LOVE PIZZA!

PLUM PUDDING

 ×2

+175 +70

RECIPE FROM TV

JAS LOVES this!

POPPYSEED MUFFIN

+150 +60

RECIPE FROM TV

Penny & Leah love these~

PUMPKIN PIE ♡

+225 +90

RECIPE FROM TV

MARNIE LOVES PUMPKIN PIE

PUMPKIN SOUP

+200   +89

RECIPE FROM ROBIN

+2 LUCK   +2 DEFENSE
SEBASTIAN LOVES IT.

RADISH SALAD

+200   +89

RECIPE FROM TV

RED PLATE

+240   +107

RECIPE FROM EMILY

Penny loves Red Plate

RHUBARB PIE

+215   +96

RECIPE FROM MARNIE

JODI & MARU LOVE IT!

RICE PUDDING

+115   +51

RECIPE FROM EVELYN

DEMETRIUS LOVES THIS

ROASTED HAZELNUTS

 ×3

+175   +78

RECIPE FROM TV

Kent loves these ♡

ROOTS PLATTER

+125   +56

LEARNED AT COMBAT LVL 3

PENNY LOVES THIS
+3 COMBAT BOOST

SALAD

+113   +50

RECIPE FROM EMILY

LEAH LOVES SALAD!

SALMON DINNER

+125   +56

RECIPE FROM GUS

ALEX LOVES SALMON DINNER
...it's packed with protein!

SASHIMI さしみ

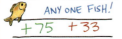 ANY ONE FISH!

+75   +33

RECIPE FROM LINUS

Sebastian loves it.

SEAFOAM PUDDING

+175   +78

+4 FISHING

SHRIMP COCKTAIL

+225   +101

+1 FISHING   +1 LUCK

SPAGHETTI

+75 +33

RECIPE FROM LEWIS

Robin loves spaghetti.

SPICY EEL

+115 +51

RECIPE FROM GEORGE

Abigail loves this!

STIR FRY

+200 +89

RECIPE FROM TV

LEAH LOVES THIS.

STRANGE BUN

+100 +44

RECIPE FROM SHANE

≡ EVERYONE HATES THIS! ≡

FITS IN THE CHEST IN VINCENT'S ROOM...

STUFFING

+170 +76

RECIPE FROM PAM

+2 DEFENSE BOOST   Evelyn loves it!
♡

SUPER MEAL

+160 +71

RECIPE FROM KENT

HARVEY LOVES THIS HEALTHY DISH ♡

SURVIVAL BURGER

+125 +56

FORAGING LVL 2

+3 FORAGING BOOST

Emily loves this burger

TOM KHA SOUP

+175 +78

RECIPE FROM SANDY

+2 FARMING BOOST

ELLIOTT & PENNY LOVE IT!

TORTILLA

+50 +22

RECIPE FROM TV

KENT & PIERRE HATE TORTILLA ☹

TRIPLE SHOT ESPRESSO

☕ ×3

+8 +3

+1 SPEED

TROUT SOUP

+100 +44

RECIPE FROM TV

+1 FISHING BOOST

WILLY SELLS THIS.

VEGETABLE MEDLEY

+165 +74

RECIPE FROM CAROLINE

JODI ♡ LEAH ♡ LEWIS love Vegetable Medley ~

Customize Your Wardrobe

After you've obtained your first piece of Cloth, Emily will stop by the Farmhouse to give you permission to use the sewing and tailoring equipment in her house. Using this equipment, you'll have the ability to tailor an outfit that's perfect for you.

By combining Cloth with other items in the sewing machine, a vast array of different pieces of clothing can be created. Hundreds of clothing options are available, many of them obtainable only via tailoring. Mix and match all of these various apparel options to assemble the outfit that best defines YOU. And of course, you can change up that outfit any way you like at any time.

In addition to the sewing machine, you'll also be able to use Emily's dyeing table to change the colors of any dyeable clothes you're currently wearing. Just remember to bring along plenty of colorful supplies to fill the dye pots.

All of your new clothing can be stored in Dressers; your wardrobe will be automatically sorted into tops, bottoms, hats, footwear and rings, so finding just the right outfit combination will take no time at all!

It's also possible to get your own Sewing Machine that you can put in your home by completing a Special Order from Emily.

You can use the dye pots to customize the colors of everything you're wearing at once. Add an item of each color into the corresponding pot, and once you've filled all six pots, pick the exact colors you want! Not all pieces of clothing can be dyed, though.

TAILORING

Creating new clothing is simple; just place a piece of Cloth (or maybe a secret item) onto the feed, and another item onto the spool, and away you go!

 +  =

Complete an outfit or costume by creating matching parts. With nearly 300 different shirts, pants, skirts and hats available, the customization options are endless!

Do you like the look of one pair of shoes or boots but find their stats lacking? You can easily transfer stats from one piece of footwear to another to create your own custom-tailored shoes and boots!

Chapter 5
Fishing

Stardew Valley is home to a whole host of different types of fish. The freshwater lakes formed by the rivers flowing down from the Mountains create a diverse marine ecosystem, teeming with life. Throughout the year, you'll encounter dozens of aquatic species; some will be easy to catch, while others will require the utmost patience and finesse.

As you hone your fishing skills, you'll learn to use bait and tackle to attract fish more quickly and catch them more easily.

And for the truly adventurous, there have been rumors of a number of incredibly rare fish that have settled in the valley's waters. Truly, they are the stuff of legends; if you can catch any of these fish—or perhaps all of them—you might go down in history as the greatest angler who ever lived!

HOW TO FISH

Cast the line, and when you've got a bite, act fast to keep the fish in your green bar! It takes some practice, but you'll be as good as Willy in no time.

1. CAST the LINE

Healthier, higher-quality fish tend to prefer deeper water, so cast the line as far as you can for the best chance to catch Silver and Gold-quality fish.

2. WAIT for a BITE   *HIT!*

3. REEL it IN!

keep the fish in the green bar to max out the catch bar

— MAX

FISHING BAR →

CATCH BAR

FISH IS CAUGHT WHEN THE METER IS FULL

If you can keep the fish in the green bar and make a perfect catch, you'll get a boost to your fishing experience... and a chance to reel in Iridium-quality fish!

Fish can be found in the ocean as well as in rivers and lakes throughout the valley. Due to variances in salt content, current and other factors, you'll find a different assortment of fish in each body of water. There are even fish that call the Sewers home!

Not all fish are equally easy to catch. Each moves according to one of five unique behavior patterns, along with a general difficulty that dictates the speed and extent of those movements. For example, a 15 Mixed fish should pose no challenge to even novice anglers, while an 85 Dart will give even experts a tough time.

MIXED	SMOOTH	FLOATER	SINKER	DART
BASIC PATTERN	STEADY MOVEMENT	FASTER UPWARD	FASTER DOWNWARD	RANDOM and ERRATIC

Catch treasure!
← APPEARS IN THE FISHING BAR
ITS BAR FILLS AS YOU REEL IT IN.
(YOU MUST ALSO CATCH the FISH!)

If you're having a lucky day, you may encounter a fish that carries a treasure! You'll need to reel in the treasure first and then the fish in order to get both. And remember: no fish, no treasure.

BUBBLY SPOTS
FISH BITE QUICKER HERE!

Bubbling spots on the water's surface indicate places with lots of fish activity that are sure to give you a series of quick bites.

Many fish species migrate as the seasons change, so you'll find different types of fish in the valley's waters during different seasons. In addition, some fish only approach the water's surface when it's raining, and others when it's warm and sunny.

Fish have daily schedules like everyone else, and can only be caught during the hours when they're actively searching for food.

FISHING EQUIPMENT

TRAINING ROD
- ✗ bait
- ✗ tackle

1000g
PURCHASE AT FISH SHOP
EASY FISHING BUT,
- NORMAL QUALITY FISH ONLY
- CATCHES DON'T COUNT AS ACHIEVEMENTS

BAMBOO POLE
- ✗ bait
- ✗ tackle

500g
GIFT FROM WILLY

FIBERGLASS ROD
- ✔ bait
- ✗ tackle

1,800g
PURCHASE AT FISH SHOP AFTER
FISHING LVL 2

IRIDIUM ROD
- ✔ bait
- ✔ tackle

7,500g
PURCHASE AT FISH SHOP AFTER
FISHING LVL 6

CRAB POT

PLACE IN THE WATER

CRAB POT USES BAIT→

CATCHES CERTAIN FISH PASSIVELY

BAIT

MAKES FISH BITE FASTER

WILD BAIT

MORE EFFECTIVE THAN NORMAL BAIT

SPINNER

INCREASES BITE RATE SLIGHTLY

DRESSED SPINNER

INCREASES BITE RATE

MAGNET BAIT

INCREASES RATE OF TREASURE, BUT LOWERS BITE RATE

BARBED HOOK

HELPS YOUR FISHING BAR <u>CLING</u> TO FISH!

TRAP BOBBER

CATCHING BAR DECREASES SLOWER

CORK BOBBER

INCREASES SIZE OF YOUR FISHING BAR

LEAD BOBBER

PREVENTS YOUR FISHING BAR FROM BOUNCING

TREASURE HUNTER

FISH DON'T ESCAPE WHILE COLLECTING TREASURE

QUALITY BOBBER
BOOSTS THE QUALITY OF FISH THAT YOU CATCH

CURIOSITY LURE
INCREASES YOUR CHANCE TO CATCH RARE FISH

CAVE FISH

These extremophile fish prefer the harsh conditions present in underground lakes and other hidden bodies of water. Unaffected by any outdoor conditions, they can be caught in any season and any time of day.

GHOSTFISH 45g

SPECIALTY FISH BUNDLE

MINES: LVL 20, 60, 100

50, MIXED

STONEFISH 300g

MINES: LVL 20

65, SINKER

ICE PIP 500g

MINES: LVL 60

85, DART

LAVA EEL 700g

MINES: LVL 100

90, MIXED

SLIMEJACK 100g

MUTANT BUG LAIR

55, DART

VOID SALMON 150g

WITCH'S SWAMP

80, MIXED

DESERT FISH

The unique species of fish found in the desert lake have evolved interesting defense mechanisms. They can be caught in any season from 6am to 10pm.

SANDFISH 75g

SPECIALTY FISH BUNDLE

65, MIXED

SCORPION CARP 150g

90, DART

OCEAN FISH

Not surprisingly, you can find a wide variety of ocean fish near the beach, by casting from the piers. What you'll find in the ocean will vary greatly depending on the time of day and season.

ALBACORE 75g
60, MIXED
FALL + WINTER
SUNNY + RAIN
6AM-11AM, 6PM-2AM

ANCHOVY 30g
30, DART
SPRING, FALL

EEL 85g
NIGHT FISHING BUNDLE
70, SMOOTH
4PM-2AM
SPRING, FALL
RAIN

FLOUNDER 100g
50, SINKER
SPRING - SUMMER
6AM - 8PM

HALIBUT 80g
50, SINKER
WINTER - SUMMER
6AM-11AM, 7PM-2AM

HERRING 30g
25, DART
WINTER - SPRING

OCTOPUS 150g
95, SINKER
SUMMER
6AM - 1PM

PUFFERFISH 200g
SPECIALTY FISH BUNDLE
80, FLOATER
SUMMER
SUNNY
12PM - 4PM

RED MULLET 75g
55, SMOOTH
SUMMER, WINTER
6AM - 7PM

RED SNAPPER 50g
OCEAN FISH BUNDLE
40, MIXED
SUMMER - FALL
RAIN
6AM - 7PM

SARDINE 40g

30, DART

OCEAN FISH BUNDLE

FALL - SPRING
6AM - 7PM

SEA CUCUMBER 75g

40, SINKER

FALL - WINTER
6AM - 7PM

SQUID 80g

75, SINKER

WINTER
6PM - 2AM

SUPER CUCUMBER 250g

80, SINKER

SUMMER - FALL
6PM - 2AM

TILAPIA 75g

50, MIXED

OCEAN FISH BUNDLE

SUMMER - FALL
6AM - 2PM

TUNA 100g

70, SMOOTH

OCEAN FISH BUNDLE

SUMMER, WINTER
6AM - 7PM

DEEP SEA FISH

These unique species prefer cold, dark waters, so they can only be found at the depths of the Gem Sea's bottom. You'll need to hitch a ride on a submarine if you even want to catch a glimpse of them.

SPOOK FISH 220g

60, DART

NIGHT MARKET ONLY

BLOBFISH 500g

75, FLOATER

NIGHT MARKET ONLY

MIDNIGHT SQUID 100g

55, SINKER

NIGHT MARKET ONLY

143

LAKE FISH

Some fish species can only be found in the lake just outside the Mines, near the foot of the Mountains.

BULLHEAD 75g

LAKE FISH BUNDLE

46, SMOOTH

LAKE OUTSIDE THE MINES

LARGE MOUTH BASS 100g

LAKE FISH BUNDLE

50, MIXED 6AM-7PM

LAKE OUTSIDE THE MINES

STURGEON 200g

LAKE FISH BUNDLE

78, MIXED SUMMER, WINTER 6AM-7PM

LAKE OUTSIDE THE MINES

CARP 30g

LAKE FISH BUNDLE

VERY COMMON

4x CARP MAKE CARP SURPRISE

15, MIXED SPRING - FALL

LAKE OUTSIDE THE MINES, POND, SEWERS, SECRET WOODS

WINTER - SEWER, SECRET WOODS

CHUB 50g

COMMON

FIELD RESEARCH BUNDLE

35, DART

LAKE OUTSIDE THE MINES, FOREST RIVER

LINGCOD 120g

TRICKY FISH!

85, MIXED WINTER

LAKE OUTSIDE THE MINES, RIVERS

MIDNIGHT CARP 150g

55, MIXED FALL-WINTER 10PM - 2AM

LAKE OUTSIDE THE MINES

RAINBOW TROUT 65g

TROUT SOUP

45, MIXED SUMMER SUNNY 6AM-7PM

LAKE OUTSIDE THE MINES, RIVERS

PERCH 55g

35, MIXED WINTER

LAKE OUTSIDE THE MINES, RIVERS, FOREST POND

WALLEYE 105g

NIGHT FISHING BUNDLE

45, SMOOTH FALL RAIN 12PM- 2AM

LAKE OUTSIDE THE MINES, RIVERS, FOREST POND

RIVER FISH

The rivers cutting through Pelican Town and Cindersap Forest are practically overflowing with fish of all types.

SUNFISH 30g
RIVER FISH BUNDLE

30 MIXED
SPRING-SUMMER
-SUNNY-
6AM-7PM

RIVERS

TIGER TROUT 150g
RIVER FISH BUNDLE

60, DART
FALL, WINTER
6AM-7PM

RIVERS

SHAD 60g
RIVER FISH BUNDLE

45, SMOOTH
SPRING-FALL
9AM-2AM
RAIN

RIVERS

BREAM 45g
NIGHT FISHING BUNDLE

35, SMOOTH
6PM-2AM

RIVERS

SALMON 75g
SALMON DINNER!

50, MIXED
FALL
6AM-7PM

RIVERS

CATFISH 200g
RIVER FISH BUNDLE

75, MIXED
RAIN
SPRING, FALL-RIVERS
SUMMER-SECRET WOODS

SMALLMOUTH BASS 50g

28, MIXED
SPRING, FALL

TOWN RIVER,
FOREST POND

PIKE 100g

60, DART
SUMMER, WINTER

RIVERS,
FOREST POND

DORADO 100g

78, MIXED
SUMMER
6AM-7PM

FOREST RIVER

WOODSKIP 75g
SPECIALTY FISH BUNDLE

50, MIXED

SECRET WOODS

145

CRAB POT

Some bottom-feeding crustaceans and mollusks can only be scooped up using a Crab Pot.
Don't forget the bait!

LOBSTER 120g
5%

CRAB 100g
10%

SHRIMP 60g
20%

OYSTER 40g
15%

CLAM 50g
15%

COCKLE 50g
30%

MUSSEL 30g
35%

CRAYFISH 75g
35%
FRESHWATER

SNAIL 65g
25%
FRESHWATER

PERIWINKLE 20g
55%
FRESHWATER

Some of these undesirable catches can be used in cooking, while others can be transformed into useful materials with the Recycler.

GREEN ALGAE 15g   JOJA COLA 20g   SEAWEED 20g   WHITE ALGAE 25g

SOGGY NEWSPAPER

BROKEN GLASSES

BROKEN CD

DRIFTWOOD
LEAH LIKES IT!

TRASH

RECYCLES INTO REFINED QUARTZ!

REMEMBER to RECYCLE your TRASH!

THE LEGENDARY FIVE

Catching these extraordinarily rare fish requires the ultimate in skill. Amateurs need not apply.

MUTANT CARP
1,000g

80, DART

FOUND IN THE MURKY SEWER WATERS. ANY SEASON, DAY OR NIGHT.

ANGLER
900g

85, SMOOTH

FOUND OFF THE PLANK BRIDGE NORTH OF JOJAMART. DEEP WATER. LVL 3 FISHING REQUIRED. FALL ONLY.

CRIMSONFISH
1,500g

95, MIXED

FOUND SOUTH OF THE TIDAL POOLS. CAST YOUR LINE SOUTHWEST OFF THE PIER. LVL 5 FISHING REQUIRED. SUMMER ONLY.

GLACIERFISH
1,000g

100, MIXED

FOUND SOUTH OF ARROWHEAD ISLAND IN CINDERSAP FOREST. DEEP WATER. LVL 6 FISHING REQUIRED. WINTER ONLY.

LEGEND
5,000g

110, MIXED

— KING OF ALL FISH —
MOUNTAIN LAKE, SOUTH OF THE GUILD. NEAR THE UNDERWATER LOG. LVL 10 FISHING REQUIRED. SPRING ONLY, RAINY.

FISH PONDS

On your farm, you can raise everything from Chickens and Pigs to Dinosaurs and Slimes, so why not try your hand at fish? Robin can build you a Fish Pond where you can raise up to 10 fish of any one kind. Most fish produce Roe, but they can also produce a number of other items, depending on the fish. Squids will give you Squid Ink, for instance.

Roe can be aged in Preserves Jars to produce Aged Roe. Sturgeon will produce Sturgeon Roe, which can be processed into famously fancy Caviar!

By crafting Wood or Stone Signs and placing them on your Fish Ponds, you'll know at a glance how many of which types of fish are in each Fish Pond.

Fish are a little different from your typical livestock; in most cases, they reproduce fairly quickly, but will make special requests as their populations grow. Different types of fish have unique personalities, ranging from polite and sweet to downright rude. Don't be surprised if your fish call you a Landlubber as they make their demands!

Keep in mind that legendary fish can't be kept in Fish Ponds. These rare fish are loners, and their wild personalities are too big to be contained!

As the fish in your Fish Ponds reproduce, many will begin requesting specific items to help them feel more comfortable in their new homes. For example, fish might ask for things commonly found in Crab Pots, like Seaweed, Green Algae or Driftwood. Desert fish will ask for Coconuts or Cactus Fruit, and Woodskips will ask for items from the Secret Woods. The first Sturgeon in a Fish Pond will have the audacity to ask for a Diamond!

When you fulfill one of these special requests, you'll increase the capacity of the Fish Pond, allowing the fish within to continue reproducing until they eventually reach a maximum of 10 fish. You can also help speed the process along by adding fish of the same type to the pond yourself.

The fish in your Fish Pond don't fight back, so they can be caught effortlessly. If you have a full Fish Pond, it can be a good idea to catch a fish every few days; they'll naturally reproduce to replace the one taken each time.

There are a few fish that are so extreme that they will change the color of the water in their Fish Ponds. Super Cucumber, Slimejack, Lava Eel and Void Salmon all impart interesting colors to their home waters!

Chapter 6
Mining & Adventuring

Mining can be a very lucrative enterprise, especially during the cold of winter when there isn't quite as much work to be done on the farm. You can instead spend your days exploring the damp, dark mountain caverns, mining for Ores and Gems while fighting monsters.

Risk and reward go hand in hand in the Mines; as you progress downward, the monsters become stronger and more dangerous while the Gems and Minerals become more plentiful and more valuable. You'll earn more powerful weapons and equipment along the way as well, turning the tides of battle in your favor.

And once you reach the very bottom, you'll find your adventure has only just begun.

INTO THE MINES!

As you make your way deeper and deeper into the Mines, you'll face increasingly tough monsters. But what doesn't kill you makes you stronger, and the more monsters you defeat, the higher your Combat Skill level will climb—and more Combat Skill means more HP to withstand attacks. Be careful, though; if the monsters manage to knock you out, you'll find yourself back at the entrance to the Mines in bad shape, with items and money missing from your backpack!

It's easy to lose track of time in the Mines, so keep an eye on the clock and give yourself plenty of time to get back home by 2am. But don't worry; you don't have to tackle the entirety of the Mines in one day. There's an elevator that stops on every fifth floor, which will activate once you reach that floor for the first time.

So get out there and start hunting for treasure!

GEODES

You can find a wealth of treasures locked away inside Geodes, including Ores, Gems and even ancient artifacts. Of course, some Geodes will only contain Stones or Coal, but the mystery is half the fun! Clint will carefully open any Geode and extract its contents for 25g.

GEODE
MINES 1-40

Stone	Jamborite
Clay	Jagoite
Coal	Limestone
Copper Ore	Mudstone
Iron Ore	Malachite
Alamite	Nekoite
Calcite	Orpiment
Celestine	Petrified Slime
Dwarvish Helm	Sandstone
Earth Crystal	Slate
Granite	Thunder Egg

FROZEN GEODE
MINES 40-80

	Frozen Tear
Stone	Geminite
Clay	Ghost Crystal
Coal	Hematite
Copper Ore	Kyanite
Iron Ore	Lunarite
Gold Ore	Marble
Aerinite	Ocean Stone
Ancient Drum	Opal
Esperite	Pyrite
Fairy Stone	Soapstone
Fluorapatite	

MAGMA GEODE
MINES 80-120

	Dolomite
Stone	Dwarf Gadget
Clay	Fire Opal
Coal	Fire Quartz
Copper Ore	Helvite
Iron Ore	Jasper
Gold Ore	Lemon Stone
Iridium Ore	Neptunite
Baryte	Obsidian
Basalt	Star Shards
Bixite	Tigerseye

OMNI GEODE   MINES and SKULL CAVERN

	Ancient Drum	Ghost Crystal	Obsidian
	Baryte	Granite	Ocean Stone
	Basalt	Helvite	Petrified Slime
Stone	Bixite	Hematite	Prismatic Shard
Clay	Calcite	Jamborite	Pyrite
Coal	Dwarvish Helm	Jagoite	Slate
Copper Ore	Dwarf Gadget	Jasper	Sandstone
Iron Ore	Fairy Stone	Limestone	Soapstone
Gold Ore	Fire Opal	Lemon Stone	Star Shards
Iridium Ore	Fire Quartz	Malachite	Thunder Egg
Aerinite	Fluorapatite	Nekoite	Marble
Alamite	Geminite	Neptunite	

MINERALS

AERINITE
125g

ALAMITE
150g

BARYTE
50g

BASALT
175g

BIXITE
300g

CALCITE
75g

CELESTINE
125g

DOLOMITE
300g

ESPERITE
100g

FAIRY STONE
250g

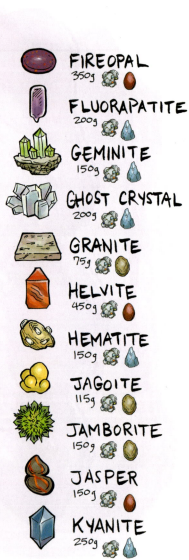

FIREOPAL
350g

FLUORAPATITE
200g

GEMINITE
150g

GHOST CRYSTAL
200g

GRANITE
75g

HELVITE
450g

HEMATITE
150g

JAGOITE
115g

JAMBORITE
150g

JASPER
150g

KYANITE
250g

A total of 41 different Minerals can be found within the Geodes you'll dig up in the Mines. Try to find them all and complete the Museum's collection!

LEMON STONE 200g

LIMESTONE 15g

LUNARITE 200g

MALACHITE 100g

MARBLE 110g

MUDSTONE 25g

NEKOITE 80g

NEPTUNITE 400g

OBSIDIAN 200g

OCEAN STONE 220g

OPAL 150g

ORPIMENT 80g

PETRIFIED SLIME 120g

PYRITE 120g

SANDSTONE 60g

SLATE 85g

SOAPSTONE 120g

STAR SHARDS 500g

THUNDER EGG 100g

TIGERSEYE 275g

GEMS

Each of the 8 precious Gems found in the Mines grows from a unique and conspicuous Node, except for the Prismatic Shard, which can occasionally be extracted from Mystic Stones and Iridium Nodes.

Some Gems have also been known to turn up every now and then along with Ores and other Minerals when panning in rivers, and a few types of Gem grow directly from the cavern floors and can be picked by hand like any other forageable resource.

TOPAZ 80g
TOPAZ + GEM NODES,
MINES LVL 1+

AMETHYST 100g
AMETHYST + GEM NODES,
MINES LVL 1+

JADE 200g
JADE + GEM NODES
MINES LVL 40+

AQUAMARINE 250g
AQUAMARINE + GEM NODES
MINES LVL 40+

EMERALD 250g
EMERALD + GEM NODES,
MINES LVL 80+

RUBY 250g
RUBY + GEM NODES
MINES LVL 80+

DIAMOND 750g
DIAMOND + GEM NODES
MINES LVL 50+

PRISMATIC SHARD 2,000g
VERY RARE.
SOME HIGH-LEVEL MONSTERS DROP IT
IRIDIUM NODE, OMNI GEODE, MYSTIC STONE.

QUARTZ 25g
COMMON IN THE MINES
CAN BE MADE INTO REFINED QUARTZ

EARTH CRYSTAL 50g
MINES LVL 1-40

FROZEN TEAR 75g
MINES LVL 40-80

FIRE QUARTZ 100g
MINES LVL 80+
CAN MAKE 3 REFINED QUARTZ

GEM NODE
CONTAINS A GEM

MYSTIC STONE
CAN CONTAIN GOLD ORE,
IRIDIUM ORE OR PRISMATIC SHARD

COPPER PAN

- USED TO GATHER
- ORE FROM STREAMS -

given to you by Willy
after the Glittering
Boulder disappears.

USE NEAR SHIMMERING LIGHTS
IN RIVERS TO PAN FOR
ORE and MINERALS!

RESOURCES

Metal Ores and Bars are important crafting ingredients for many of the machines you'll use to create artisan goods; Clint can also use Bars to upgrade your farm tools. Ores can be smelted into Bars using the Furnace, along with a little Coal to get the fire going.

COAL 15g
COMMON IN MINES, USED IN SMELTING BARS IN THE FURNACE

REFINED QUARTZ 50g
1 QUARTZ, 1 COAL, 1.5 HRS
1 FIRE QUARTZ, 1 COAL, 1.5 HRS

COPPER ORE 5g
MOST COMMON IN MINES LVLS 30-39

COPPER BAR 60g
5 COPPER ORE, 1 COAL, ½ HR

IRON ORE 10g
MINES LVL 40+

IRON BAR 120g
5 IRON ORE, 1 COAL, 2 HRS

GOLD ORE 25g
MINES LVL 80+

GOLD BAR 250g
5 GOLD ORE, 1 COAL, 5 HRS

IRIDIUM ORE
SKULL CAVERN 100g

IRIDIUM BAR 1,000g
5 IRIDIUM ORE, 1 COAL, 8 HRS

RADIOACTIVE ORE 300g
THE MINES & SKULL CAVERN, UNDER SPECIAL QUESTS ONLY

RADIOACTIVE BAR 3,000g
5 RADIOACTIVE ORE, 1 COAL, 10 HRS

These rare and dangerous materials can only be obtained under equally dangerous circumstances. A certain someone in a faraway place holds the key.

THE MINES

elevator

Dwarf

MINE CART

ENTRANCE
obtain the
Rusty Sword

TAKE OUT
GRUBS
QUICKLY

10

CHEST:
Leather
boots

GHOSTFISH
↓ and
STONEFISH

20

CHEST:
Steel
Smallsword

30

Copper
ore
abundant

DARK
AREA

BRING
TORCHES

BEWARE of
STONE
GOLEMS!

40

CHEST:
Slingshot

Frozen
geodes
common

50

CHEST:
Tundra Boots

DUST SPRITES
DROP COAL

IRON ORE
MORE COMMON

60

CHEST:
Crystal Dagger

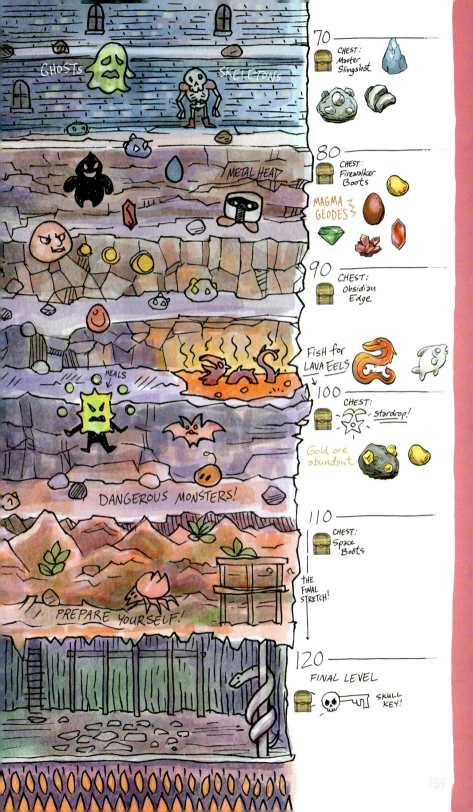

GHOSTS

SKELETONS

70

CHEST:
Master
Slingshot

80

CHEST:
Firewalker
Boots

MAGMA
GEODES

90

CHEST:
Obsidian
Edge

METAL HEAD

Fish for
LAVA EELS

100

CHEST:
Stardrop!

Gold ore
abundant

HEALS

DANGEROUS MONSTERS!

110

CHEST:
Space
Boots

THE
FINAL
STRETCH!

PREPARE YOURSELF!

120

FINAL LEVEL

SKULL
KEY!

ADVENTURING

The Mines and caverns can be quite dangerous, so be sure to pack some food for the journey. You might happen upon a Cave Carrot or two along the way, but it never hurts to bring a few extra meals to keep your strength up as you explore and battle. They may take up space in your backpack, but it's better to leave behind some monster loot than to be knocked unconscious and lose something much more valuable.

Unlike farming tools or even the Pickaxe, using weapons doesn't deplete your energy. So don't be afraid to swing madly when the monsters get too close for comfort!

If you do happen to lose a tool or other item that can't be replaced, don't worry; someone is bound to find it and return it safely to your mailbox by morning. The Adventurer's Guild also offers an Item Recovery Service; for a nominal fee, Marlon will venture down and quickly recover a single lost item for you.

MONSTER LOOT

5g

SLIME

15g

BAT WING

8g

BUG MEAT
MAKES BAIT

40g

SOLAR
ESSENCE

WIZARD
LOVES
ESSENCES

50g

VOID
ESSENCE

12g

BONE FRAGMENT

At first glance, the bits and pieces left behind by vanquished monsters might just look like disgusting trash. But they're all surprisingly valuable crafting ingredients, and you can always cash them out at the Adventurer's Guild if you have more than you need.

MONSTERS

THE MINES, LVLS 1-40

BAT HP 24

SHRIEKS BEFORE ATTACKING

WEAK! BUG HP 1

FLIES IN A FIXED PATH, EASY TO AVOID

CAVE FLY HP 22

TURNS INTO A CAVE FLY →

VERY AGGRESSIVE, FLIES DIRECTLY AT YOU

GRUB HP 20

DEFEAT QUICKLY!

GREEN SLIME HP 24

LOOKS CUTE, BUT DON'T BE FOOLED

DUGGY HP 40

ATTACKS FROM UNDERGROUND IN SANDY AREAS

USING A HOE CAN BLOCK THEM FROM BURROWING UP

ROCK CRAB HP 30

SURPRISE! THAT IS NO ROCK! CAN DROP A <u>CRAB</u>

162

THE MINES, LVLS 40-80

FROST BAT
HP 36

DRESSED FOR
CHILLY CONDITIONS

DUST SPRITE
HP 40

DROPS COAL

STONE GOLEM
HP 45

...WHAT'S THAT
MOVING IN
THE SHADOWS?

NOT A HUGE
THREAT

FROST JELLIES
HP 106

A BIT TOUGHER

SKELETON
HP 140

ATTACKS
AND THROWS
BONES!

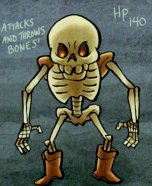

GHOST
HP 96

LIGHT
AS A
FEATHER

MIGHT DROP A SOLAR ESSENCE
OR GHOSTFISH

THE MINES, LVLS 80-120

LAVA BAT HP 80

STILL SHRIEKY!

SQUID KID HP 1

SHOOTS FIREBALLS, BUT WEAK

SLUDGE HP 205

TOUGHER YET!

LAVA CRAB HP 120

EEK! STILL NOT A ROCK

METAL HEAD HP 40

HIGH DEFENCE

RESISTS KNOCKBACK

SHADOW SHAMAN HP 80

MAGIC USER

CAN HEAL!

CAN JINX!

USE CAUTION!

SHADOW BRUTE HP 160

RELATED TO SHADOW SHAMAN, BUT DOESN'T USE MAGIC

NO FRIENDLY SHADOW BRUTES EXIST IN THE MINES

QUARRY MINE

COPPER SLIME HP 102

HAUNTED SKULL HP 80

THESE SKULLS SWARM!

IRON SLIME HP 205

164

☠ SKULL CAVERN

ARMORED BUG

IMPERVIOUS TO DAMAGE,
BUT PREDICTABLE
AND NOT AGGRESSIVE

PURPLE SLIME

HP 410

THE TOUGHEST
SLIMES!

IRIDIUM BAT

HP 300

STARTS APPEARING
ON LEVEL 50

CARBON GHOST

HP 190

ONLY ON FLOORS
WITH MUMMIES

BIG SLIME

HP 60-240

DEPENDING ON COLOR

WILL OFTEN BURST
INTO SEVERAL SLIMES
UPON DEFEAT

SERPENT

HP 150

MAKES
SCARY
SOUNDS!

DROPS TREASURE SUCH AS
BOMBS, SPICY EEL,
RABBIT'S FOOT + PRISMATIC SHARD

MUMMY

ONLY
~BOMBS~
WILL DEFEAT
THEM
FOR GOOD

HP 260,
OVER
AND
OVER...

WHEN
KNOCKED
DOWN,
THEY'LL
ARISE
AFTER 10
SECONDS

PEPPER REX

HP 300

SHOOTS FIRE!
CAN DROP PREHISTORIC
ARTIFACTS, DINO EGGS

IRIDIUM CRAB

HP 240

TRICKY IRIDIUM NODE!

CAN DROP IRIDIUM ORE
AND CRAB CAKES

WEAPONS

Many weapons, both sharp and blunt, are available to wield against the hordes of monsters in the Mines and caves. By examining the power, speed, weight and other statistics of each, you can choose the weapon that best suits your fighting style.

SCYTHE
1-3 DMG

GOLDEN SCYTHE
13 DMG

RUSTY SWORD
2-5 DMG

WOODEN BLADE
3-7 DMG

STEEL SMALLSWORD
4-8 DMG
+2 SPEED

SILVER SABER
4-8 DMG
+1 DEFENSE

PIRATE'S SWORD
8-14 DMG
+2 SPEED

IRON EDGE
12-25 DMG
+2 SPEED
+1 DEFENSE
+3 WEIGHT

FOREST SWORD
8-18 DMG
+2 SPEED
+1 DEFENSE

CUTLASS
9-17 DMG
+2 SPEED

HOLY BLADE
18-24 DMG
+3 WEIGHT

INSECT HEAD
10-20 DMG
+2 SPEED
+2 CRIT CHANCE

CLAYMORE
20-32 DMG
-4 SPEED
+2 DEFENSE
+3 WEIGHT

BONE SWORD
20-30 DMG
+4 SPEED
+2 WEIGHT

TEMPLAR'S BLADE
22-29 DMG
+1 DEFENSE

NEPTUNE'S GLAIVE
18-35 DMG
-1 SPEED
+2 DEFENSE
+4 WEIGHT

OSSIFIED BLADE
26-42 DMG
-2 SPEED
+2 DEFENSE
+1 WEIGHT

OBSIDIAN EDGE
30-45 DMG
-1 SPEED
+10 CRIT POWER

YETI TOOTH
26-42 DMG
+4 DEFENSE
+10 CRIT POWER

STEEL FALCHION
28-46 DMG
+4 SPEED
+20 CRIT POWER

DARK SWORD
30-45 DMG
-5 SPEED
+5 WEIGHT
+2 CRIT CHANCE

LAVA KATANA
55-64 DMG
+3 DEFENSE
+3 WEIGHT
+25 CRIT POWER

GALAXY SWORD
60-80 DMG
+4 SPEED

CARVING KNIFE
1-3 DMG
+2 CRIT CHANCE

WIND SPIRE
1-5 DMG
+5 WEIGHT
+1 CRIT CHANCE
+10 CRIT POWER

IRON DIRK
2-4 DMG
+2 CRIT CHANCE

ELF BLADE
3-5 DMG
+2 CRIT CHANCE

CRYSTAL DAGGER
4-10 DMG
+5 WEIGHT
+2 CRIT CHANCE
+50 CRIT POWER

BURGLAR'S SHANK
7-12 DMG
+2 CRIT CHANCE
+25 CRIT POWER

SHADOW DAGGER
10-20 DMG
+2 CRIT CHANCE

BROKEN TRIDENT
15-26 DMG
+1 CRIT CHANCE

WICKED KRIS
24-30 DMG
+4 CRIT CHANCE

IRIDIUM NEEDLE
20-35 DMG
+6 CRIT CHANCE
+200 CRIT POWER

GALAXY DAGGER
30-40 DMG
+1 SPEED
+5 WEIGHT
+1 CRIT CHANCE

FEMUR
6-11 DMG
+2 SPEED

WOOD CLUB
9-16 DMG

WOOD MALLET
15-24 DMG
+2 SPEED
+3 WEIGHT

LEAD ROD
18-27 DMG
-4 SPEED

KUDGEL
27-40 DMG
-1 SPEED
+2 WEIGHT
+4 CRIT POWER

THE SLAMMER
40-55 DMG
-2 SPEED

GALAXY HAMMER
70-90 DMG
+2 SPEED
+5 WEIGHT

SLINGSHOT
1-3 DMG

MASTER SLINGSHOT
2-6 DMG

The damage dealt by slingshots depends on the ammunition; Stones and Ores can be used, and you can craft Explosive Ammo to clear out groups of monsters. You can even shoot Eggs and some fruits and vegetables!

RINGS

Some Rings are earned from Quests or dropped by slain monsters, while others must be crafted or purchased from Marlon at the Adventurer's Guild. You can wear two at once, combining their effects.

SMALL GLOW RING
EMITS LIGHT
the mines

GLOW RING
EMITS MORE LIGHT!
the mines

GLOWSTONE RING
GLOWS AND ATTRACTS ITEMS!
crafting

SMALL MAGNET RING
INCREASES RADIUS FOR COLLECTING ITEMS (MAGNETISM UP!)
the mines

MAGNET RING
MAGNETISM UP MORE!
the mines

AMETHYST RING
+10% KNOCKBACK
1,000g

TOPAZ RING
+10% PRECISION
1,000g

AQUAMARINE RING
+10% CRIT CHANCE
2,500g

JADE RING
+10% CRIT POWER
2,500g

EMERALD RING
+10% WEAPON SPEED
5,000g

RUBY RING
+10% ATTACK
5,000g

SLIME CHARMER RING
SLIMES WON'T HURT YOU
eradication goal

WARRIOR RING
SOMETIMES GIVES TEMP +10 ATTACK AFTER DEFEATING A MONSTER
crafting

VAMPIRE RING
RESTORES 2 HEALTH AFTER DEFEATING A MONSTER
eradication goal

THORNS RING
ENEMIES TAKE DAMAGE WHEN THEY DAMAGE YOU
crafting

CRABSHELL RING
+5 DEFENSE
eradication goal

IMMUNITY BAND
+4 IMMUNITY
skull cavern, mines lvl 100+

SAVAGE RING
SPEED BOOST AFTER DEFEATING A MONSTER
eradication goal

STURDY RING
NEGATIVE STATUS EFFECTS LAST HALF AS LONG
crafting

BURGLAR'S RING
DEFEATED MONSTERS DROP MORE LOOT
eradication goal

LUCKY RING
+1 LUCK
skull cavern

NAPALM RING
MAKES ENEMIES EXPLODE UPON DEFEAT
eradication goal

RING OF YOBA
AFTER TAKING DAMAGE, IT MAY BESTOW A SHORT PERIOD OF INVINCIBILITY
crafting

IRIDIUM BAND
ALL-IN-ONE
GLOW + MAGNET + RUBY RING
+GLOW, +MAGNETISM, +10% ATTACK
crafting

WEDDING RING
MARRY A FELLOW FARMER
crafting

FOOTWEAR

Quality footwear will aid you in combat, providing a boost to both defense and resistance to status ailments. Most footwear must either be earned or purchased from Marlon at the Adventurer's Guild, though a rare few may be found elsewhere or even received as gifts. Some cannot be purchased until a pair is first found in a chest in the Mines.

SNEAKERS
+1 DEFENSE

500g

RUBBER BOOTS
+1 IMMUNITY

LEATHER BOOTS
+1 DEFENSE
+1 IMMUNITY

500g

COMBAT BOOTS
+3 DEFENSE

1,250g

TUNDRA BOOTS
+2 DEFENSE
+1 IMMUNITY

750g

THERMAL BOOTS
+1 DEFENSE
+2 IMMUNITY

DARK BOOTS
+4 DEFENSE
+2 IMMUNITY

2,500g

FIREWALKER BOOTS
+3 DEFENSE
+3 IMMUNITY

lvl 80 the mines   2,500g

SPACE BOOTS
+4 DEFENSE
+4 IMMUNITY

lvl 110 the mines   5,000g

GENIE SHOES
+1 DEFENSE
+6 IMMUNITY

skull cavern drop

LEPRECHAUN SHOES
+2 DEFENSE
+1 IMMUNITY

trains

CRYSTAL SHOES
+3 DEFENSE
+5 IMMUNITY

skull cavern drop

EMILY'S MAGIC BOOTS
+4 DEFENSE
+4 IMMUNITY

Emily 14-heart event

HATS

Celebrate your Achievements with an array of fancy headwear! Though a few Hats are obtained during special events, most must either be made via Tailoring, or be purchased from the mouse in southern Cindersap Forest for 1,000g after earning the relevant Achievement. A few are earned by completing Monster Eradication Goals for the Adventurer's Guild as well; those hats can then be purchased from Marlon again at any time.

20,000g
ARCANE HAT
defeat 100 mummies

1,000g
ARCHER'S CAP
cook every recipe

BEANIE
tree seed + cloth

BLOBFISH MASK
blobfish + cloth

1,000g
BLUE BONNET
donate 40 different items

BLUE COWBOY HAT
treasure floor in skull cavern

1,000g
BOWLER HAT
1,000,000g earned

BRIDAL VEIL
pearl + cloth

1,000g
BUTTERFLY BOW
5-heart friendship

1,000g
CAT EARS
10-hearts with 8 people

1,000g
CHEF HAT
cook every recipe

1,000g
CHICKEN MASK
complete 40 quests

CONE HAT
buy at night market

1,000g
COOL CAP
250,000g earned

COPPER PAN
just wear it as a hat!

COWBOY HAT
complete the museum

1,000g
COWGAL HAT
ship 300 of one crop

1,000g
COWPOKE HAT
ship 15 of each crop

DARK COWBOY HAT
treasure floor in skull cavern

1,000g
DAISY
craft 15 items

1,000g
DELICATE BOW
cook 10 different recipes

DINOSAUR HAT
dinosaur egg + cloth

1,000g
EARMUFFS
5-hearts with 20 people

1,000g
ELEGANT TURBAN
earn every achievement!

EMILY'S MAGIC HAT
Emily's 14-heart event

1,000g
EYE PATCH
catch every fish

FASHION HAT
caviar + cloth

1,000g
FEDORA
500 tokens at the fair

FISHING HAT
various fish + cloth

FLAT TOPPED HAT
sauce / stuffing + cloth

FLOPPY BEANIE
tree sap + cloth

GARBAGE HAT
rare drop, check trash

GOGGLES
cloth + bug steak

GNOME'S CAP 1,000g
craft every item

GOBLIN MASK 1,000g
ship every item

GOLDEN MASK
golden mask + cloth

GOOD OL' CAP 1,000g
15,000g earned

GREEN TURBAN
desert trader, 50 omni geodes

HAIR BONE
prehistoric tibia + cloth

HARD HAT 20,000g
defeat 30 duggies

HUNTER'S CAP 1,000g
upgrade house twice

KNIGHT'S HELMET
defeat 50 pepper rex

LIVING HAT
wilderness golem / weeds

LOGO CAP
lava eel + cloth

LUCKY BOW 1,000g
50,000g earned

MAGIC COWBOY HAT
desert trader, 333 omni geodes

MAGIC TURBAN
desert trader, 333 omni geodes

MOUSE EARS 1,000g
10-heart friendship

MUSHROOM CAP
rare drop, fell a mushroom tree

OFFICIAL CAP 1,000g
catch 20 different fish

PARTY HAT
pizza + cloth

PARTY HAT
chocolate cake + cloth

PARTY HAT 1,000g
fish taco + cloth

PIRATE HAT
treasure chest + cloth

PLUM CHAPEAU 1,000g
cook 25 different recipes

POLKA BOW 1,000g
complete 10 quests

PROPELLER HAT
miner's treat + cloth

PUMPKIN MASK
jack-o-lantern + cloth

RED COWBOY HAT
treasure floor in skull cavern

SAILOR'S CAP
win the winter fishing competition

SANTA HAT 1,000g
5 hearts with 10 people

SKELETON MASK 20,000g
defeat 50 skeletons

SOMBRERO 1,000g
10,000,000g earned

SOU'WESTER 1,000g
catch 10 different fish

SPOTTED HEADSCARF
red mushroom + cloth

SQUIRE'S HELMET
metal head rare drop

STRAW HAT
win the egg hunt

TIARA 1,000g
5 hearts with 5 people

TOP HAT 8,000 Qi Coins
buy in Qi's casino

TOTEM MASK
any totem + cloth

TROPICLIP 1,000g
upgrade your home

TRUCKER HAT 1,000g
craft 30 different items

WATERMELON BAND 1,000g
catch 100 fish

WEARABLE DWARF HELM
dwarvish helm/gadget + cloth

WHITE TURBAN
sweet gem berry + cloth

WITCH HAT
golden pumpkin + cloth

✵ Chapter 7 ✵
Community Involvement
and Advanced Goals

Beyond the obvious objective of nurturing a successful and productive farm, there are a number of other long-term goals that you can choose to pursue. These goals can lead to a richer, more fulfilling life experience.

You came to the valley to escape the soul-crushing tedium, the deadlines and the pressure of city life. But even out here, there are people who depend on you. In this small, tightly-knit community, everyone has something to contribute, and everyone has a need that you can fill. Strengthening ties, both to the community and to its people, is an important part of the experience of living in such a small, isolated town.

Once some time has passed, and Stardew Valley truly begins to feel like home, perhaps you'll find yourself looking for ways to give back to the community that welcomed you with open arms so many long seasons ago.

Rebuilding the Museum

Donate Minerals, Gems and artifacts to the Museum to expand its collection; you'll earn one-of-a-kind rewards as you reach certain donation milestones.

In addition, a number of books that were checked out long ago have gone missing. Perhaps you'll be the one to return them to their shelves! You could uncover some Stardew Valley history and practical advice by perusing the pages of these Lost Books.

Rewards for Donation Milestones

9 Cauliflower Seeds	5 items donated
9 Melon Seeds	10 items donated
1 Starfruit Seed	15 items donated
'A Night on Eco Hill' Painting	20 items donated
'Jade Hills' Painting	25 items donated
Large Futan Bear	30 items donated
9 Pumpkin Seeds	35 items donated
Rarecrow #8	40 items donated
Bear Statue	50 items donated
Rusty Key	60 items donated
3 Triple Shot Espresso	70 items donated
5 Warp Totem: Farm	80 items donated
Magic Rock Candy	90 items donated
Stardrop	All Items! 95 items donated

Rewards for Number of Minerals Donated

Standing Geode	11
Singing Stone	21
Obsidian Vase	31
Crystal Chair	41
Crystalarium	50

YOU DON'T NEED TO DONATE THE FIRST OF EACH ITEM!

HATCH YOUR DINOSAUR EGG IN YOUR INCUBATOR AND YOU'LL END UP WITH MANY MORE DINO EGGS!

KEEP A PRISMATIC SHARD TO TAKE TO THE 3 POINTS IN THE DESERT. THERE WILL BE OTHERS!

DONATED MINERALS CHECKLIST ✓

- [ ] AERINITE
- [ ] ALAMITE
- [ ] AMETHYST
- [ ] AQUAMARINE
- [ ] BARYTE
- [ ] BASALT
- [ ] BIXITE
- [ ] CALCITE
- [ ] CELESTINE
- [ ] DIAMOND
- [ ] DOLOMITE
- [ ] EARTH CRYSTAL
- [ ] EMERALD
- [ ] ESPERITE
- [ ] FAIRY STONE
- [ ] FIREOPAL
- [ ] FIRE QUARTZ
- [ ] FLUORAPATITE
- [ ] FROZEN TEAR
- [ ] GEMINITE
- [ ] GHOST CRYSTAL
- [ ] GRANITE
- [ ] HELVITE
- [ ] HEMATITE
- [ ] JADE
- [ ] JAGOITE
- [ ] JAMBORITE

- [ ] JASPER
- [ ] KYANITE
- [ ] LEMON STONE
- [ ] LIMESTONE
- [ ] LUNARITE
- [ ] MALACHITE
- [ ] MARBLE
- [ ] MUDSTONE
- [ ] NEKOITE
- [ ] NEPTUNITE
- [ ] OBSIDIAN
- [ ] OCEAN STONE
- [ ] OPAL
- [ ] ORPIMENT
- [ ] PETRIFIED SLIME
- [ ] PRISMATIC SHARD
- [ ] PYRITE
- [ ] QUARTZ
- [ ] RUBY
- [ ] SANDSTONE
- [ ] SLATE
- [ ] SOAPSTONE
- [ ] STAR SHARDS
- [ ] THUNDER EGG
- [ ] TIGERSEYE
- [ ] TOPAZ

ARTIFACTS

There are 42 different artifacts to be found by slaying monsters, fishing for treasure chests and digging in the dirt. You can learn more about each from Gunther by donating it to the Museum; you'll also earn rewards as you fill out the collection.

DWARF SCROLL I 1g
☐

DINOSAUR EGG 350g
☐

DWARF SCROLL II 1g
☐

RARE DISC 300g
☐

DWARF SCROLL III 1g
☐

ANCIENT SWORD 100g
☐

DWARF SCROLL IV 1g
☐ Reward for all Scrolls:
Dwarvish Translation Guide

RUSTY SPOON 25g
☐

CHIPPED AMPHORA 40g
☐

RUSTY SPUR 25g
☐

ARROWHEAD 40g
☐

RUSTY COG 25g
☐

ANCIENT DOLL 60g
☐

CHICKEN STATUE 50g
☐ Reward:
Chicken Statue Furniture

ELVISH JEWELRY 200g
☐

ANCIENT SEED 5g
☐ Reward: Ancient Seed &
Crafting Recipe

CHEWING STICK 50g
☐

PREHISTORIC TOOL 50g
☐

ORNAMENTAL FAN 300g
☐

DRIED STARFISH 40g
☐

ANCHOR
☐ 100g

GLASS SHARDS
☐ 20g

BONE FLUTE
☐ Reward: 100g
Flute Block

PREHISTORIC HANDAXE
☐ 50g

DWARVISH HELM
☐ 100g

DWARF GADGET
☐ 200g

ANCIENT DRUM
☐ Reward: 100g
Drum Block

GOLDEN MASK
☐ 500g

GOLDEN RELIC
☐ 250g

STRANGE DOLL
☐ 1,000g

STRANGE DOLL
☐ 1,000g

PREHISTORIC SKULL
☐ 100g

PREHISTORIC SCAPULA
☐ 100g

SKELETAL HAND 100g
☐ Skull/Scapula/Hand Reward:
Sloth Skeleton L

PREHISTORIC RIB
☐ 100g

PREHISTORIC VERTEBRA
☐ 100g
Rib/Vertebra Reward:
Sloth Skeleton M

PREHISTORIC TIBIA 100g
☐

SKELETAL TAIL 100g
☐ Tibia/Tail Reward:
Sloth Skeleton R

NAUTILUS FOSSIL
☐ 80g

AMPHIBIAN FOSSIL
☐ 150g

PALM FOSSIL
☐ 100g

TRILOBITE
☐ 50g

Revitalizing the Community Center!

The old Community Center has certainly seen better days. The people of Pelican Town used to be more connected, more united. They've forgotten that closeness in recent years, but you have the power to change things.

Bringing the community back together, fostering togetherness and rekindling friendships can seem like impossible tasks, but working alongside the Junimos, there's nothing you can't do!

In order to revive the Community Center—and the community itself—you need only complete the Bundles the Junimos have requested by contributing certain items:

CRAFTS ROOM	Provide new crafting supplies foraged from around the valley.
PANTRY	Restock the shelves with an assortment of crops and other foods.
FISH TANK	Fill the tank with a variety of different fish.
BULLETIN BOARD	Satisfy the personal requests of your fellow townsfolk.
VAULT	Refill the town's coffers with some very generous donations.
BOILER ROOM	Fuel the furnace with materials gathered from the Mines.

Completing a set of Bundles immediately reawakens the room; each of the six areas of the Community Center will spring to life as the Junimos work their magic. Once all six areas have been restored and the Community Center has been completely rejuvenated, the whole town will gather to celebrate a return to the peaceful way of life they used to know.

And with everyone in the community standing in solidarity, you'll finally rid the valley of the scourge of JojaMart once and for all!

When you are first setting up your new Farm, you'll have the option to select either the Standard Bundles or Remixed Bundles. The Standard Bundles are the same for every Farm, but the Remixed Bundles provide an additional challenge for more experienced Farmers. The Bundles you'll be asked to fulfill—and the items required to complete those Bundles—may differ from Farm to Farm, and Farmer to Farmer.

The Bundle listings on the following pages represent the Standard Bundles.

COMPLETING THE BUNDLES QUICKLY

 The Crafts Room Bundles can be filled a little quicker if you spend some time in the Mines, since some of the late-year forageables are occasionally dropped by monsters.

 The Boiler Room Bundles should be easy to fill quickly as you explore the Mines, since both Minerals and Ores become common as you venture deeper. If you get lucky, you might even get an Iron or Gold Bar early, especially if you have a good rapport with Clint.

 Upgrade your Axe to a Steel Axe as soon as possible to gain access to the Secret Woods; some items, like the Fiddlehead Fern, can be found there at different times of year.

 Fruit bats can bring you the fruits needed for the Artisan Bundle; if you instead choose to have Demetrius set up mushrooms in the cave on your farm, you'll need to plant trees to gather these fruits yourself.

 The Chef's Bundle can be tricky, since it requires a Truffle, which requires a Pig, which requires the Deluxe Barn. Likewise, the Enchanter's Bundle requires a Rabbit's Foot and therefore a Deluxe Coop.

 Sometimes, you'll find an item you need for a Bundle at the Travelling Cart. Though you'll likely pay quite a bit, it can be worth the price to get a difficult Bundle completed early.

 The Quality Crops Bundle can be tough to fill during the first year, since Basic Fertilizer only gives you a 33% chance of growing Gold-star crops. Once you have access to Quality Fertilizer, it becomes much easier.

Crafts Room

SPRING FORAGING
— 30 SPRING SEEDS —

Wild Horseradish, Daffodil, Leek, Dandelion

SUMMER FORAGING
— 30 SUMMER SEEDS —

Sweet Pea, Grapes, Spice Berry

FALL FORAGING
— 30 FALL SEEDS —

Common Mushroom, Wild Plum, Hazelnut, Blackberry

WINTER FORAGING
— 30 WINTER SEEDS —

Winter Root, Crystal Fruit, Snow Yam, Crocus

CONSTRUCTION
— CHARCOAL KILN —

99 Wood, 99 Wood, 99 Stone, 10 Hardwood

EXOTIC FORAGING
— 5 AUTUMN'S BOUNTY —

Coconut, Cactus Fruit, Cave Carrot, Red Mushroom, Purple Mushroom, Maple Syrup, Oak Resin, Pine Tar, Morel

Bridge Repair

Pantry

SPRING CROPS
— 20 SPEED-GRO —

☐ ☐ ☐ ☐

Parsnip, Green Bean, Cauliflower, Potato

SUMMER CROPS
— QUALITY SPRINKLER —

☐ ☐ ☐ ☐

Tomato, Hot Pepper, Blueberry, Melon

FALL CROPS
— BEE HOUSE —

☐ ☐ ☐ ☐

Corn, Eggplant, Pumpkin, Yam

QUALITY CROPS
— PRESERVES JAR —

☐ ☐ ☐

Gold-quality: 5 Parsnips, 5 Melons, 5 Pumpkins, 5 Corn

ANIMAL BUNDLE
— CHEESE PRESS —

☐ ☐ ☐ ☐ ☐

Large Milk, Large Brown Egg, Large White Egg,
Large Goat Milk, Wool, Duck Egg

ARTISAN BUNDLE
— KEG —

☐ ☐ ☐ ☐ ☐ ☐

Truffle Oil, Cloth, Goat Cheese, Cheese, Honey, Jelly, Apple,
Apricot, Orange, Peach, Pomegranate, Cherry

Greenhouse

Fish Tank

RIVER FISH
— 30 BAIT —

☐ ☐ ☐ ☐

Sunfish, Catfish, Shad, Tiger Trout

NIGHT FISH
— SMALL GLOW RING —

☐ ☐ ☐

Walleye, Bream, Eel

LAKE FISH
— DRESSED SPINNER —

☐ ☐ ☐ ☐

Largemouth Bass, Carp, Bullhead, Sturgeon

OCEAN FISH
— 5 BEACH WARP TOTEM —

☐ ☐ ☐ ☐

Sardine, Tuna, Red Snapper, Tilapia

SPECIALTY FISH
— 5 DISH O' THE SEA —

☐ ☐ ☐ ☐

Pufferfish, Ghostfish, Sandfish, Woodskip

CRAB POT
— 3 CRAB POTS —

☐ ☐ ☐ ☐ ☐

Lobster, Crayfish, Crab, Cockle, Mussel, Shrimp, Snail, Periwinkle, Oyster, Clam

Glittering Boulder Removed

Boiler Room

BLACKSMITH'S
— FURNACE —

☐ ☐ ☐

Copper Bar, Iron Bar, Gold Bar

GEOLOGIST'S
— 5 OMNI GEODES —

☐ ☐ ☐ ☐

Quartz, Earth Crystal, Frozen Tear, Fire Quartz

ADVENTURER'S
— SMALL MAGNET RING —

☐ ☐

99 Slime, 10 Bat Wing, Solar Essence, Void Essence

Mine Carts Repaired

Bulletin Board

CHEF'S
— 3 PINK CAKES —

☐ ☐ ☐ ☐ ☐ ☐

Maple Syrup, Fiddlehead Fern, Truffle,
Poppy, Maki Roll, Fried Egg

DYE
— SEED MAKER —

☐ ☐ ☐ ☐ ☐ ☐

Red Mushroom, Sea Urchin, Sunflower,
Duck Feather, Aquamarine, Red Cabbage

FIELD RESEARCH
— RECYCLING MACHINE —

☐ ☐ ☐ ☐

Purple Mushroom, Nautilus Shell, Chub, Frozen Geode

FODDER
— HEATER —

☐ ☐ ☐

10 Hay, 10 Wheat, 3 Apples

ENCHANTER'S
— 5 GOLD BARS —

☐ ☐ ☐ ☐

Oak Resin, Wine, Rabbit's Foot, Pomegranate

Friendship

Vault

2,500g
— 3 CHOCOLATE CAKES —

5,000g
— 30 QUALITY FERTILIZER —

10,000g
— LIGHTNING ROD —

25,000g
— CRYSTALARIUM —

Bus Repair

Joja Membership

For just 5,000g, you can purchase a JojaMart membership and contribute to the improvement of your community. As a JojaMart member, you'll receive storewide discounts on all purchases. And with your membership, the Joja Corporation will be able to establish a warehouse on the grounds of the old Community Center.

The Joja warehouse is just that: a warehouse, with nothing of value. No Bundles, no Junimos, no warmth. Just shelves full of boxes.

Instead of gathering sets of items to complete Bundles, you'll invest directly in the improvement of the community with cold, hard cash. The major improvement milestones are the same, but with set prices.

Joja
Join Us. Thrive.

"Community Development" Projects

Location:

Pelican Town

Projects:

☐ **Bus:** 40,000g
All the necessary repairs will be made to the bus, restoring service to Calico Desert.

☐ **Minecarts:** 15,000g
The minecarts throughout the valley will be repaired, allowing you to travel quickly to a number of destinations.

☐ **Bridge:** 25,000g
The broken bridge east of the mines will be repaired, granting access to the Quarry.

☐ **Greenhouse:** 35,000g
The Greenhouse on your farm will be rebuilt.

☐ **Panning:** 20,000g
The boulder near the mines will be removed; ores and minerals will begin to flow into the rivers, enabling panning.

Prepared by:

Morris

Once all of the improvement goals have been met and checked off Morris's handy checklist, the employees of the local JojaMart will gather to celebrate your accomplishment. To commemorate the event, Joja management will reward you with your very own Joja Cola vending machine.

Congratulations.

You're the hero of the Joja Corporation.

187

THE SECRET NOTES

On a cold, crisp Winter morning, you might catch a glimpse of a shadowy figure lurking in the distance as you head toward town. Use the expert tracking skills you've no doubt developed over the past seasons on the farm to find his hiding place, and he'll hand over the Magnifying Glass he found.

With the Magnifying Glass, you'll be able to uncover Secret Notes as you farm, forage, mine and battle. Secret Notes lead to all sorts of treasure, goodies, and even new adventures! Try to find them all!

STATUE of UNCERTAINTY

In the depths of the Sewers stands a strange statue, a monument to a powerful guardian spirit of uncertainty and clouded judgment. If one were to make an offering of, say, 10,000g to this statue, it might be possible to alter one's career path by changing one's specializations in one of the five skills (Farming, Mining, Foraging, Fishing or Combat).

YEAR 3

If you'll recall, Grandpa left a note for you at the shrine on your farm letting you know he'd return on the dawn of the third year. When his spirit appears before you on the first of Spring, he'll evaluate your progress, both on the farm and in life.

If your evaluation score is especially high, you may earn a very valuable gift. If not, don't despair; you can request a re-evaluation from Grandpa at any time by placing a Diamond on the shrine altar.

IRIDIUM ORE
✦ x2-8
PER DAY

SCORE 12 or higher
out of 21 potential points
and you'll receive the
⋛ STATUE of PERFECTION ⋚

	ACHIEVEMENT	POINTS
THESE ARE CUMULATIVE — 1,000,000 EARNED = 7 TOTAL POINTS	50,000g EARNED	1
	100,000g EARNED	1
	200,000g EARNED	1
	300,000g EARNED	1
	500,000g EARNED	1
	1,000,000g EARNED	2
	30+ levels in Skills	1
	Level 10 in every Skill	1
	Complete Museum Collection	1
	Catch Every Fish	1
	Ship Every Item	1
	Fully Upgraded House	1
	8+ Hearts with 5+ Villagers	1
	8+ Hearts with 10+ Villagers	1
	4+ Hearts with your pet	1
	Completed Community Center	3
	Skull Key obtained	1
	Rusty Key obtained	1

THE SUMMER LUAU
How to Improve Soup and Influence Governors

On the 11th of Summer, Pelican Town plays host to the annual beach Luau. This festive summer event even invites a visit from the Governor, who is always eager to sample the fresh delicacies the valley has to offer. The main attraction at the Luau is the communal soup pot; every villager adds an ingredient that they feel will help balance the complex flavor of the soup.

But now that you're here, things are a little different. By adding just the right special ingredient, you can take the soup's flavor to the next level and win everyone's respect and admiration. You can earn up to 120 friendship points with every villager with the right ingredient!

If you're not able to add something impressive to the mix, it's best to add nothing at all; after all, the soup was passable to begin with. And a truly terrible ingredient could cost you as much as 100 friendship points with EVERYONE!

These ingredients will get you a **GOOD** reaction!
+ 60 pts

Cauliflower	Super Cucumber	⭐ Winter Root
Cheese	Artichoke	Coffee
Fairy Rose	Red Cabbage	Milk
Goat Cheese	Crystal Fruit	Maple Syrup
Melon	⭐ Grape	Truffle Oil
Truffle	⭐ Hazelnut	Beer
Yam	Snow Yam	Oil
Catfish	⭐ Spice Berry	Rice
Sturgeon	⭐ Wild Plum	Vinegar

...In a pinch? Pick these up the day before from Pierre's or the Saloon!

These will get you the <u>BEST</u> reaction:

IRIDIUM OR GOLD STAR ONLY
+ 120 pts

⭐ Cauliflower	⭐ Yam
⭐ Cheese	⭐ Catfish
⭐ Fairy Rose	⭐ Sturgeon
⭐ Goat Cheese	⭐ Super Cucumber
⭐ Melon	⭐ Artichoke
⭐ Truffle	⭐ Red Cabbage

THE STARDEW VALLEY FAIR

Rockin' the Grange Display

On the 16th of Fall, come to the Town Square with nine of your finest goods that showcase your farming and other skills. These nine items should represent at least six of the following categories:

- Animal Products
- Artisan Goods
- Cooking
- Fish
- Foraging (including Flowers/Tree Saps)
- Fruits
- Minerals
- Vegetables

You get 5 points automatically for participating, 2 points for each item placed and 5 points per category displayed (up to 30 points). Each item you submit will earn you up to 8 points based on its quality and value.

NUMBER OF POINTS GIVEN PER ITEM

5   PARTICIPATION ✓
18   NINE ITEMS (2pts each) ✓
+ 30   SIX CATEGORIES (5pts each) ✓
___
53   *90 TOTAL POINTS NEEDED FOR FIRST PLACE!*

THAT LEAVES...
37 points needed from NINE total items

ITEM VALUE	NO STAR	SILVER STAR	GOLD STAR	IRIDIUM STAR
0g+	1	2	3	5
20g+	2	3	4	6
90g+	3	4	5	7
200g+	4	5	6	8
300g+	5	6	6	8
400g+	6	6	6	8

90 total points will get you first place and 1,000 Star Tokens! There's a booth here that sells a Stardrop for 2,000 Star Tokens, so you'll have to gamble or fish for the rest. FYI, they say that green is a pretty lucky color.

THE WINTER NIGHT MARKET

WINTER 15-17, 5PM - CLOSE

For three days in the middle of Winter, merchants and artisans gather from all across the Gem Sea to share their wares with the fine folks of Pelican Town. On these nights, cozy up with a FREE cup of hot Coffee and peruse the unique and sometimes mysterious items on display.

Not one to miss an opportunity, the Travelling Cart vendor makes an appearance. As usual, the items available (and their prices) are random.

Embark on the deep-sea fishing tour for only 1,000g; unique fish and other treasures await your hook at the bottom of the sea! Or relax and watch the Mermaid Show, where the mermaids dance and sing their mesmerizing song. They say the mermaids enjoy hearing others play their song as well; why not give it a try?

Seasonal Decor Vendor

🎍 Big Green Cane	200g		🎁 Seasonal Decor	500g
🌿 Green Canes	200g		🎄 Seasonal Plant	500g
🍬 Mixed Canes	200g		🌲 Seasonal Plant	500g
🍭 Red Canes	200g		🪴 Seasonal Plant	500g
🎏 Big Red Cane	200g		🌱 Seasonal Plant	500g
🕯 Plain Torch	800g		🌸 Seasonal Plant	500g
🪵 Stump Torch	800g		🪴 Seasonal Plant	500g
🎌 Clouds Banner	1,000g			

Strange Goods Vendor

🪦 Grave Stone (15th)	200g		🦉 Stone Owl (17th)	500g
🗿 Stone Frog (15th)	500g		🔺 Cone Hat	2,500-10,000g
🛡 Suit of Armor (16th)	200g		🔥 Iridium Fireplace	15,000g
🦜 Stone Parrot (16th)	500g		🎃 Rarecrow #7	5,000g
🪵 Log Section (17th)	200g		🎃 Rarecrow #8	5,000g

The Strange Goods Vendor also offers a wide variety of seeds and starters from a particular season each night of the market.

The famous painter Lupini displays his works and you can own his latest piece for just 1,200g. Be sure to visit more than once, since he'll have a different painting available each night of the market, and new pieces each year!

If you lose track of time and don't think you'll make it back home by 2am, not to worry! For only 250g, the mysterious Shrouded Figure outside Willy's shop will allow you to use a Farm Warp Totem; you'll be instantly transported back to the farm, safe and sound.

COLLECTING RARECROWS

Rarecrows work just like normal Scarecrows, including their crow protection radius of roughly 8 tiles, but add a little fun to your fields. Collect them all!

SOLD DURING the STARDEW VALLEY FAIR FOR 800 ☆

SOLD DURING SPIRIT'S EVE FOR 5,000 g

SOLD AT THE CASINO for ⓒ 10,000

SOLD RANDOMLY DURING FALL/WINTER AT THE TRAVELLING CART FOR 4,000g

SOLD DURING the FLOWER DANCE FOR 2,500g

DWARF SELLS FOR 2,500g

20 ARTIFACTS DONATED TO the MUSEUM

40 ITEMS DONATED TO the MUSEUM

The Zuzu City Rarecrow Society has been known to reward those who complete the whole collection with an exclusive scarecrow crafting recipe. This heavy-duty Deluxe Scarecrow has an amazing 16-tile crow protection radius!

OBTAINING EVERY STARDROP FRUIT

Its flavor is strangely reminiscent of _____.

Eating this fruit is a life-altering experience. It gives you a permanent spring in your step and more energy to take on each day!

 Show your best wares at the Stardew Valley Fair and purchase a Stardrop for 2,000 Star Tokens.

 Make your way to the treasure chest at level 100 of the Mines.

 Catch every different fish there is to catch and Willy will reach out to show his admiration.

 Make your spouse the happiest spouse in all the land by attaining 13 out of 14 hearts!

 Feed a Sweet Gem Berry to a certain statue hidden away in forested ruins.

 Befriend a friendly shadow in the Sewers and purchase a Stardrop for 20,000g.

 Complete the entire Museum collection by donating 95 unique items.

THE DARK TALISMAN

Once you've completed the full set of community revitalization goals, Wizard will contact you with a request to retrieve a bottle of Magic Ink from the lair of his ex-wife, the Witch. With this ink, Wizard will be able to summon arcane structures to aid you on the farm. The path to the Witch's lair is blocked by an enchanted stone sentry; you'll need the Dark Talisman to remove the enchantment and dismiss the sentry. Krobus is known to have been in possession of such an artifact.

Krobus did indeed have the talisman, but he dropped it while exploring the strange tunnel nearby, and sealed the tunnel's entrance as a precaution. He'll unseal it and allow you access, where you'll battle hordes of mutant grubs and flies as you search for the Dark Talisman.

VAMPIRE RING RECOMMENDED

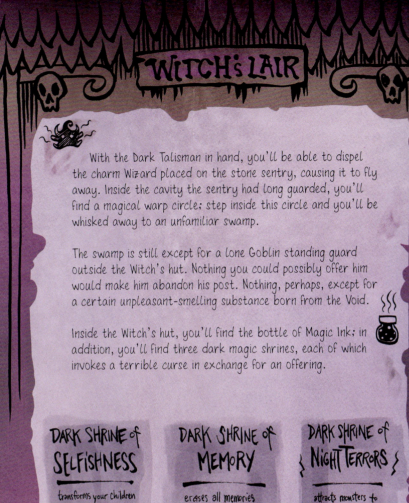

WITCH'S LAIR

With the Dark Talisman in hand, you'll be able to dispel the charm Wizard placed on the stone sentry, causing it to fly away. Inside the cavity the sentry had long guarded, you'll find a magical warp circle; step inside this circle and you'll be whisked away to an unfamiliar swamp.

The swamp is still except for a lone Goblin standing guard outside the Witch's hut. Nothing you could possibly offer him would make him abandon his post. Nothing, perhaps, except for a certain unpleasant-smelling substance born from the Void.

Inside the Witch's hut, you'll find the bottle of Magic Ink; in addition, you'll find three dark magic shrines, each of which invokes a terrible curse in exchange for an offering.

DARK SHRINE of SELFISHNESS

transforms your children into doves, setting them free and wiping your spouse's memories of them.

offering:
PRISMATIC SHARD

DARK SHRINE of MEMORY

erases all memories between you and your ex-spouse, making you complete strangers again.

offering:
30,000g

DARK SHRINE of NIGHT TERRORS

attracts monsters to your farm at night. Can be disabled with a second offering.

offering:
STRANGE BUN

Abandoned Jojamart

On a dark and stormy night, shortly after the
revitalization of the Community Center, a powerful
blast of lightning rocks the abandoned ruins of the
JojaMart. Inside, one lone Junimo remains, separated
from its kin and yearning to return home...

MISSING BUNDLE
— MOVIE TICKET —

☐ ☐ ☐ ☐ ☐

5 Ancient Fruit (Gold-quality), Wine (Silver-quality), Dinosaur Mayonnaise,
Caviar, Prismatic Shard, Void Salmon (Gold-quality)

Many of the items required to fulfill this Bundle
and send the little one on its way can be difficult
to obtain. But with patience and perseverance come
a great reward that everyone in Pelican Town can
enjoy together!

Movie Theater

MOVIE THEATER

Once reunited with their lost one, the Junimos will express their gratitude by using their magic to transform the JojaMart into a brand new Movie Theater!

Once per week, you can visit alone or invite a friend or that special someone to watch the season's big hit movie. Treat your guest to a delicious snack at the concession counter as well.

The Movie Theater also features a Crane Game; for 500g, you get three plays and three chances to win fabulous prizes. A number of unique items can only be found here, including movie posters and special seasonal decorations.

WILLY'S BOAT

Once the Community Center has been completely revitalized and Willy has the time to pursue his own personal projects, he'll invite you to the back room of his shop to show off one such project: a dilapidated old boat he inherited from his father. It'll take a lot of work to get the boat back into working order, and Willy lacks the materials: 200 pieces of Hardwood, 5 Iridium Bars and 5 Battery Packs. If you can round up the supplies, Willy will enlist Robin's help, and the two of them will work through the night to make all the needed repairs and prepare the boat for a voyage across the Gem Sea!

As soon as the boat is once again seaworthy, Willy will happily take you on a tour of the Fern Islands, all the way south to Ginger Island, a tropical paradise at the foot of a volcano. You can visit any time you like—as long as the Fish Shop is open—by buying a ticket for just 1,000g!

GOLDEN WALNUTS

Ginger Island is home to a unique species of tree that bears mystical and valuable Golden Walnuts. The colorful birds of the island are especially fond of these strange walnuts, and will greatly reward anyone kind enough to bring them a handful of the delicious treats by building and repairing buildings and other useful structures all over the place!

These elusive seeds can be found in the strangest of places; though some are still waiting to be picked from their trees, many have been buried around the island, taken by the monsters of the nearby volcano and hoarded by creatures who will only part with them in exchange for your help.

By seeking out peculiar spots in the ground to dig, solving riddles in unlikely places and braving the dungeon in the volcano on the north side of the island, you'll soon find you have more Golden Walnuts than you know what to do with, which suits the parrots just fine!

If you're having trouble finding those last few Golden Walnuts to complete your collection, a certain parrot who asked for you very first walnut might know where they all are.

Ginger Island

A Dock
B Leo's Nest
C Volcano
D Parrot Express
E Resort
F Gem Bird Shrine
G Tiger Slime Grove
H Birdie's Hut
I Island Field Office
J Sleeping Turtle

T

D

C

B

D

I

F

K

J

Q

E

D

A

R

ISLAND INHABITANTS

Ginger Island is far from deserted, it would seem. Not only is the island home to countless colorful parrots, dangerous striped Tiger Slimes and a host of volcanic villains, but a surprising number of friendly faces await as well. From shops and traders to explorers and talking frogs, there's never a lonely day in this island paradise.

And who knows? Maybe with enough persistence and the right gifts, you'll be able to invite a certain island inhabitant to come live in Stardew Valley!

LEO

Good Bird Boy
Leo's Nest, Cliff West of the Volcano, Island Beach

Duck Feather, Mango, Ostrich Egg, Poi

Dragon Tooth, Nautilus Shell, Quartz, Rainbow Shell, Sea Urchin, Spice Berry

Cooked Foods, Pickles, Triple Shot Espresso, Coffee, Alcoholic Drinks

SUMMER 26

Family: The birds of Ginger Island

BIRDIE After her husband was lost at sea, this pirate's widow spent years searching for him. Now all she wants is to find a memento to bring peace to her soul, though she certainly doesn't mind a bit of company now and then.

PROF. SNAIL This intrepid explorer and archaeologist may have bitten off a bit more than he can chew for once; after rescuing him from his subterranean confines, you can help him collect fossils and survey the island's natural features.

GOURMAND A gargantuan frog who pines for a time when fruits, vegetables and other crops were plentiful on the island. If you can grow some of those crops to help him reminisce, he'll reward you with Golden Walnuts aplenty!

ISLAND TRADER

The Island Trader offers a wide variety of rare and exotic goods, trading for other items of value from around Ginger Island.

Open all day, every day once unlocked for 10 Golden Walnuts.

Everyday stock:			
Warp Totem: Farm	5 Taro Root	(Mon) Small Cap	30 Taro Root
Taro Tuber	2 Bone Fragment	(Tues) Palm Wall Ornament	Pineapple
Pineapple Seeds	Magma Cap	(Wed) Bluebird Mask	30 Taro Root
Tropical TV	30 Taro Root	(Thu) 'Volcano' Photo	5 Mango
Jungle Torch	5 Cinder Shard	(Fri) Deluxe Cowboy Hat	30 Taro Root
Banana Sapling	5 Dragon Tooth	(Sat) Oceanic Rug	3 Blue Discus
Mango Sapling	75 Mussel	(Sun) Tropical Double Bed	5 Banana
Wild Double Bed	100 Cinder Shard	(Even Days) Tropical Chair	Lionfish
Tropical Bed	20 Ginger	Golden Coconut (after Clint opens one)	10 Coconut
Mahogany Seed	Stingray		
Luau Skirt	50 Taro Root	Galaxy Soul (last day of each season)	10 Radioactive Bar
Banana Pudding Recipe	30 Bone Fragment		
Deluxe Retaining Soil Recipe	50 Cinder Shard		

SLEEP HUT

On the western expanse of Ginger Island lie the ruins of an old thatched-roof hut, collapsed and broken. In exchange for 20 Golden Walnuts, the island parrots will quickly rebuild the hut into a spacious tropical Farmhouse, complete with kitchen and enough beds for all the farmhands on your Farm!

Once the hut is complete, you'll be able to farm, explore and adventure without worrying about making the trek all the way back to Stardew Valley at the end of the day. The parrots will also happily build a mailbox next to the hut for an additional 5 Golden Walnuts; you'll be able to access your mail from your tropical home away from home. If you do start to feel homesick, a special Farm Warp Obelisk can be constructed for 20 Golden Walnuts... and it doubles as a bird nest!

ISLAND OBELISK

After your first visit to Ginger Island, Wizard will be able to conjure the Island Obelisk on your farm, allowing you to quickly return at any time.

1,000,000g, 10 Iridium Bar, 10 Dragon Tooth, 10 Banana

ISLAND RESORT

You can't keep an island paradise like this a secret forever, so why not share its beauty with the people of Pelican Town? For just 20 Golden Walnuts, the parrots will turn the heaps of wood scrap on the southern beach into a cozy beach Resort! Then your fellow townsfolk can visit all they like to enjoy the warm sunshine and the relaxing sound of the waves, weather permitting.

On days when Gus can bring himself to step out from behind the bar at the Stardrop Saloon, you'll find him tending bar here instead, offering a selection of tasty beverages, including a few tropical-inspired concoctions.

GUS's BAR

Piña Colada	600g
Beer	500g
Pale Ale	1,000g
Mead	800g
Cranberry Candy	400g
Mango Wine ⭐	5,000g
Tropical Curry Recipe	2,000g

GINGER ISLAND'S RICHES

300g

BOTH CAN GROW ON YOUR FARM IN SUMMER

14 days; 7 days

PINEAPPLE

20g

TARO TUBER

GROWS FASTER NEAR WATER, LIKE RICE SHOOTS

100g

→ **TARO ROOT**

10 days

7 days w/ irrigation

130g

BOTH CAN GROW ON YOUR FARM IN SUMMER

150g

TREES

100g

Harvest trees for hardwood

MANGO

BANANA

MAHOGANY SEED

FORAGING

60g

CURES NAUSEA

GINGER

100g

COCONUT

2/6

CLINT CAN OPEN THEM

GOLDEN COCONUT

LIONFISH 100g

50, SMOOTH

STINGRAY 180g

PIRATE COVE

80, SINKER

BLUE DISCUS 120g

60, DART

OMNI GEODE NODE
VOLCANO

CLAY NODE
ISLAND QUARRY

MUSSEL NODE
WEST BEACH

BONE NODE
BONE FRAGMENT 12g
ISLAND QUARRY

CINDER SHARD NODE
CINDER SHARD 50g
VOLCANO

ISLAND FIELD OFFICE FOSSILS

Professor Snail is in need of someone to help him hunt down fossils, as well as to perform a survey of the island's flora and fauna.

Once the collection and survey are complete, he'll reward you with a recipe for crafting the Ostrich Incubator, allowing you to hatch and raise Ostriches on your Farm!

OSTRICH INCUBATOR
50 BONE FRAGMENT
50 CINDER SHARD
50 HARDWOOD

FITS IN BARNS

WARP TOTEM: ISLAND

5 HARDWOOD
1 DRAGON TOOTH
1 GINGER

VOLCANO DWARF

WARP TO GINGER ISLAND

FAIRY DUST

1 DIAMOND
1 FAIRY ROSE

BIRDIE'S QUEST

MAKES KEGS, FURNACES AND OTHER
MACHINES FINISH THEIR CYCLE

MAGIC BAIT

1 RADIOACTIVE ORE
3 BUG MEAT

×5

WALNUT ROOM

CATCH FISH FROM ANY
TIME, WEATHER AND SEASON

DELUXE RETAINING
SOIL

5 STONE
3 FIBER
1 CLAY

ISLAND TRADER

GUARANTEES SOIL STAYS
WATERED OVERNIGHT

HYPER SPEED-GRO

1 RADIOACTIVE ORE
3 BONE FRAGMENT
1 SOLAR ESSENCE

WALNUT ROOM

INCREASES GROWTH RATE BY >33%

×5

DELUXE FERTILIZER

1 IRIDIUM BAR
40 SAP

WALNUT ROOM

CHANCE FOR IRIDIUM-QUALITY CROPS

HEAVY TAPPER

30 HARDWOOD
1 RADIOACTIVE BAR

WALNUT ROOM

HARVESTS PRODUCTS FROM
TREES IN HALF THE TIME

HOPPER

10 HARDWOOD
1 IRIDIUM BAR
1 RADIOACTIVE BAR

WALNUT ROOM

LOADS ITEMS INTO
MACHINES AUTOMATICALLY

BANANA PUDDING

+125   +56

ISLAND TRADER

MINING +1, LUCK +1, DEFENSE +1

ABIGAIL LOVES THIS

GINGER ALE

 ×3

+63   +28

VOLCANO DWARF

LUCK +1

VINCENT LOVES THIS!

MANGO STICKY RICE

+113   +50

LEO ♡7+

DEFENSE +3

SANDY'S FAVORITE

POI

 ×4

+75   +33

LEO ♡3+

LEO LOVES POI

TROPICAL CURRY

+150   +67

GUS RESORT

FORAGING +4

CAROLINE AND GUS
LOVE THIS DISH

SQUID INK RAVIOLI

+125   +56

COMBAT LVL 9

MINING +1

INTO THE VOLCANO

The north side of the island rises high above the rest, its sandy soil giving way to the volcanic rock of a mountain peak. Within that mountain, rivers and pools of magma flow through an ever-shifting, ever-changing cavern full of ferocious beasts and Dwarvish ruins.

In the depths of the volcano, a lone Dwarvish shopkeeper peddles wares and offers respite from the dangers above and below. Some of the offerings here vary from day to day, but many can be lifesavers in this treacherous place, assuming you have the ability to communicate with Dwarves.

Cinderclown Shoes	100 Cinder Shard
Cherry Bomb	300g
Bomb	600g
Mega Bomb	1,000g
(50%) Roots Platter	1,200g
(50%) Super Meal	1,200g
(25%) Pink Bow	10,000g
Warp Totem: Island Recipe	10,000g
Ginger Ale Recipe	1,000g

MAGMA SPRITE

HP 220

DROPS CINDER SHARDS

MAGMA SPARKER

HP 310

DROPS CINDER SHARDS

HP 415

FOUND IN WEST ISLAND

TIGER SLIME

LAVA LURK

HP 220

SHOOTS FIREBALLS

MAY DROP DRAGON TEETH

MAGMA DUGGY

HP 380

MAY DROP TARO ROOT

FALSE MAGMA CAP

HP 290

DROPS REAL MAGMA CAPS

DWARVISH SENTRY

HP 300

MAY DROP GEMS

HOT HEAD

HP 250

CAN EXPLODE WHEN ANGRY!

213

GOLDEN HELMET

golden coconut

DELUXE PIRATE HAT

volcano dungeon chest

PINK BOW

volcano dwarf,
10,000g

FROG HAT

gourmand's cave fishing

BLUEBIRD MASK

island trader,
30 taro root

SMALL CAP

island trader,
30 taro root

DELUXE COWBOY HAT

island trader, 30 taro root

STAR HELMET

mushroom tree seed
+ cloth

RADIOACTIVE GOGGLES

radioactive bar
+ cloth

SWASHBUCKLER HAT

dragon tooth
+ cloth

SUNGLASSES

cinder shard + cloth

TIGER HAT

dropped by tiger slimes

WARRIOR HELMET

ostrich egg + cloth

FORAGER'S HAT

ginger + cloth

???'S HAT

walnut room

??? MASK

??? fruit + cloth

???

volcano caldera,
perfection

CINDERCLOWN SHOES

+6 DEFENSE
+5 IMMUNITY

volcano
dwarf shop

MERMAID BOOTS

+5 DEFENSE
+8 IMMUNITY

volcano
chest

DRAGONSCALE BOOTS

+7 DEFENSE

volcano
chest

SOUL SAPPER RING

RECOVER ENERGY WHEN SLAYING MONSTERS

volcano chest

PHOENIX RING

ONCE PER DAY, IF YOU'RE KNOCKED OUT, YOU'LL BE RESTORED

volcano chest

HOT JAVA RING

MONSTERS MAY DROP COFFEE!

volcano chest

PROTECTION RING

INVINCIBILITY PERIOD UP

volcano chest

DWARF SWORD

65-75 DMG

+2 SPEED
+4 DEFENSE

volcano chest

DWARF DAGGER

32-38 DMG

+1 SPEED
+6 DEFENSE
+5 WEIGHT
+6 CRIT CHANCE

volcano chest

DWARF HAMMER

75-85 DMG

+2 DEFENSE
+5 WEIGHT

volcano chest

DRAGONTOOTH CUTLASS

75-90 DMG
+50 CRIT POWER

volcano chest

DRAGONTOOTH SHIV

40-50 DMG
+5 WEIGHT
+3 CRIT CHANCE
+100 CRIT POWER

volcano chest

DRAGONTOOTH CLUB

80-100 DMG

+3 WEIGHT
+50 CRIT POWER

volcano chest

THE FORGE

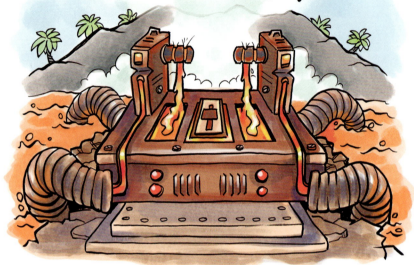

Long ago, the Dwarves who lived on Ginger Island built a massive Forge in the volcano's caldera, harnessing the power of the volcano itself—as well as the energy condensed within the mountain's Cinder Shards—to forge mighty weapons and tools. And to this day, that Forge still stands, waiting for someone new to come along and breathe new life into their equipment.

By forging gems into your weapons, you'll be able to make them more powerful, adding damage, speed, knockback, and even additional chances for a critical hit! And, should you change your mind, any weapon can be unforged at any time, restoring it to its original condition and recovering some of the Cinder Shards used in the forging process.

Weapons and tools can be enchanted with the power of a Prismatic Shard; it can be hard to predict just what sort of enchantment might result, and only one enchantment can affect an item at any time, but you can reforge the item to change the enchantment as long as you have another Prismatic Shard.

Two different rings can also be combined into one, granting the effects of both. Weapons can be merged as well, creating a custom weapon with the appearance of one and the statistics of another.

You can enchant weapons and tools by infusing the magical energy of Prismatic Shards into them.
Each enchantment costs 20 Cinder Shards.

Artful:	Faster special move cooldown.
Bug Killer:	Extra damage to bugs, kills Armored Bugs.
Crusader:	Extra damage to undead & shadows, Mummies don't revive.
Vampiric:	Steal a bit of health when hitting monsters.
Haymaker:	Get more Fiber and harvest Hay when cutting weeds.

Auto-Hook:	Automatically hooks fish when they bite. (Rod)
Archaeologist:	Doubles chance of digging up Artifacts. (Hoe)
Bottomless:	Unlimited water. (Watering Can)
Efficient:	Uses no energy. (All tools)
Generous:	Chance of digging up twice as many items. (Hoe)
Master:	Increases effective Fishing level by one. (Rod)
Powerful:	Break rocks and chop trees in fewer swings. (Pickaxe, Axe)
Preserving:	Chance of not depleting Bait or Tackle. (Rod)
Reaching:	Adds 5x5 tile area of effect when charging. (Hoe, Watering Can)
Shaving:	Get extra Wood, Hardwood and Crops when chopping. (Axe)
Swift:	Tool can be swung and charged much faster. (Pickaxe, Axe, Hoe)

 Each weapon can be forged with up to three gems for three different effects. Forging the first gem costs 10 Cinder Shards, the second 15, and the third 20. A Diamond results in a set of random upgrades.

| WEIGHT UP | CRIT CHANCE UP | SPEED UP | CRIT DAMAGE UP | DAMAGE UP | DEFENSE UP | RANDOM THREE EFFECTS |

And for those who crave power, you'll find it by infusing 3 Galaxy Souls into each of the Galaxy weapons to forge the ultimate weapons:

INFINITY BLADE

80-100 DMG

+4 SPEED
+2 DEFENSE

INFINITY DAGGER

60-70 DMG

+1 SPEED
+3 SPEED
+5 WEIGHT
+4 CRIT CHANCE

INFINITY GAVEL

100-120 DMG

+2 SPEED
+1 DEFENSE
+5 WEIGHT

THE MYSTERIOUS WALNUT ROOM

Far along the western shore of Ginger Island, nestled in the cliffside, a strange monolithic door stands bearing these words: "Only the greatest walnut hunters may enter here." And indeed, the door will only open to those who have managed to truck down and collect at least 100 of the elusive Golden Walnuts scattered across the island.

Inside, secrets will be revealed, challenges will be undertaken, and great prizes will be awarded. By completing challenges, you can earn valuable Gems that aren't available anywhere else in the world. From the Walnut Room's vending machine, strange and powerful items can be obtained in exchange for these rare Gems.

Junimo Chest ×2	30 Gems	Seasoning ×10	10 Gems
Horse Flute	50 Gems	???'s Hat	5 Gems
Pierre's Missing Stocklist	50 Gems	Aquatic Sanctuary	20 Gems
Hopper	10 Gems	Heavy Tapper Recipe	20 Gems
Enricher ×4	20 Gems	Hyper Speed-Gro Recipe	30 Gems
Pressure Nozzle ×4	20 Gems	Deluxe Fertilizer Recipe	20 Gems
Deconstructor	20 Gems	Hopper Recipe	50 Gems
Key To The Town	20 Gems	Magic Bait Recipe	20 Gems
Galaxy Soul	40 Gems	Exotic Double Bed	50 Gems
Mushroom Tree Seed	5 Gems	Gem ×2	1 Golden Walnut
Magic Bait ×20	5 Gems	Golden Egg	100 Gems

Much like the Community Request and Special Orders boards, the Walnut Room provides its own unique challenges. From achieving a high score in Junimo Kart to shipping large amounts of a special crop within a single season, these requests will put your skills and wits to the test.

Some challenges require delving back into the Mines or Skull Cavern, but with added dangers; anyone brave enough to face these challenges may find nodes full of Radioactive Ore along the way down.

the Quest for Perfection

For the ultimate challenge seeker, the Walnut Room also features a progress tracker toward perfection. Here, only the most challenging tasks matter: shipping every crop, cooking every recipe, crafting every item... and these are just some of the feats that must be achieved in order to become an elite among elites.

Those who complete the list and reach absolute perfection can stand atop the Summit and celebrate their accomplishment.

- Produce & Forage Shipped
- Obelisks on Farm
- Golden Clock on Farm
- Monster Slayer Hero
- Great Friends
- Farmer Level
- Found All Stardrops
- Cooking Recipes Made
- Crafting Recipes Made
- Fish Caught
- Golden Walnuts Found

DANGERS IN THE DEEP

CAN DROP
SQUID INK

SHOOTS WEAKENING BUBBLES

COOL BUT
DANGEROUS

THREE
CAN
STACK

SNEAKY
ROCKS

RADIOACTIVE ORE

QUICK
AND
JUMPY

RARE

STICK
BUG!

FLY

GRUB

FAST
GHOST!

SNEAKY
STICKS

CAUSES
NAUSEA
PREVENTS YOU FROM EATING
(GINGER CURES IT)

220

ICE MAGIC STOPS YOU COLD!

MORE HP

FAST

HEALS MORE

TOUGHER THAN NORMAL

SHOOTS BLINDING ARROWS

SHOOTS 4X FIREBALLS

FAKE GOLD NODE

LOOOOOONG

SKULL CAVERN

THE LONGER THEY ARE, THE MORE HP THEY HAVE

These fearsome foes only appear during special quests, or after you've activated the Shrine of Challenge upon completing such a quest.

Chapter 8
Appendix & Farmer's Almanac

The world of Stardew Valley is filled with many different sorts of people, places, events and items. It can be difficult to keep track of villagers' gift preferences, cooking and crafting ingredients, crop growing cycles, and the myriad other tidbits of information you'll use in your day-to-day affairs on the farm and in the valley.

The following section serves as a quick reference guide for many of these pieces of data. Much like a condensed farmer's almanac, it provides a wealth of information, arranged into a set of handy charts:

Detailed crop info
Crafting
Cooking ingredients
Artisan goods
Villager gift preferences
...and much, much more!

You can refer to this info-packed section at any time when you need facts quickly.

SKILLS

Farming

Level 1	Level 2	Level 3	Level 4	Level 5	
Crafting Recipes	Crafting Recipes:	Crafting Recipes:	Crafting Recipes:	Choose a profession:	
Scarecrow Basic Fertilizer	Mayonnaise Machine Stone Fence Sprinkler	Bee House Speed-Gro Farmer's Lunch	Preserves Jar Basic Retaining Soil Iron Fence	**Rancher:** Animal products worth 20% more. **Tiller:** Crops worth 10% more.	

Mining

Level 1	Level 2	Level 3	Level 4	Level 5	
Crafting Recipes:	Crafting Recipes:	Crafting Recipes:	Crafting Recipes:	Choose a profession:	
Cherry Bomb	Staircase	Miner's Treat	Glowstone Ring Transmute (Fe)	**Miner:** +1 Ore per vein. **Geologist:** Chance for Gems to appear in pairs.	

Foraging

Level 1	Level 2	Level 3	Level 4	Level 5	
Crafting Recipes:	Crafting Recipes:	Crafting Recipes:	Crafting Recipes:	Choose a profession:	
Wild Seeds (Sp) Field Snack	Survival Burger	Tapper	Charcoal Kiln Wild Seeds (Su)	**Forester:** Chopping down trees produces 25% more Wood. **Gatherer:** Chance for double harvest of foraged items.	
Trees sometimes drop seeds.			+1 Wild berry harvesting		

Combat

Level 1	Level 2	Level 3	Level 4	Level 5	
Crafting Recipes:	Crafting Recipes:	Crafting Recipes:	Crafting Recipes:	Choose a profession:	
Bug Steak Sturdy Ring	Life Elixir	Roots Platter	Warrior Ring	**Fighter:** All attacks deal 10% more damage. +15 HP **Scout:** Critical strike chance increased by 50%.	

Fishing

Level 1	Level 2	Level 3	Level 4	Level 5	
Crafting Recipes:	Crafting Recipes:	Crafting Recipes:	Crafting Recipes:	Choose a profession:	
-	Bait	Crab Pot Dish O' The Sea	Recycling Machine	**Fisher:** Fish worth 25% more. **Trapper:** Resources required to craft Crab Pots reduced.	

	Level 6	Level 7	Level 8	Level 9	Level 10
Crafting Recipes:	Crafting Recipes:	Crafting Recipes:	Crafting Recipes:	Crafting Recipes:	Choose a profession:
	Cheese Press Hardwood Fence Quality Sprinkler	Loom Quality Retaining Soil	Oil Maker Keg Deluxe Speed-Gro	Seed Maker Iridium Sprinkler Quality Fertilizer	*If you chose Rancher at Level 5:* **Coopmaster:** Befriend Coop animals quicker. Incubation time cut in half. **Shepherd:** Befriend Barn animals quicker. Sheep produce Wool faster.
					If you chose Tiller at Level 5: **Artisan:** Artisan goods worth 40% more. **Agriculturist:** All crops grow 10% faster.

	Level 6	Level 7	Level 8	Level 9	Level 10
Crafting Recipes:	Crafting Recipes:	Crafting Recipes:	Crafting Recipes:	Crafting Recipes:	Choose a profession:
	Bomb	Transmute (Au)	Mega Bomb	Crystalarium	*If you chose Miner at Level 5:* **Blacksmith:** Metal Bars worth 50% more. **Prospector:** Coal find doubled.
					If you chose Geologist at Level 5: **Excavator:** Geode find doubled. **Gemologist:** Gems worth 30% more.

	Level 6	Level 7	Level 8	Level 9	Level 10
Crafting Recipes:	Crafting Recipes:	Crafting Recipes:	Crafting Recipes:	Crafting Recipes:	Choose a profession:
	Lightning Rod Wild Seeds (Fa) Warp Totem: Beach	Tree Fertilizer Wild Seeds (Wi) Warp Totem: Mountains	Warp Totem: Farm	Cookout Kit Rain Totem	*If you chose Forester at Level 5:* **Lumberjack:** Normal trees occasionally drop Hardwood. **Tapper:** Syrup is worth 25% more.
			+1 Wild berry harvesting		*If you chose Gatherer at Level 5:* **Botanist:** Foraged items are always highest quality, Iridium-star. **Tracker:** Locations of foragable items are revealed.

	Level 6	Level 7	Level 8	Level 9	Level 10
Crafting Recipes:	Crafting Recipes:	Crafting Recipes:	Crafting Recipes:	Crafting Recipes:	Choose a profession:
	Slime Egg-Press Oil of Garlic	Ring of Yoba Thorns Ring	Slime Incubator Explosive Ammo	Iridium Band	*If you chose Fighter at Level 5:* **Brute:** Damage is increased by 15%. **Defender:** HP is increased by 25.
				Cooking Recipe: Squid Ink Ravioli	*If you chose Scout at Level 5:* **Acrobat:** Cooldown on special moves is cut in half. **Desperado:** Critical hits are deadlier.

	Level 6	Level 7	Level 8	Level 9	Level 10
Crafting Recipes:	Crafting Recipes:	Crafting Recipes:	Crafting Recipes:	Crafting Recipes:	Choose a profession:
	Spinner Trap Bobber	Cork Bobber Treasure Hunter	Worm Bin Barbed Hook Dressed Spinner	Magnet Seafoam Pudding	*If you chose Fisher at Level 5:* **Angler:** Fish worth 50% more. **Pirate:** Chance to find treasure doubled.
					If you chose Trapper at Level 5: **Mariner:** Crab Pots never catch trash. **Luremaster:** Crab Pots no longer need to be baited.

Skill professions can be changed by the Statue of Uncertainty in the Sewers for 10,000g.

Pierre's vs. JojaMart

Name	Price (Pierre's)	Price (JojaMart)*
Amaranth Seeds	70g	87g
Apple Sapling	4,000g	-
Apricot Sapling	2,000g	-
Artichoke Seeds	30g	-
Auto-Petter (Available After Completing the Joja Warehouse)	-	50,000g
Basic Fertilizer	100g	-
Basic Retaining Soil	100g	-
Bean Starter	60g	75g
Blueberry Seeds	80g	-
Bok Choy Seeds	50g	62g
Bouquet	200g	-
Catalogue	30,000g	-
Cauliflower Seeds	80g	100g
Cherry Sapling	3,400g	-
Corn Seeds	150g	187g
Cranberry Seeds	240g	300g
Deluxe Speed-Gro	150g	-
Eggplant Seeds	20g	25g
Fairy Seeds	200g	250g
Flooring	100g	250g
Garlic Seeds	40g	-
Grape Starter	60g	75g
Grass Starter	100g	125g
Grass Starter Recipe	1,000g	-
Hops Starter	60g	75g
J. Cola Light	-	500g
Jazz Seeds	30g	37g
Joja Cola	-	75g
Joja Wallpaper	-	20g
Kale Seeds	70g	87g
Melon Seeds	80g	100g
Oil	200g	-
Orange Sapling	4,000g	-
Parsnip Seeds	20g	25g
Peach Sapling	6,000g	-
Pepper Seeds	40g	50g
Pomegranate Sapling	6,000g	-
Poppy Seeds	100g	125g
Potato Seeds	50g	62g
Pumpkin Seeds	100g	125g
Quality Fertilizer	150g	-
Quality Retaining Soil	150g	-
Radish Seeds	40g	50g
Red Cabbage Seeds	100g	-
Rice	200g	250g
Rice Shoot	40g	-
Spangle Seeds	50g	62g
Speed-Gro	100g	-
Sugar	100g	125g
Sunflower Seeds	200g	125g
Tomato Seeds	50g	62g
Tulip Bulb	20g	25g
Vinegar	200g	-
Wallpaper	100g	250g
Wheat Flour	100g	125g
Wheat Seeds	10g	12g
Yam Seeds	60g	75g

*JojaMart prices will be reduced to match Pierre's with membership; Sunflower Seeds will be reduced to 100g.

Carpenter's Shop

Robin carries a daily rotating stock of furniture items in addition to the following.

Name	Requirements			Price
Barrel Brazier Recipe	Stump Brazier Recipe	-	-	800g
Basic Log	-	-	-	250g
Basic Window	-	-	-	300g
Bed	-	-	-	500g
Brick Fireplace	-	-	-	1,000g
Brick Floor Recipe	-	-	-	500g
Budget TV	-	-	-	750g
Calendar	-	-	-	2,000g
Carved Brazier Recipe	Gold Brazier Recipe	-	-	2,000g
Child Bed	House Upgrade 2	-	-	2,000g
Crystal Path Recipe	-	-	-	200g
Deluxe Red Double Bed	Special Order	-	-	6,000g
Double Bed	House Upgrade 1	-	-	2,000g
Floor TV	-	-	-	700g
Furniture Catalogue	House Upgrade 1	-	-	200,000g
Gold Brazier Recipe	Barrel Brazier Recipe	-	-	1,000g
Iron Lamp-post Recipe	-	-	-	1,000g
Log Section	-	-	-	350g
Marble Brazier Recipe	Skull Brazier Recipe	-	-	5,000g
Mini-Fridge	House Upgrade 1	-	-	3,000g
Plasma TV	House Upgrade 1	-	-	4,500g
Rustic Plank Floor Recipe	-	-	-	200g
Seasonal Plant	-	-	-	400g
Skull Brazier Recipe	Carved Brazier Recipe	-	-	3,000g
Small Window	-	-	-	300g
Stepping Stone Path Recipe	-	-	-	100g
Stone*	-	-	-	20g / 100g
Stone Brazier Recipe	Wooden Brazier Recipe	-	-	400g
Stone Fireplace	-	-	-	1,500g
Stone Floor Recipe	-	-	-	100g
Stone Walkway Floor Recipe	-	-	-	200g
Stove Fireplace	-	-	-	3,000g
Straw Floor Recipe	-	-	-	200g
Stump Brazier Recipe	Stone Brazier Recipe	-	-	800g
Telephone	-	-	-	2,000g
Wood*	-	-	-	10g / 50g
Wood Chipper	Mail on Winter 2nd	-	-	1,000g
Wood Floor Recipe	-	-	-	100g
Wood Lamp-post Recipe	-	-	-	500g
Wooden Brazier Recipe	-	-	-	250g
Workbench	-	-	-	2,000g
Farm Buildings:				
Barn	Wood (350)	Stone (150)	-	6,000g
Big Barn	Wood (450)	Stone (200)	-	12,000g
Big Coop	Wood (400)	Stone (150)	-	10,000g
Coop	Wood (300)	Stone (100)	-	4,000g
Deluxe Barn	Wood (550)	Stone (300)	-	25,000g
Deluxe Coop	Wood (500)	Stone (200)	-	20,000g
Cabin	Stone (10)	-	-	100g
Cabin	Wood (5)	Fiber (10)	-	100g
Cabin	Wood (10)	-	-	100g
Fish Pond	Stone (200)	Seaweed (5)	Green Algae (5)	5,000g
Mill	Wood (150)	Stone (50)	Cloth (4)	2,500g
Shed	Wood (300)	-	-	15,000g
Big Shed	Wood (550)	Stone (300)	-	20,000g
Shipping Bin	Wood (150)	-	-	250g
Silo	Stone (100)	Clay (10)	Copper Bar (5)	100g
Slime Hutch	Stone (500)	Refined Quartz (10)	Iridium Bar (1)	10,000g
Stable	Hardwood (100)	Iron Bar (5)	-	10,000g
Well	Stone (75)	-	-	1,000g
House & Community Upgrades:				
House Upgrade 1	Wood (450)	-	-	10,000g
House Upgrade 2	Hardwood (150)	-	-	50,000g
House Upgrade 3	-	-	-	100,000g
Community Upgrade 1	Wood (950)	-	-	500,000g
Community Upgrade 2 (Shortcuts)	Community Upgrade 1	-	-	300,000g

*The prices of Wood & Stone increase from year 2 onward.

Store Hours

	Mon	Tue	Wed	Thu	Fri	Sat	Sun	Closed for festivals?
Pierre's General Store	9a - 5p	9a - 5p	*	9a - 5p	9a - 5p	9a - 5p	9a - 5p	yes
JojaMart	9a - 11p	9a - 11p	9a - 11p	9a - 11p	9a - 11p	9a - 11p	9a - 11p	yes
Carpenter's Shop	9a - 5p	-	9a - 5p	9a - 5p	9a - 4p	9a - 5p	9a - 5p	yes
Marnie's Ranch	-	-	9a - 4p	9a - 4p	9a - 4p	9a - 4p	9a - 4p	yes
The Stardrop Saloon	12p - 12a	12p - 12a	12p - 12a	12p - 12a	12p - 12a	12p - 12a	12p - 12a	yes
Harvey's Clinic	9a - 3p	9a - 3p	9a - 3p	9a - 3p	9a - 3p	9a - 3p	9a - 3p	yes
Blacksmith	9a - 4p	9a - 4p	9a - 4p	9a - 4p	closed if community center is complete	9a - 4p	9a - 4p	yes
Fish Shop	9a - 5p	9a - 5p	9a - 5p	9a - 5p	9a - 5p	closed if not raining	9a - 5p	yes
Wizard's Tower	6a - 11p	6a - 11p	6a - 11p	6a - 11p	6a - 11p	6a - 11p	6a - 11p	only flower dance & festival of ice
Travelling Cart	-	-	-	-	6a - 8p	-	6a - 8p	-
Oasis & Casino	9a - 11:50p	9a - 11:50p	9a - 11:50p	9a - 11:50p	9a - 11:50p	9a - 11:50p	9a - 11:50p	yes

*Pierre's General Store is open Wednesdays from 9a - 5p if the Community Center is completed.

Marnie's Ranch

	Name	Requirements			Price
	Auto-Grabber	Farming Level 10	-	-	25,000g
	Golden Egg	Perfection	-	-	100,000g
	Hay	-	-	-	50g
	Heater	-	-	-	2,000g
	Milk Pail	-	-	-	1,000g
	Ornamental Hay Bale	-	-	-	250g
	Shears	-	-	-	1,000g
	Chicken	Coop	-	-	800g
	Cow	Barn	-	-	1,500g
	Duck	Big Coop	-	-	1,200g
	Goat	Big Barn	-	-	4,000g
	Pig	Deluxe Barn	-	-	16,000g
	Rabbit	Deluxe Coop	-	-	8,000g
	Sheep	Deluxe Barn	-	-	8,000g

The Stardrop Saloon

	Name	Energy	Health	Price
	Beer	50	22	400g
	Bread	50	22	120g
	Coffee	3	1	300g
	Joja Cola (From Vending Machine)	13	5	75g
	Pizza	150	67	600g
	Salad	113	50	220g
	Spaghetti	75	33	240g
	Bread Recipe	50	22	100g
	Cookie Recipe (If not received from Evelyn's 4-Heart Event)	90	40	300g
	Hashbrowns Recipe	90	40	50g
	Maki Roll Recipe	100	45	300g
	Omelet Recipe	100	45	100g
	Pancakes Recipe	90	40	100g
	Pizza Recipe	150	67	150g
	Tortilla Recipe	50	22	100g
	Triple Shot Espresso Recipe	8	3	5,000g

Harvey's Clinic

Name	Energy	Health	Price
Energy Tonic	500	200	1,000g
Muscle Remedy	50	20	1,000g

Blacksmith

Name	Ingredients	Price
Coal*	-	150g / 250g
Copper Ore*	-	75g / 150g
Gold Ore*	-	400g / 750g
Iron Ore*	-	150g / 250g
Copper Tool Upgrade (Watering Can, Axe, Hoe, Pickaxe, Trash Can)	Copper Bar (5)	2,000g
Gold Tool Upgrade (Watering Can, Axe, Hoe, Pickaxe, Trash Can)	Gold Bar (5)	10,000g
Iridium Tool Upgrade (Watering Can, Axe, Hoe, Pickaxe, Trash Can)	Iridium Bar (5)	25,000g
Steel Tool Upgrade (Watering Can, Axe, Hoe, Pickaxe, Trash Can)	Iron Bar (5)	5,000g
Geode Processing (Including Artifact Troves and Golden Coconuts)	-	25g

*The prices of Coal & Ores increase from year 2 onward.

Fish Shop

Name	Requirements	Price
Bait	Fishing Level 2	5g
Bamboo Pole	-	500g
Barbed Hook	Fishing Level 8	1,000g
Copper Pan	Fish Tank Bundles	2,500g
Cork Bobber	Fishing Level 7	750g
Crab Pot	Fishing Level 3	1,500g
Dressed Spinner	Fishing Level 8	1,000g
Fiberglass Rod	Fishing Level 2	1,800g
Fisher Double Bed	-	25,000g
Iridium Rod	Fishing Level 6	7,500g
Large Fish Tank	-	2,000g
Lead Bobber	Fishing Level 6	200g
Magnet	Fishing Level 9	1,000g
Small Fish Tank	-	500g
Spinner	Fishing Level 6	500g
Training Rod	-	1,000g
Trap Bobber	Fishing Level 6	500g
Treasure Hunter	Fishing Level 7	750g
Trout Soup	-	250g

Wizard's Tower

Name	Requirements			Price
Desert Obelisk	Iridium Bar (20)	Coconut (10)	Cactus Fruit (10)	1,000,000g
Earth Obelisk	Iridium Bar (10)	Earth Crystal (10)	-	500,000g
Gold Clock	-	-	-	10,000,000g
Island Obelisk	Iridium Bar (10)	Dragon Tooth (10)	Banana (10)	1,000,000g
Junimo Hut	Stone (200)	Starfruit (9)	Fiber (100)	20,000g
Water Obelisk	Iridium Bar (5)	Clam (10)	Coral (10)	500,000g

229

SHOPS

Krobus's Shop

Name	Available	Price
Bat Wing	Sun. (Ltd. Qty.)	30g
Crystal Floor Recipe	Only One	500g
Iridium Sprinkler	Fri. (1/Week)	10,000g
Mixed Seeds	Thu. (10/Week)	30g
Monster Fireplace	Always	20,000g
Omni Geode	Tue. (1/Week)	350g
Random Fish or Fishing Gear	Wed. (Ltd. Qty.)	Varies
Random Food	Sat. (Ltd. Qty.)	Varies
Return Scepter	Only One	2,000,000g
Sign of the Vessel	Always	350g
Slime	Mon. (50/Week)	10g
Solar Essence	Always (10/Day)	80g
Stardrop	Only One	20,000g
Void Egg	Always	5,000g
Void Essence	Always (10/Day)	100g
Wicked Statue Recipe	Only One	1,000g

Dwarf's Shop

Name	Energy	Health	Price
Bomb	-	-	600g
Cherry Bomb	-	-	300g
Life Elixir	200	80	2,000g
Mega Bomb	-	-	1,000g
Miner's Treat	125	50	1,000g
Oil of Garlic	200	80	3,000g
Rarecrow #6	-	-	2,500g
Stone Cairn	-	-	200g
Weathered Floor Recipe	-	-	500g

Travelling Cart

The Travelling Cart sells a random assortment of items; the following are only sold here.

Name	Requirements				Price
Coffee Beans	-	-	-	-	2,500g
Rare Seed	-	-	-	-	1,000g
Rarecrow #4	-	-	-	-	4,000g
Wedding Ring Recipe*	-	-	-	-	500g

*Available only in multiplayer.

Oasis

	Name	Available	Price
	Beet Seeds	Every Day	20g
	Cactus Fruit	Tuesdays	150g
	Cactus Seeds	Every Day	150g
	Coconut	Mondays (Max. 10)	200g
	Deluxe Speed-Gro	Thursdays	80g
	Honey	Fridays	200g
	Ice Cream	Sundays	240g
	'Jade Hills Extended'	Wednesdays	5,000g
	Large Brown Couch	Sundays	3,000g
	Large Cottage Rug	Mondays	2,000g
	Large Green Rug	Fridays	2,500g
	Old World Rug	Thursdays	2,500g
	Omni Geode	Wednesdays	1,000g
	Quality Retaining Soil	Saturdays	200g
	Rhubarb Seeds	Every Day	100g
	Seasonal Plant	Every Day	100g
	Shirt (Random)	Every Day	1,000g
	Starfruit Seeds	Every Day	400g
	Wall Cactus	Every Day	700g
	Wall Sconce	Tuesdays (25%)	500g
	Wall Sconce	Tuesdays (25%)	500g
	Wall Sconce	Tuesdays (25%)	500g
	Wall Sconce	Tuesdays (25%)	500g
	Wall Sconce	Saturdays (50%)	500g
	Wall Sconce	Saturdays (50%)	500g

Casino

	Name	Price
	Burnt Offering	4,000 Qi Coins
	Hardwood Fence	100 Qi Coins
	Highway 89	4,000 Qi Coins
	Magnet	1,000 Qi Coins
	Modern Double Bed	8,000 Qi Coins
	Primal Motion	5,000 Qi Coins
	Rarecrow #3	10,000 Qi Coins
	Spires	3,000 Qi Coins
	Statue of Endless Fortune	1,000,000g
	Top Hat	8,000 Qi Coins
	Warp Totem: Farm	500 Qi Coins

Desert Trader

The Desert Trader operates every day except for Winter 15-17 (The Night Market)

Name	Available	Trade For
Artifact Trove	Always	5 Omni Geodes
Birch Double Bed	Always	1 Pearl
Bomb	Always	5 Quartz
Butterfly Hutch	Always	200 Bat Wings
Cheese	Fridays	1 Emerald
Cloth	Wednesdays	3 Aquamarines
Fall Seeds	Saturdays	2 Winter Seeds
Fiber	Always	5 Stone
Green Turban	Always	50 Omni Geodes
Hay x3	Mondays	1 Omni Geode
Magic Cowboy Hat	Odd-numbered days	333 Omni Geodes
Magic Rock Candy	Thursdays	3 Prismatic Shards
Magic Turban	Even-numbered days	333 Omni Geodes
Mega Bomb	Always	5 Iridium Ore
Spicy Eel	Always	1 Ruby
Spring Seeds	Saturdays	2 Summer Seeds
Staircase	Sundays	1 Jade
Summer Seeds	Saturdays	2 Fall Seeds
Triple Shot Espresso	Always	1 Diamond
Void Ghost Pendant	After reaching 10 hearts with Krobus	200 Void Essence
Warp Totem: Desert	Always	3 Omni Geodes
Warp Totem: Desert (Recipe)	Always	10 Iridium Bars
Winter Seeds	Saturdays	2 Spring Seeds

Island Trader

The Island Trader operates all day, every day once unlocked for 10 Golden Walnuts.

Name	Available	Trade For
Banana Pudding Recipe	Always	30 Bone Fragments
Banana Sapling	Always	5 Dragon Teeth
Bluebird Mask	Wednesdays	30 Taro Roots
Deluxe Cowboy Hat	Fridays	30 Taro Roots
Deluxe Retaining Soil Recipe	Always	50 Cinder Shards
Galaxy Soul	Last Day of Month	10 Radioactive Bars
Golden Coconut	After Breaking One Open	10 Coconuts
Jungle Torch	Always	5 Cinder Shards
Luau Skirt	Always	50 Taro Roots
Mahogany Seed	Always	1 Stingray
Mango Sapling	Always	75 Mussels
Oceanic Rug	Saturdays	3 Blue Discus
Palm Wall Ornament	Tuesdays	1 Pineapple
Pineapple Seeds	Always	1 Magma Cap
Small Cap	Mondays	30 Taro Roots
Taro Tuber	Always	2 Bone Fragments
Tropical Bed	Always	20 Ginger
Tropical Chair	Even-numbered Days	1 Lionfish
Tropical Double Bed	Sundays	5 Bananas
Tropical TV	Always	30 Taro Roots
'Volcano' Photo	Thursdays	5 Mangoes
Warp Totem: Farm	Always	5 Taro Roots
Wild Double Bed	Always	100 Cinder Shards

Volcano Dwarf

Name		Availability	Price
	Bomb	Always	600g
	Cherry Bomb	Always	300g
	Cinderclown Shoes	Always	100 Cinder Shards
	Ginger Ale Recipe	Only One	1,000g
	Mega Bomb	Always	1,000g
	Pink Bow	25% Chance	10,000g
	Roots Platter	50% Chance	1,200g
	Super Meal	50% Chance	1,200g
	Warp Totem: Island Recipe	Only One	1,000g

Walnut Room

Name		Price
	Aquatic Sanctuary	20
	Deconstructor	20
	Deluxe Fertilizer Recipe	20
	Enricher x4	20
	Exotic Double Bed	50
	Galaxy Soul	40
	Golden Egg	100
	Heavy Tapper Recipe	20
	Hopper	10
	Hopper Recipe	50
	Horse Flute	50
	Hyper Speed-Gro Recipe	30
	Junimo Chest (2)	30
	Key To The Town	20
	Magic Bait (20)	5
	Magic Bait Recipe	20
	Mr. Qi's Hat	5
	Mushroom Tree Seed	5
	Pierre's Missing Stocklist	50
	Pressure Nozzle x4	20
	Qi Gem (2)	1
	Qi Seasoning (10)	10

A different design is available each day at Pierre's for 100g, or JojaMart for 250g.
Or purchase the Catalogue for 30,000g for unrestricted access to the entire collection!

Name	Obtained		Purchase Price
1000 Years From Now	Winter Night Market		1,200g
A Night on Eco Hill	Museum (20 Donations)		-
Anchor	Carpenter's Shop Travelling Cart	•	750g 250 - 2,500g
Aquatic Sanctuary	Walnut Room		20 Qi Gems
Artist Bookcase	Carpenter's Shop Travelling Cart	•	1,200g 250 - 2,500g
Bamboo Mat	Carpenter's Shop Travelling Cart	•	250g 250 - 2,500g
Basic Log	Carpenter's Shop		250g
Basic Window	Carpenter's Shop Travelling Cart	•	300g 250 - 2,500g
Bear Statue	Museum (50 Donations)		-
Bed	Carpenter's Shop	•	500g
Big Green Cane	Winter Night Market		200g
Big Red Cane	Winter Night Market		200g
Birch Bench	Carpenter's Shop Travelling Cart	•	750g 250 - 2,500g
Birch Chair	Carpenter's Shop Travelling Cart		350g 250 - 2,500g
Birch Double Bed	Desert Trader		Pearl
Birch Dresser	Carpenter's Shop Travelling Cart	•	5,000g 250 - 2,500g
Birch End Table	Carpenter's Shop Travelling Cart	•	500g 250 - 2,500g
Birch Table	Carpenter's Shop Travelling Cart		750g 250 - 2,500g
Birch Tea-Table	Carpenter's Shop Travelling Cart	•	750g 250 - 2,500g
Blossom Rug	Furniture Catalogue Only	•	-
Blue Armchair	Carpenter's Shop Travelling Cart	•	1,000g 250 - 2,500g
Blue City	Carpenter's Shop Travelling Cart	•	250g 250 - 2,500g
Blue Couch	Carpenter's Shop Travelling Cart	•	1,750g 250 - 2,500g
Blue Diner Chair	Carpenter's Shop Travelling Cart	•	750g 250 - 2,500g
Blue Stool	Carpenter's Shop Travelling Cart	•	350g 250 - 2,500g
Blueberries	Carpenter's Shop Travelling Cart	•	250g 250 - 2,500g
Boarded Window	Carpenter's Shop Travelling Cart	•	400g 250 - 2,500g
Boat	Fishing from Beach Farm secret spot		-
Bobo Statue	Movie Theater Crane Game		-
Bone Rug	Penny's 14-Heart Event	•	-
Bonsai Tree	Carpenter's Shop Travelling Cart	•	800g 250 - 2,500g
Box Lamp	Carpenter's Shop Travelling Cart	•	750g 250 - 2,500g
Breakfast Chair	Carpenter's Shop Travelling Cart	•	750g 250 - 2,500g
Brick Fireplace	Carpenter's Shop	•	1,000g
Brown Armchair	Carpenter's Shop Travelling Cart	•	1,000g 250 - 2,500g
Brown Couch	Carpenter's Shop Travelling Cart	•	1,750g 250 - 2,500g
Budget TV	Carpenter's Shop	•	750g
Burlap Rug	Carpenter's Shop Travelling Cart	•	350g 250 - 2,500g
Burnt Offering	Museum (11 Artifacts) Casino		- 4,000 Qi Coins
Butterfly Hutch	Desert Trader		200 Bat Wings
Calendar	Carpenter's Shop	•	2,000g
Calico Falls	Carpenter's Shop Travelling Cart	•	750g 250 - 2,500g
Candle Lamp	Carpenter's Shop	•	1,000g
Candy Table	Carpenter's Shop Travelling Cart	•	1,000g 250 - 2,500g
Carved Window	Carpenter's Shop Travelling Cart	•	900g 250 - 2,500g
Ceiling Flags	Carpenter's Shop Travelling Cart	•	50g 250 - 2,500g
Ceiling Leaves	Flower Dance	•	400g
Ceiling Leaves	Flower Dance	•	400g
Ceiling Leaves	Luau	•	400g

Purchase the Furniture Catalogue for 200,000g and get
unrestricted access to nearly every furniture item available!

	Name		Obtained	Purchase Price
	Ceiling Leaves	•	Luau	400g
	Ceiling Leaves	•	Luau	400g
	Ceramic Pillar	•	Carpenter's Shop Travelling Cart	250g 250 - 2,500g
	Chest		Crafting	-
	Chicken Statue		Museum (Donate Chicken Statue)	-
	Child Bed	•	Carpenter's Shop	2,000g
	China Cabinet	•	Carpenter's Shop Travelling Cart	6,000g 250 - 2,500g
	Classic Lamp	•	Carpenter's Shop Travelling Cart	1,000g 250 - 2,500g
	Cloud Decal		Dance of the Moonlight Jellies	1,200g
	Cloud Decal		Dance of the Moonlight Jellies	1,200g
	Clouds		Winter Night Market	1,200g
	Clouds Banner	•	Winter Night Market	1,000g
	Coffee Maker		Evelyn's Special Order	-
	Coffee Table	•	Carpenter's Shop Travelling Cart	1,250g 250 - 2,500g
	Colorful Set	•	Carpenter's Shop Egg Festival	500g 500g
	Country Chair	•	Carpenter's Shop Travelling Cart	750g 250 - 2,500g
	Country Lamp	•	Carpenter's Shop Travelling Cart	500g 250 - 2,500g
	Crystal Chair		Museum (41 Minerals)	-
	Cute Chair	•	Carpenter's Shop Travelling Cart	1,200g 250 - 2,500g
	Dancing Grass	•	Carpenter's Shop Travelling Cart	400g 250 - 2,500g
	Dark Bookcase	•	Carpenter's Shop Travelling Cart	2,000g 250 - 2,500g
	Dark Couch	•	Carpenter's Shop Travelling Cart	2,500g 250 - 2,500g
	Dark Rug	•	Carpenter's Shop Travelling Cart	2,000g 250 - 2,500g
	Dark Table	•	Carpenter's Shop Travelling Cart	2,000g 250 - 2,500g
	Dark Throne	•	Carpenter's Shop Travelling Cart	2,000g 250 - 2,500g
	Decorative Axe	•	Feast of the Winter Star	1,000g
	Decorative Bowl	•	Carpenter's Shop Travelling Cart	250g 250 - 2,500g
	Decorative Lantern	•	Carpenter's Shop Travelling Cart	500g 250 - 2,500g
	Decorative Pitchfork	•	Egg Festival	1,000g
	Decorative Trash Can	•	Fishing in the Community Center fountain	-
	Deluxe Fish Tank	•	Willy's Special Order Fish Shop (After Special Order)	- 5,000g
	Deluxe Red Double Bed		Carpenter's Shop (After Special Order)	6,000g
	Deluxe Tree		Movie Theater Crane Game	-
	Dining Chair	•	Carpenter's Shop Travelling Cart	1,200g 250 - 2,500g
	Dining Chair	•	Carpenter's Shop Travelling Cart	1,200g 250 - 2,500g
	Diviner Table	•	Carpenter's Shop Travelling Cart	2,250g 250 - 2,500g
	Double Bed	•	Carpenter's Shop (After House Upgrade 1)	2,000g
	Dried Sunflowers		Stardew Valley Fair	100 Star Tokens
	Drum Block		Robin (Six-Heart Event) Museum (Donate Ancient Drum)	-
	Elegant Fireplace	•	Penny's 14-Heart Event	-
	Exotic Double Bed		Walnut Room	50 Qi Gems
	Exotic Tree		Movie Theater Crane Game	-
	Farm Computer		Crafting (Recipe from Demetrius)	-
	Festive Dining Table	•	Carpenter's Shop Travelling Cart	3,500g 250 - 2,500g
	Fisher Double Bed		Fish Shop	25,000g
	Floor Divider L	•	Furniture Catalogue Only	-
	Floor Divider R	•	Furniture Catalogue Only	-
	Floor Divider L	•	Furniture Catalogue Only	-
	Floor Divider R	•	Furniture Catalogue Only	-
	Floor Divider L	•	Furniture Catalogue Only	-

FURNITURE

Name		Obtained	Purchase Price
Floor Divider R	•	Furniture Catalogue Only	-
Floor Divider L	•	Furniture Catalogue Only	-
Floor Divider R	•	Furniture Catalogue Only	-
Floor Divider L	•	Furniture Catalogue Only	-
Floor Divider R	•	Furniture Catalogue Only	-
Floor Divider L	•	Furniture Catalogue Only	-
Floor Divider R	•	Furniture Catalogue Only	-
Floor Divider L	•	Furniture Catalogue Only	-
Floor Divider R	•	Furniture Catalogue Only	-
Floor Divider L	•	Furniture Catalogue Only	-
Floor Divider R	•	Furniture Catalogue Only	-
Floor TV	•	Carpenter's Shop	700g
Flute Block		Robin (Six-Heart Event) Museum (Donate Bone Flute)	-
Foliage Print		Fishing in north Ginger Island secret spot	-
??Foroguemon??		Secret place, secret item, Secret Note	-
Frozen Dreams	•	Festival of Ice	2,000g
Fruit Salad Rug		Penny's 14-Heart Event	-
Funky Rug	•	Spirit's Eve	4,000g
Futan Bear	•	Carpenter's Shop Travelling Cart	1,500g 250 - 2,500g
Futan Rabbit		Movie Theater Crane Game	-
Globe	•	Carpenter's Shop Travelling Cart	750g 250 - 2,500g
Gold Pillar	•	Carpenter's Shop Travelling Cart	450g 250 - 2,500g
Gourmand Statue		Fishing in Pirate Cove	-
Grandmother End Table	•	Carpenter's Shop Travelling Cart	1,000g 250 - 2,500g
Grave Stone		Winter Night Market (Winter 15th)	200g
Green Armchair	•	Carpenter's Shop Travelling Cart	1,000g 250 - 2,500g
Green Canes		Winter Night Market	200g
Green Cottage Rug	•	Furniture Catalogue	-
Green Couch	•	Carpenter's Shop Travelling Cart	1,750g 250 - 2,500g
Green Office Stool	•	Carpenter's Shop Travelling Cart	350g 250 - 2,500g
Green Plush Seat	•	Carpenter's Shop Travelling Cart	750g 250 - 2,500g
Green Serpent Statue		Movie Theater Crane Game	-
Green Stool	•	Carpenter's Shop Travelling Cart	350g 250 - 2,500g
Groovy Chair	•	Carpenter's Shop Travelling Cart	750g 250 - 2,500g
Hanging Shield	•	Carpenter's Shop Travelling Cart	500g 250 - 2,500g
Highway 89		Casino Travelling Cart	4,000 Qi Coins 250 - 2,500g
??HMTGF??		Secret place, secret item, Secret Note	-
House Plant	•	Carpenter's Shop Travelling Cart	250g 250 - 2,500g
House Plant	•	Carpenter's Shop Travelling Cart	250g 250 - 2,500g
House Plant	•	Carpenter's Shop Travelling Cart	250g 250 - 2,500g
House Plant	•	Carpenter's Shop Travelling Cart	250g 250 - 2,500g
House Plant	•	Carpenter's Shop Travelling Cart	250g 250 - 2,500g
House Plant	•	Carpenter's Shop Travelling Cart	250g 250 - 2,500g
House Plant	•	Carpenter's Shop Travelling Cart	250g 250 - 2,500g
House Plant	•	Carpenter's Shop Travelling Cart	250g 250 - 2,500g
House Plant	•	Carpenter's Shop Travelling Cart	250g 250 - 2,500g
House Plant	•	Carpenter's Shop Travelling Cart	250g 250 - 2,500g
House Plant	•	Carpenter's Shop Travelling Cart	250g 250 - 2,500g
House Plant	•	Carpenter's Shop Travelling Cart	250g 250 - 2,500g

Name		Obtained	Purchase Price
House Plant	•	Carpenter's Shop Travelling Cart	250g 250 - 2,500g
House Plant	•	Carpenter's Shop Travelling Cart	250g 250 - 2,500g
House Plant	•	Carpenter's Shop Travelling Cart	250g 250 - 2,500g
Icy Banner		Festival of Ice	800g
Icy Rug	•	Festival of Ice	4,000g
Indoor Hanging Basket		Movie Theater Crane Game	-
Indoor Palm	•	Carpenter's Shop Travelling Cart	600g 250 - 2,500g
Industrial Pipe	•	Carpenter's Shop Travelling Cart	300g 250 - 2,500g
Iridium Fireplace		Winter Night Market	15,000g
Iridium Krobus		Fishing south of Forest entrance to Sewers	-
It Howls in the Rain		Movie Theater Crane Game	-
J. Cola Light	•	JojaMart	500g
Jack-O-Lantern		Spirit's Eve Festival	750g (Recipe: 2,000g)
Jade Hills		Museum (25 Donations)	-
Jade Hills Extended	•	Oasis (Wednesdays)	5,000g
Journey of the Prairie King: The Motion Picture		Movie Theater Crane Game	-
Journey of the Prairie King Arcade System		Complete Journey of the Prairie King	-
Jungle Decal	•	Luau	800g
Jungle Decal	•	Luau	800g
Jungle Decal	•	Luau	800g
Jungle Decal	•	Luau	800g
Jungle Torch		Island Trader	5 Cinder Shards
Junimo Chest		Walnut Room (Purchased as a pair)	30 Qi Gems
Junimo Kart Arcade System		Complete Progress Mode in Junimo Kart	-
Junimo Plush		Secret place, secret day, Secret Note	-
King Chair	•	Carpenter's Shop Travelling Cart	3,000g 250 - 2,500g
Kitemaster 95	•	Carpenter's Shop Travelling Cart	600g 250 - 2,500g
L. Light String	•	Carpenter's Shop Travelling Cart	400g 250 - 2,500g
Land Of Clay		Winter Night Market	1,200g
Large Brown Couch	•	Oasis (Sundays)	3,000g
Large Cottage Rug	•	Oasis (Mondays)	2,000g
Large Fish Tank	•	Fish Shop	2,000g
Large Green Rug	•	Oasis (Fridays)	2,500g
Large Red Rug	•	Feast of the Winter Star	1,000g
Lawn Flamingo		Egg Festival	400g
Leah's Sculpture		Leah (Six-Heart Event)	-
Lg. Futan Bear		Museum (30 Donations)	-
Lifesaver		Fishing in Willy's Boathouse	-
Light Green Rug	•	Stardew Valley Fair	500 Star Tokens
Little Photos	•	Carpenter's Shop Travelling Cart	250g 250 - 2,500g
Little Tree	•	Carpenter's Shop Travelling Cart	350g 250 - 2,500g
Log Panel	•	Feast of the Winter Star	500g
Log Panel	•	Feast of the Winter Star	700g
Log Section		Carpenter's Shop Winter Night Market (Winter 17th)	350g 200g
Long Cactus		Movie Theater Crane Game	-
Long Palm		Movie Theater Crane Game	-
Luau Table	•	Carpenter's Shop Travelling Cart	1,000g 250 - 2,500g
Luxury Bookcase	•	Carpenter's Shop Travelling Cart	2,000g 250 - 2,500g
Luxury Table	•	Carpenter's Shop Travelling Cart	2,000g 250 - 2,500g

Name		Obtained	Purchase Price
Mahogany Bench	•	Carpenter's Shop Travelling Cart	2,000g 250 - 2,500g
Mahogany Chair	•	Carpenter's Shop Travelling Cart	1,000g 250 - 2,500g
Mahogany Dining Table	•	Carpenter's Shop Travelling Cart	3,000g 250 - 2,500g
Mahogany Dresser	•	Carpenter's Shop Travelling Cart	7,500g 250 - 2,500g
Mahogany End Table	•	Carpenter's Shop Travelling Cart	1,000g 250 - 2,500g
Mahogany Table	•	Carpenter's Shop Travelling Cart	1,500g 250 - 2,500g
Mahogany Tea-Table	•	Carpenter's Shop Travelling Cart	1,500g 250 - 2,500g
Manicured Pine	•	Carpenter's Shop Travelling Cart	500g 250 - 2,500g
Metal Chair	•	Carpenter's Shop Travelling Cart	800g 250 - 2,500g
Metal Window	•	Carpenter's Shop Travelling Cart	800g 250 - 2,500g
Miner's Crest	•	Carpenter's Shop Travelling Cart	1,000g 250 - 2,500g
Mini-Fridge		Carpenter's Shop	3,000g
Mini-Jukebox		Gus's 5-Heart Event	-
Mixed Canes		Winter Night Market	200g
Model Ship	•	Carpenter's Shop Travelling Cart	750g 250 - 2,500g
Modern Bench	•	Carpenter's Shop Travelling Cart	2,000g 250 - 2,500g
Modern Bookcase	•	Carpenter's Shop Travelling Cart	1,600g 250 - 2,500g
Modern Dining Table	•	Carpenter's Shop Travelling Cart	2,700g 250 - 2,500g
Modern Double Bed	•	Casino	8,000 Qi Coins
Modern End Table	•	Carpenter's Shop Travelling Cart	800g 250 - 2,500g
Modern Fish Tank	•	Fish Shop	500g
Modern Lamp	•	Carpenter's Shop Travelling Cart	750g 250 - 2,500g
Modern Rug	•	Dance of the Moonlight Jellies	4,000g
Modern Table	•	Carpenter's Shop Travelling Cart	1,250g 250 - 2,500g
Modern Tea-Table	•	Carpenter's Shop Travelling Cart	1,000g 250 - 2,500g
Monster Danglers	•	Carpenter's Shop Travelling Cart	1,000g 250 - 2,500g
Monster Fireplace	•	Krobus	20,000g
Monster Rug	•	Carpenter's Shop Travelling Cart	1,250g 250 - 2,500g
Moonlight Jellies Banner	•	Dance of the Moonlight Jellies	800g
Moon Table	•	Carpenter's Shop Travelling Cart	2,500g 250 - 2,500g
My First Painting		Leah's 14-Heart Event	-
Mysterium		Movie Theater Crane Game	-
Mystic Rug	•	Penny's 14-Heart Event	-
Natural Wonders: Exploring Our Vibrant World		Movie Theater Crane Game	-
Nautical Rug	•	Carpenter's Shop Travelling Cart	1,250g 250 - 2,500g
Needlepoint Flower	•	Carpenter's Shop Travelling Cart	500g 250 - 2,500g
Neolithic Table	•	Carpenter's Shop Travelling Cart	1,800g 250 - 2,500g
Oak Bench	•	Carpenter's Shop Travelling Cart	750g 250 - 2,500g
Oak Chair	•	Carpenter's Shop Travelling Cart	350g 250 - 2,500g
Oak Dresser	•	Carpenter's Shop Travelling Cart	5,000g 250 - 2,500g
Oak End Table	•	Carpenter's Shop Travelling Cart	500g 250 - 2,500g
Oak Table	•	Carpenter's Shop Travelling Cart	750g 250 - 2,500g
Oak Tea-Table	•	Carpenter's Shop Travelling Cart	750g 250 - 2,500g
Obsidian Vase		Museum (31 Minerals)	-
Oceanic Rug	•	Carpenter's Shop Island Trader	1,250g 3 Blue Discus
Old World Rug	•	Oasis (Thursdays)	2,500g
Orange Office Stool	•	Carpenter's Shop Travelling Cart	350g 250 - 2,500g
Ornamental Hay Bale	•	Marnie's Ranch	250g
Ornate Lamp	•	Carpenter's Shop Travelling Cart	1,050g 250 - 2,500g
Ornate Window	•	Carpenter's Shop Travelling Cart	900g 250 - 2,500g

Name		Obtained	Purchase Price
Palm Wall Ornament		Island Trader (Thursdays)	Pineapple
Pastel Banner		Egg Festival	1,000g
Patchwork Rug	•	Carpenter's Shop Travelling Cart	800g 250 - 2,500g
Pathways	•	Carpenter's Shop Travelling Cart	750g 250 - 2,500g
Physics 101		Fishing in the Volcano's caldera	-
Pink Office Chair	•	Carpenter's Shop Travelling Cart	500g 250 - 2,500g
Pink Plush Seat	•	Carpenter's Shop Travelling Cart	750g 250 - 2,500g
??Pinky Lemon??		Secret place, secret item, Secret Note	-
Pirate Double Bed	•	Furniture Catalogue Only	-
Pirate Rug		Penny's 14-Heart Event	-
Plain Torch	•	Luau Winter Night Market	700g 800g
Plasma TV	•	Carpenter's Shop (After House Upgrade)	4,500g
Plush Bunny		Egg Festival	2,000g
Porthole	•	Carpenter's Shop Travelling Cart	700g 250 - 2,500g
Portrait of a Mermaid		Winter Night Market	1,200g
Primal Motion	•	Casino Travelling Cart	5,000 Qi Coins 250 - 2,500g
Pub Table	•	Carpenter's Shop Travelling Cart	800g 250 - 2,500g
Purple Office Chair	•	Carpenter's Shop Travelling Cart	500g 250 - 2,500g
Purple Serpent Statue		Movie Theater Crane Game	-
Puzzle Table	•	Carpenter's Shop Travelling Cart	1,500g 250 - 2,500g
Pyramid Decal		Fishing in southern waters in Calico Desert	-
Queen of the Gem Sea	•	Carpenter's Shop Travelling Cart	1,200g 250 - 2,500g
Red Armchair	•	Carpenter's Shop Travelling Cart	1,000g 250 - 2,500g
Red Canes		Winter Night Market	200g
Red Cottage Rug	•	Comes with the Standard Farmhouse Penny's 14-Heart Event	-
Red Couch	•	Carpenter's Shop Travelling Cart	1,750g 250 - 2,500g
Red Diner Chair	•	Carpenter's Shop Travelling Cart	750g 250 - 2,500g
Red Eagle		Winter Night Market	1,200g
Red Rug	•	Carpenter's Shop Travelling Cart	1,000g 250 - 2,500g
S. Pine	•	Carpenter's Shop Travelling Cart	500g 250 - 2,500g
S. Wall Flower	•	Flower Dance	800g
Sam's Boombox		Sam's 14-Heart Event	-
Seasonal Decor		Flower Dance Winter Night Market	350g 500g
Seasonal Plant		Egg Festival Winter Night Market	350g 500g
Seasonal Plant		Egg Festival Winter Night Market	350g 500g
Seasonal Plant		Flower Dance Winter Night Market	350g 500g
Seasonal Plant		Oasis Winter Night Market	100g 500g
Seasonal Plant		Carpenter's Shop Winter Night Market	400g 500g
Seasonal Plant		Flower Dance Winter Night Market	350g 500g
Sewing Machine		Emily's Special Order	-
Sign of the Vessel		Krobus	350g
Singing Stone		Museum (21 Minerals)	-
Skeleton		Museum (15 Artifacts)	-
Skull Poster	•	Carpenter's Shop Travelling Cart	500g 250 - 2,500g
Sloth Skeleton L		Museum (Donate Prehistoric Skull & Scapula, and Skeletal Hand)	-
Sloth Skeleton M		Museum (Donate Prehistoric Rib & Prehistoric Vertebra)	-
Sloth Skeleton R		Museum (Donate Prehistoric Tibia & Skeletal Tail)	-
Small Crystal	•	Carpenter's Shop Travelling Cart	750g 250 - 2,500g
Small Fish Tank	•	Fish Shop	500g
Small Junimo Plush		Movie Theater Crane Game	-

Name		Obtained	Purchase Price
Small Junimo Plush		Movie Theater Crane Game	-
Small Junimo Plush		Movie Theater Crane Game	-
Small Junimo Plush		Movie Theater Crane Game	-
Small Plant	•	Carpenter's Shop / Travelling Cart	250g / 250 - 2,500g
Small Wall Pumpkin		Movie Theater Crane Game	-
Small Window	•	Carpenter's Shop / Travelling Cart	300g / 250 - 2,500g
Snowy Rug	•	Penny's 14-Heart Event	-
Soda Machine		Complete Joja Community Development	-
Solar Kingdom		Winter Night Market	1,200g
Solar Panel		Crafting (Recipe from Caroline)	-
Solid Gold Lewis		Secret Note	-
Spires	•	Casino / Travelling Cart	4,000 Qi Coins / 250 - 2,500g
Squirrel Figurine		Fishing outside Volcano secret exit	-
Standing Geode		Museum (11 Minerals)	-
Stardew Hero Trophy		Reward for Rebuilding Community Center	-
Starport Decal	•	Dance of the Moonlight Jellies	1,000g
Starry Double Bed	•	Furniture Catalogue Only	-
Statue Of Endless Fortune		Casino	1,000,000g
Statue of Perfection		Reward from Grandpa's Evaluation	-
Statue of True Perfection		Achieve 100% Perfection	-
Stone Cairn		Dwarf	200g
Stone Chest		Crafting (Recipe from Robin)	-
Stone Fireplace	•	Carpenter's Shop	1,500g
Stone Frog		Winter Night Market (Winter 15th)	500g
Stone Owl		Random Overnight Event	-
Stone Owl		Winter Night Market (Winter 17th)	500g
Stone Parrot		Winter Night Market (Winter 16th)	500g
Stone Slab	•	Carpenter's Shop / Travelling Cart	1,000g / 250 - 2,500g
Stove Fireplace		Carpenter's Shop	3,000g
Strange Capsule		Random Overnight Event	-
Strawberry Decal		Penny's 14-Heart Event	-
Strawberry Double Bed	•	Furniture Catalogue Only	-
Stump Seat	•	Carpenter's Shop / Travelling Cart	2,000g / 250 - 2,500g
Stump Torch	•	Winter Night Market	800g
Suit of Armor		Winter Night Market (Winter 16th)	500g
Sun 44	•	Carpenter's Shop / Travelling Cart	800g / 250 - 2,500g
Sun 45	•	Carpenter's Shop / Travelling Cart	350g / 250 - 2,500g
Sun Table	•	Carpenter's Shop / Travelling Cart	2,500g / 250 - 2,500g
Table Plant	•	Carpenter's Shop / Travelling Cart	250g / 250 - 2,500g
Tea Set		Feast of the Winter Star	-
Telephone		Carpenter's Shop	2,000g
The Brave Little Sapling		Movie Theater Crane Game	-
The Miracle at Coldstar Ranch		Movie Theater Crane Game	-
The Muzzamaroo	•	Carpenter's Shop / Travelling Cart	1,000g / 250 - 2,500g
The Serpent		Winter Night Market	1,200g
The Zuzu City Express		Movie Theater Crane Game	-
Three Trees		Winter Night Market	1,200g
Topiary Tree	•	Carpenter's Shop / Travelling Cart	500g / 250 - 2,500g
Totem Pole	•	Carpenter's Shop / Travelling Cart	750g / 250 - 2,500g
Tree Column	•	Carpenter's Shop / Travelling Cart	1,000g / 250 - 2,500g

	Name		Obtained	Purchase Price
	Tree of the Winter Star	•	Carpenter's Shop Travelling Cart	5,000g 250 - 2,500g
	Tropical Bed	•	Island Trader	20 Ginger
	Tropical Chair		Island Trader (Even-numbered days)	Lionfish
	Tropical Double Bed	•	Island Trader	5 Bananas
	Tropical Fish #173		Winter Night Market	1,200g
	Tropical TV		Island Trader	30 Taro Roots
	Tub o' Flowers		Flower Dance	250g (Recipe 1,000g)
	Vanilla Villa	•	Carpenter's Shop Travelling Cart	500g 250 - 2,500g
	VGA Paradise	•	Carpenter's Shop Travelling Cart	1,200g 250 - 2,500g
	Vista		Fishing outside the Spa	-
	Volcano Photo		Island Trader (Thursdays)	5 Mangoes
	Wall Basket		Fishing in Secret Woods Pond	-
	Wall Cactus	•	Oasis	700g
	Wall Flower	•	Flower Dance	800g
	Wallflower Pal	•	Carpenter's Shop Travelling Cart	500g 250 - 2,500g
	Wall Palm	•	Luau	1,000g
	Wall Pumpkin		Movie Theater Crane Game	-
	Wall Sconce	•	Oasis (Tuesdays - Random)	500g
	Wall Sconce	•	Oasis (Tuesdays - Random)	500g
	Wall Sconce	•	Oasis (Tuesdays - Random)	500g
	Wall Sconce	•	Oasis (Tuesdays - Random)	500g
	Wall Sconce	•	Oasis (Saturdays)	500g
	Wall Sconce	•	Festival of Ice	1,000g
	Wall Sconce	•	Oasis (Saturdays)	500g
	Walnut Bench	•	Carpenter's Shop Travelling Cart	750g 250 - 2,500g
	Walnut Chair	•	Carpenter's Shop Travelling Cart	350g 250 - 2,500g
	Walnut Dresser	•	Carpenter's Shop Travelling Cart	5,000g 250 - 2,500g
	Walnut End Table	•	Carpenter's Shop Travelling Cart	500g 250 - 2,500g
	Walnut Table	•	Carpenter's Shop Travelling Cart	750g 250 - 2,500g
	Walnut Tea-Table	•	Carpenter's Shop Travelling Cart	750g 250 - 2,500g
	Wicked Statue		Crafting (Recipe from Krobus)	1,000g
	Wild Double Bed		Island Trader	100 Cinder Shards
	Winter Banner		Feast of the Winter Star	1,000g
	Winter Chair	•	Carpenter's Shop Travelling Cart	750g 250 - 2,500g
	Winter Dining Table	•	Carpenter's Shop Travelling Cart	3,500g 250 - 2,500g
	Winter End Table	•	Carpenter's Shop Travelling Cart	800g 250 - 2,500g
	Winter Table	•	Carpenter's Shop Travelling Cart	1,250g 250 - 2,500g
	Winter Tree Decal		Movie Theater Crane Game	-
	Wizard Couch	•	Carpenter's Shop Travelling Cart	4,000g 250 - 2,500g
	Wood Chipper		Carpenter's Shop	1,000g
	Woodcut Rug	•	Carpenter's Shop Travelling Cart	800g 250 - 2,500g
	Wood Panel	•	Feast of the Winter Star	500g
	Woodsy Couch	•	Carpenter's Shop Travelling Cart	3,000g 250 - 2,500g
	Workbench		Carpenter's Shop	3,000g
	World Map	•	Carpenter's Shop Travelling Cart	500g 250 - 2,500g
	Wumbus		Movie Theater Crane Game	-
	Wumbus Statue		Movie Theater Crane Game	-
	Yellow Armchair	•	Carpenter's Shop Travelling Cart	1,000g 250 - 2,500g
	Yellow Couch	•	Carpenter's Shop Travelling Cart	1,750g 250 - 2,500g

Purchase the Furniture Catalogue for 200,000g and get
unrestricted access to nearly every furniture item available!

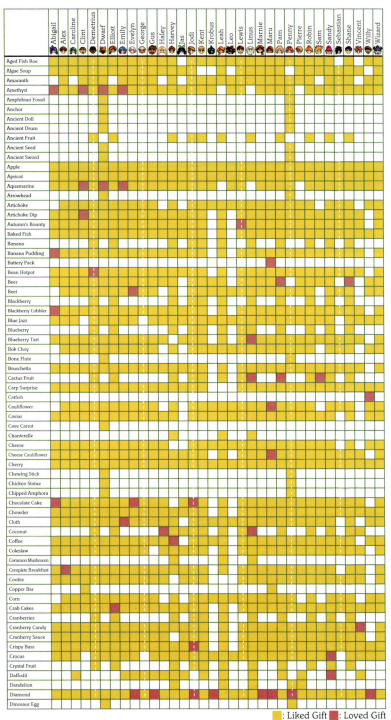

■ : Liked Gift ■ : Loved Gift

	Abigail	Alex	Caroline	Clint	Demetrius	Dwarf	Elliott	Emily	Evelyn	George	Gus	Haley	Harvey	Jas	Jodi	Kent	Krobus	Leah	Leo	Lewis	Linus	Marnie	Maru	Pam	Penny	Pierre	Robin	Sam	Sandy	Sebastian	Shane	Vincent	Willy	Wizard
Dinosaur Mayo	Y	Y	Y	Y	Y		Y	Y	Y	Y	Y	Y	Y		Y	Y		Y		Y		Y	Y	Y	Y	Y	Y	Y	Y	Y	Y		Y	Y
Dish O' The Sea				Y			Y		Y	Y	Y				Y					Y	R			Y		Y							Y	
Dragon Tooth																			Y	Y														
Dried Starfish					Y													Y							Y									
Driftwood																		Y																
Duck Egg	Y		Y	Y	Y		Y	Y	Y	Y	Y		Y		Y	Y		Y		Y		Y	Y	Y	Y	Y	Y	Y	Y	Y	Y		Y	Y
Duck Feather						R		Y										Y			R													
Duck Mayonnaise	Y		Y	Y	Y		Y	Y	Y	Y	Y	Y	Y		Y	Y		Y		Y		Y	Y	Y	Y	Y	Y	Y	Y	Y	Y		Y	Y
Dwarf Gadget						Y																	Y											
Dwarf Scroll I						Y																	Y											
Dwarf Scroll II						Y																	Y											
Dwarf Scroll III						Y																	Y											
Dwarf Scroll IV						Y																	Y											
Dwarvish Helm						Y																	Y											
Earth Crystal	Y			Y		Y		Y										Y					Y							Y				Y
Egg	Y		Y	Y	Y		Y	Y	Y	Y	Y		Y		Y	Y		Y		Y		Y	Y	Y	Y	Y	Y	Y	Y	Y	Y		Y	Y
Eggplant	Y		Y	Y	Y		Y	Y	Y	Y	Y		Y		Y	Y		Y		Y		Y	Y	Y	Y	Y	Y	Y	Y	Y	Y		Y	Y
Eggplant Parmesan	Y		Y	Y	Y		Y	Y	Y	Y	Y	Y	Y	R	Y	Y		Y		Y		Y	Y	Y	Y	Y	Y	Y	Y	Y	Y		Y	Y
Elvish Jewelry																																		
Emerald	Y		R	Y	R	R	Y	Y																	R									
Escargot	Y		Y	Y	Y		Y	Y	Y	Y	Y		Y		Y	Y		Y		Y		Y	Y	Y	Y	Y	Y	Y	Y	Y	Y		Y	Y
Fairy Rose			Y	Y	Y		R	Y	Y		Y	R	Y		Y			Y		Y		R	Y		Y	Y	Y	Y	Y	Y				Y
Farmer's Lunch	Y		Y	Y	Y		Y	Y	Y	Y	Y		Y		Y	Y		Y		Y		Y	R	Y	Y	Y	Y	Y	Y	Y	Y		Y	Y
Fiddlehead Fern	Y		Y	Y	Y		Y	Y	Y	Y	Y		Y		Y	Y		Y		Y		Y	Y	Y	Y	Y	Y	Y	Y	Y	Y		Y	Y
Fiddlehead Risotto	Y	R	Y	Y	Y		Y	Y	Y	Y	Y		Y		Y	R	Y	Y		Y		Y	Y	Y	Y	Y	Y	Y	Y	Y	Y		Y	Y
Fire Quartz	Y			Y		Y		Y															Y							Y				Y
Fish Stew	Y		Y	Y	Y		Y	Y	Y	Y	Y		Y		Y	Y		Y		Y		Y	Y	Y	Y	Y	Y	Y	Y	Y	Y		Y	Y
Fish Taco	Y		Y	Y	Y		Y	Y	Y	Y	Y		R	Y	Y	Y		Y		Y		Y	Y	Y	Y	Y	Y	Y	Y	Y	Y		Y	Y
Flounder																																		
Fried Calamari	Y		Y	Y	Y		Y	Y	Y	Y	Y		Y		Y	Y		Y		Y		Y	Y	Y	Y	Y	Y	Y	Y	Y	R		Y	Y
Fried Eel	Y		Y	Y	Y		Y	Y	Y	Y	Y		Y	R	Y	Y		Y		Y		Y	Y	Y	Y	Y	Y	Y	Y	Y	Y		Y	Y
Fried Mushroom	Y		Y	Y	Y		Y	Y	Y	Y	Y		Y	R	Y	Y		Y		Y		Y	Y	Y	Y	Y	Y	Y	Y	Y	Y		Y	Y
Frozen Tear	Y			Y		Y		Y															Y						R				Y
Fruit Salad	Y		Y	Y	Y		Y	Y	Y	Y	Y		Y		Y	Y		Y		Y		Y	Y	Y	Y	Y	Y	Y	Y	Y	Y		Y	Y
Garlic	Y		Y	Y	Y		Y	Y	Y	Y	Y		Y		Y	Y		Y		Y		Y	Y	Y	Y	Y	Y	Y	Y	Y	Y		Y	Y
Ginger																																		
Ginger Ale	Y		Y	Y	Y		Y	Y	Y	Y	Y		Y		Y	Y		Y		Y		Y	Y	Y	Y	Y	Y	Y	Y	Y	Y		Y	Y
Glass Shards																																		
Glazed Yams	Y		Y	Y	Y		Y	Y	Y	Y	Y		Y		Y	Y		R		R		Y	Y	Y	Y	Y	Y	Y	Y	Y	Y		Y	Y
Goat Cheese	Y		Y	Y	Y		Y	Y	Y	Y	Y		Y		Y	Y	R	Y		Y		Y	Y	Y	Y	Y	R	Y	Y	Y	Y		Y	Y
Goat Milk	Y		Y	Y	Y		Y	Y	Y	Y	Y		Y		Y	Y		Y		Y		Y	Y	Y	Y	Y	Y	Y	Y	Y	Y		Y	Y
Gold Bar				R		Y																												
Golden Egg	Y		Y																															
Golden Mask																																			
Golden Pumpkin	R	R	R	R	R	R	R	R	R	R	R	R	R	R	R	R	R	R	R	R	R	R	R	R	R	R	R	R	R	R	R	R	R	R
Golden Relic																																			
Grape	Y		Y	Y	Y		Y	Y	Y	Y	Y		Y		Y	Y		Y		Y		Y	Y	Y	Y	Y	Y	Y	Y	Y	Y		Y	Y
Green Bean	Y		Y	Y	Y		Y	Y	Y	Y	Y		Y		Y	Y		Y		Y		Y	Y	Y	Y	Y	Y	Y	Y	Y	Y		Y	Y
Green Tea	Y	R	Y	Y	Y		Y	Y	Y	Y	Y		Y		Y	Y		R	Y	Y		Y	Y	Y	Y	Y	Y	Y	Y	Y	Y		Y	Y
Hardwood																																		
Hashbrowns	Y		Y	Y	Y		Y	Y	Y	Y	Y		Y		Y	Y		Y		Y		Y	Y	Y	Y	Y	Y	Y	Y	Y	Y		Y	Y
Hazelnut																																		
Holly																																		
Honey	Y		Y	Y	Y		Y	Y	Y	Y	Y		Y		Y	Y		Y		Y		Y	Y	Y	Y	Y	Y	Y	Y	Y	Y		Y	Y
Hot Pepper	Y		Y	Y	Y		Y	Y	Y	Y	Y		Y		Y	Y		R	Y	Y		Y	Y	Y	Y	Y	Y	Y	Y	Y	R		Y	Y
Ice Cream	Y		Y	R	Y		Y	Y	Y	Y	Y		Y		Y	Y		Y		Y		Y	Y	Y	Y	Y	Y	Y	Y	Y	Y		Y	Y
Iridium Bar				Y		Y										R							Y											
Iron Bar				Y		Y																	Y											
Jade	Y	R		Y	R	R	Y	R																										
Jelly	Y		Y	Y	Y		Y	Y	Y	Y	Y		Y		Y	Y		Y		Y		Y	Y	Y	Y	Y	Y	Y	Y	Y	Y		Y	Y
Joja Cola																																		
Juice	Y		Y	Y	Y		Y	Y	Y	Y	Y		Y		Y	Y		Y		Y		Y	Y	Y	Y	Y	Y	Y	Y	Y	Y		Y	Y
Kale	Y		Y	Y	Y		Y	Y	Y	Y	Y		Y		Y	Y		Y		Y		Y	Y	Y	Y	Y	Y	Y	Y	Y	Y		Y	Y
Leek	Y		Y	Y	Y		Y	Y	R	Y	Y		Y		Y	Y		Y		Y		Y	Y	Y	Y	Y	Y	Y	Y	Y	Y		Y	Y
Lemon Stone					R																													
Life Elixir	Y		Y	Y	Y		Y	Y	Y	Y	Y		Y		Y	Y		Y		Y		Y	Y	Y	Y	Y	Y	Y	Y	Y	Y		Y	Y
Lingcod																																		
Lobster				R																														

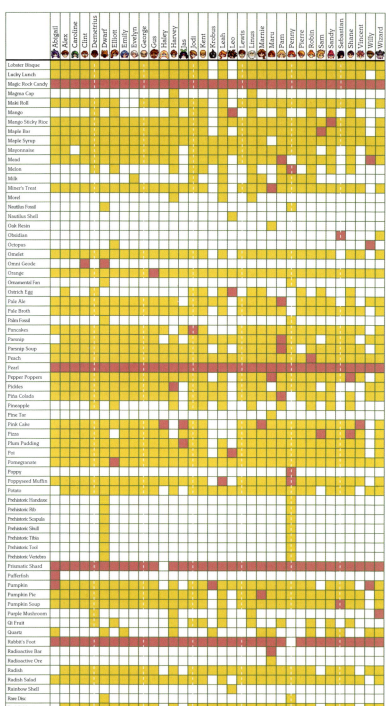

Columns (villagers): Abigail, Alex, Caroline, Clint, Demetrius, Dwarf, Elliott, Emily, Evelyn, George, Gus, Haley, Harvey, Jas, Jodi, Kent, Krobus, Leah, Leo, Lewis, Linus, Marnie, Maru, Pam, Penny, Pierre, Robin, Sam, Sandy, Sebastian, Shane, Vincent, Willy, Wizard

Rows (gifts): Lobster Bisque, Lucky Lunch, Magic Rock Candy, Magma Cap, Maki Roll, Mango, Mango Sticky Rice, Maple Bar, Maple Syrup, Mayonnaise, Mead, Melon, Milk, Miner's Treat, Morel, Nautilus Fossil, Nautilus Shell, Oak Resin, Obsidian, Octopus, Omelet, Omni Geode, Orange, Ornamental Fan, Ostrich Egg, Pale Ale, Pale Broth, Palm Fossil, Pancakes, Parsnip, Parsnip Soup, Peach, Pearl, Pepper Poppers, Pickles, Piña Colada, Pineapple, Pine Tar, Pink Cake, Pizza, Plum Pudding, Poi, Pomegranate, Poppy, Poppyseed Muffin, Potato, Prehistoric Handaxe, Prehistoric Rib, Prehistoric Scapula, Prehistoric Skull, Prehistoric Tibia, Prehistoric Tool, Prehistoric Vertebra, Prismatic Shard, Pufferfish, Pumpkin, Pumpkin Pie, Pumpkin Soup, Purple Mushroom, Qi Fruit, Quartz, Rabbit's Foot, Radioactive Bar, Radioactive Ore, Radish, Radish Salad, Rainbow Shell, Rare Disc, Red Cabbage

	Abigail	Alex	Caroline	Clint	Demetrius	Dwarf	Elliott	Emily	Evelyn	George	Gus	Haley	Harvey	Jas	Jodi	Kent	Krobus	Leah	Leo	Lewis	Linus	Marnie	Maru	Pam	Penny	Pierre	Robin	Sam	Sandy	Sebastian	Shane	Vincent	Willy	Wizard
Red Plate																									R									
Rhubarb																																		
Rhubarb Pie														R											R									
Rice Pudding					R																													
Roasted Hazelnuts																R																		
Roots Platter																									R									
Ruby					R																													
Rusty Cog																																		
Rusty Spoon					R																													
Rusty Spur																																		
Salad		R																																
Salmon Dinner		R																																
Salmonberry																																		
Sandfish																	R																	
Sashimi																														R				
Sea Cucumber																																		
Seafoam Pudding																																		
Sea Urchin																																		
Shrimp Cocktail																																		
Skeletal Hand																																		
Skeletal Tail																																		
Snail																																	R	
Snow Yam																																		
Solar Essence																																		R
Spaghetti																																		
Spice Berry																																		
Spicy Eel	R																																	
Spring Onion																																		
Squid					R																													
Squid Ink					R																													
Squid Ink Ravioli																																		
Starfruit																																		
Stir Fry																		R																
Strange Doll																																		
Strange Doll																																		
Strawberry					R																				R									
Stuffing							R																											
Sturgeon																																	R	
Summer Spangle		R																																
Sunflower																																		
Super Cucumber																																		R
Super Meal														R																				
Survival Burger																																		
Sweet Pea																								R										
Taro Root																																		
Tea Leaves																																		
Tiger Trout																																		
Tigerseye																																		
Tom Kha Soup																									R									
Tomato																																		
Topaz				R		R																												
Tortilla																																		
Trilobite																																		
Triple Shot Espresso																																		
Tropical Curry			R														R																	
Trout Soup																																		
Truffle																	R																	
Truffle Oil													R																					
Tulip																																		
Vegetable Medley														R									R											
Void Egg																														R				
Void Essence																																		R
Void Mayonnaise																																		
Wild Horseradish																																		
Wild Plum																																		
Wine																																		
Winter Root																																		
Wool						R																												
Yam																								R										

247

Abigail

	Event Trigger Conditions
2 ❤	Enter Pierre's General Store when Abigail is there, any day except Saturday.
4 ❤	Visit the Mountain between noon and 7pm on a rainy day, any season except Winter.
6 ❤	Enter Pelican Town between 9pm and midnight on a sunny day.
8 ❤	After receiving a letter from Abigail, enter Pierre's General Store between 8pm and 9pm when she's there.
10 ❤	Enter the Mines between 5pm and midnight prior to marrying Abigail.
14 🗡	Enter the Backwoods before 5pm.

Alex

	Event Trigger Conditions
2 ❤	On a sunny summer day, visit the beach when Alex is there.
4 ❤	Enter Pelican Town between 9am and 4pm.
5 ❤	Enter Alex's house when he's there.
6 ❤	Enter Alex's house when he's there.
8 ❤	On a sunny summer day, visit the beach when Alex is there.
10 ❤	Enter the Saloon between 7pm and 10pm once you've received a letter from Alex asking you to meet him there.
14 🗡	Enter the Farm on a sunny day other than Sunday in Year 2+ before 8:20am with at least 5,000g. Starts a series of events.

Caroline

	Event Trigger Conditions
3 ❤	Caroline sends you a recipe for Parsnip Soup in the mail.
6 ❤	Enter Pierre's General Store when Caroline and Abigail are there.
7 ❤	Caroline sends you a recipe for Vegetable Medley in the mail.

Clint

	Event Trigger Conditions
3 ❤	Visit the Saloon between 7pm and 11pm on Monday. He also sends you a recipe for Algae Soup in the mail.
4 ❤	Clint randomly mails you a Copper Bar, Iron Bar or Gold Bar.
6 ❤	Enter Pelican Town from Cindersap Forest between 9am and 6:30pm, after viewing his 3-heart event.
7 ❤	Clint sends you a recipe for Bean Hotpot in the mail.

Demetrius

	Event Trigger Conditions
3 ❤	Demetrius sends you a recipe for Fried Mushroom in the mail.
6 ❤	Enter the Carpenter's Shop when he and Robin are there.
7 ❤	Demetrius sends you a recipe for Autumn's Bounty in the mail, and gifts like Rainbow Shells, Amethysts and Bream.

Dwarf

	Event Trigger Conditions
0 ❤	Enter the Sewers after you've purchased the Stardrop from Krobus and possess the Dwarvish Translation Guide.

Elliott

	Event Trigger Conditions
2 ❤	Enter Elliott's cabin when he is home.
4 ❤	Enter the Saloon between 3pm and 10pm when Gus is there.
6 ❤	Enter Elliott's cabin when he is home.
8 ❤	After receiving a letter from Elliott, visit the Museum between 1pm and 7pm.
10 ❤	After receiving a letter from Elliott, go to the beach on a sunny day between 7am and 1pm.
14 🗡	Enter the Farm before 3pm while Elliott is there with no festivals in the coming week. Starts a series of events.

Emily

	Event Trigger Conditions
2 ❤	Enter Emily's house when she is home.
3 ❤	Emily sends you a recipe for Salad in the mail, and may also send Cloth or Sea Urchin.
4 ❤	Enter Pelican Town on a sunny day during the Spring, Summer or Fall before 5pm.
6 ❤	Visit Emily's house when she's there.
7 ❤	Emily sends you a recipe for Red Plate in the mail.
8 ❤	Enter the Mayor's house after receiving an invitation from Emily in the mail.
10 ❤	Enter the Secret Woods after 10pm after receiving an invitation from Emily in the mail.
14 🗡	Enter the Farm before 8:20am. Starts a series of events.

Evelyn

	Event Trigger Conditions
4 ❤	Visit Evelyn while she is at home.
7 ❤	Evelyn sends you a recipe for Rice Pudding in the mail, as well as Chocolate Cake or Bread.

George

	Event Trigger Conditions
3 ❤	George sends you a recipe for Fried Eel in the mail.
6 ❤	Enter George's house when he is home.
7 ❤	George sends you a recipe for Spicy Eel in the mail.
8 ❤	George randomly mails you Stone for crafting.

Gus

	Event Trigger Conditions
3 ❤	Gus sends you a recipe for Salmon Dinner in the mail.
4 ❤	Enter the Saloon during open hours. (This event also requires 2 hearts with Pam)
5 ❤	Enter the Farm before 11:30am on a sunny day.
7 ❤	Gus sends you a recipe for Cranberry Sauce in the mail, as well as food like Baked Fish, Bean Hotpot and Pancakes.

Haley

	Event Trigger Conditions
2 ❤	Enter Haley's house when she and Emily are both home.
4 ❤	Enter Haley's house when she's home.
6 ❤	Go to the beach between 10am and 4pm during any season except Winter.
8 ❤	On a sunny day during any season except Winter, enter Cindersap Forest between 10am and 4pm.
10 ❤	Enter Haley's house when she's home.
14 ⚔	Enter Pelican Town on a sunny day between 8am and 3pm. Starts a series of events.

Harvey

	Event Trigger Conditions
2 ❤	Enter George's house when George is home.
4 ❤	Enter the Clinic when Harvey is there.
6 ❤	Enter Pierre's General Store between 11am and 3pm.
8 ❤	Enter the Clinic.
10 ❤	Harvey sends you a letter asking to meet at the railroad tracks. Go there between 9am and 5pm.
14 ⚔	Enter the Farmhouse between 8pm and midnight when Harvey's there.

Jas

	Event Trigger Conditions
8 ❤	Enter Cindersap Forest on a sunny day in Spring before 5pm.

Jodi

	Event Trigger Conditions
3 ❤	Jodi sends you a recipe for Fried Calamari in the mail.
4 ❤	Jodi will visit your farm before 9:30am on a Monday to invite you to dinner. You will need to bring a Largemouth Bass.
7 ❤	Jodi sends you a recipe for Ice Cream, and will randomly mail you Basic or Quality Fertilizer for farming.

Kent

	Event Trigger Conditions
3 ❤	Enter Kent and Jodi's house while they are both home. Kent will also send you a recipe for Crispy Bass in the mail.
4 ❤	Kent begins to—with helpful and kindly intentions, you assume—randomly mail you explosives.
7 ❤	Kent sends you a recipe for Super Meal in the mail.

Krobus

	Event Trigger Conditions
14 ⚔	Enter the Beach on a sunny day between 8pm and 1am.

Leah

	Event Trigger Conditions
2 ❤	Enter Leah's Cottage when she's home. Your conversation here will affect future events.
4 ❤	Enter Leah's Cottage when she's home.
6 ❤	Enter Cindersap Forest when Leah is there, in any season except Winter. Leah will also visit you with a gift at your farmhouse on a sunny day between 6am and 11:30am.
8 ❤	Enter Pelican Town between 3pm and 5pm after Leah visits your farmhouse, or enter Leah's Cottage when she is home if you suggested the "website" option.
10 ❤	Enter Cindersap Forest between 11am and 4pm, in any season except winter.
14	Enter the Farm on a sunny non-Winter day other than Sunday before 8:20am. Starts a series of events.

Leo

	Event Trigger Conditions
2 ❤	Enter the western region of Ginger Island on a sunny day between 6am and 6pm.
3 ❤	Leo sends you a recipe for Poi in the mail.
4 ❤	Enter the northern region of Ginger Island on a sunny day between 6am and 6pm.
6 ❤	Enter the southern region of Ginger Island on a sunny day between 6am and 6pm.
7 ❤	Leo sends you a recipe for Mango Sticky Rice in the mail.
9 ❤	Enter the Mountains on a sunny day between 6am and 7pm.

Lewis

	Event Trigger Conditions
3 ❤	Lewis sends you a recipe for Spaghetti in the mail.
6 ❤	Enter Pelican Town on a sunny day between 7pm and 11pm. (This event also requires 6 hearts with Marnie)
7 ❤	Lewis sends you a recipe for Eggplant Parmesan in the mail.

Linus

	Event Trigger Conditions
0 ❤	Enter Pelican Town between 8pm and 12am on a sunny day.
3 ❤	Linus sends you a recipe for Sashimi in the mail.
4 ❤	Enter the Mountains between 8pm and 12am on a sunny day.
7 ❤	Linus sends you a recipe for Fish Taco in the mail, and randomly mails you Largemouth Bass, Catfish or Maki Roll.
8 ❤	Exit the Carpenter's Shop on a sunny day before 5pm.

Marnie

	Event Trigger Conditions
3 ❤	Marnie greets you at your farmhouse between 6:30am and 9:30am. She'll also send you a recipe for Pale Broth in the mail, and will begin sending you Hay as well.
6 ❤	On a sunny day between 7pm and 11pm, enter Pelican Town. (This event also requires 6 hearts with Lewis)
7 ❤	Marnie sends you a recipe for Rhubarb Pie in the mail.

Maru

	Event Trigger Conditions
2 ❤	Enter the Carpenter's Shop when Maru is home.
4 ❤	Enter the Clinic when Maru is there.
6 ❤	Enter the Mountains on a sunny day, between 9pm and 11:40pm.
8 ❤	Enter the Carpenter's Shop when Maru is home.
10	Enter the Carpenter's Shop between 9am and 4pm.
14	Enter the Farmhouse between 6am & 5pm. Starts a series of events.

Pam

	Event Trigger Conditions
3 ❤	Pam sends you a recipe for Cheese Cauliflower in the mail, as well as Energy Tonic, Battery Pack or Beer.
7 ❤	Pam sends you a recipe for Stuffing in the mail.
9 ❤	Enter Pam and Penny's House a few days after it's built.

Penny

	Event Trigger Conditions
2 ❤	Enter Pelican Town on a sunny day between 9am and 2pm.
4 ❤	Enter Pam and Penny's Trailer when Penny is home.
6 ❤	Enter Pam and Penny's Trailer when Penny is home.
8 ❤	Enter Cindersap Forest between 9am and 4pm.
10	After receiving a letter from Penny, enter the pool area of the Spa between 7pm and midnight.
14	Enter the Farmhouse between 3pm and 7pm.

Pierre

	Event Trigger Conditions
3 ♥	Pierre sends you a recipe for Blueberry Tart in the mail.
6 ♥	Enter Pierre's General Store.

Robin

	Event Trigger Conditions
6 ♥	Enter the Carpenter's Shop when Robin is there.
7 ♥	Robin sends you a recipe for Pumpkin Soup in the mail, and may also randomly send you Wood for crafting.

Sam

	Event Trigger Conditions
2 ♥	Enter Sam's house when he's home.
3 ♥	Spring through Fall of Year 1, enter the beach on a sunny day between 7am and 3pm.
4 ♥	Enter Sam's house when he's home.
6 ♥	Enter Pelican Town on a sunny day between noon and 4pm.
8 ♥	Enter the Bus Stop after 4pm once Sam greets you at your Farmhouse in the morning. (Requires viewing his 2-heart event)
10 ♥	After receiving a letter from Sam, enter Pelican Town on a sunny day between 8pm and midnight.
14 ⚔	Enter the Farmhouse before 5pm. Starts a series of events.

Sandy

	Event Trigger Conditions
4 ♥	Sandy randomly mails you Cactus Fruit.
7 ♥	Sandy sends you a recipe for Tom Kha Soup in the mail.

Sebastian

	Event Trigger Conditions
2 ♥	Enter Sebastian's room when he's there.
4 ♥	Enter the Mountain area between 11am and 5pm.
6 ♥	Enter Sebastian's room when he's there.
8 ♥	Enter the Beach on a rainy day between noon and 11pm.
10 ♥	Enter the Mountains between 8pm and midnight.
14 ⚔	Enter the Mountains on a rainy day before 7pm. Starts a series of events.

Shane

	Event Trigger Conditions
2 ♥	Enter Cindersap Forest between 8pm and midnight.
3 ♥	Shane sends you a recipe for Pepper Poppers in the mail.
4 ♥	Enter Marnie's Ranch while Shane is home.
6 ♥	Enter Cindersap Forest between 9am and 8pm on a rainy day. Then, enter Marnie's Ranch while Shane is home.
7 ♥	Enter Pelican Town between 10am and 4pm on a sunny day. (This event requires 2 hearts with Clint and Emily). Shane also sends you a recipe for Strange Bun in the mail.
8 ♥	Enter Marnie's Ranch while Shane is home.
10 ♥	After receiving an invitation from Shane, go to the Bus Stop between 4pm and 6pm.
14 ⚔	Enter Pelican Town any day other than Friday between 8am and 5pm. Starts a series of events.

Vincent

	Event Trigger Conditions
8 ♥	Enter Cindersap Forest on a sunny day in Spring before 5pm.

Willy

	Event Trigger Conditions
3 ♥	Willy sends you a recipe for Chowder in the mail.
5 ♥	Willy sends you a recipe for Escargot in the mail.
6 ♥	Enter the Beach before 5:10pm.
7 ♥	Willy sends you a recipe for Fish Stew in the mail.
9 ♥	Willy sends you a recipe for Lobster Bisque in the mail.

Wizard

	Event Trigger Conditions
4 ♥	Wizard will randomly send you Minerals in the mail; you'll also be able to enter his basement, where you can make an offering of 500g to change your appearance.

CROPS & FORAGING

Name	Season	Growth Phases (in Days)	Total	Reharvest	Energy	Health	Seed Price	Sell Price
Amaranth	Fa	1 2 2 2	7	-	50	20	70g (P) 87g (J)	150g
Ancient Fruit	Sp-Fa	2 7 7 5	28	7 Days	-	-	-	550g
Artichoke	Fa	2 2 2 1	8	-	30	12	30g (P)	160g
Beet	Fa	1 1 2 2	6	-	30	12	20g (O)	100g
Blue Jazz	Sp	1 2 2 2	7	-	45	18	30g (P) 37g (J)	50g
Blueberry	Su	1 3 3 4 2	13	4 Days	25	10	80g (P) 100g (J)	50g
Bok Choy	Fa	1 1 1 1	4	-	25	10	50g (P) 62g (J)	80g
Cactus	Sp-Wi*	2 2 3 3	12	3 Days	75	33	150g (O)	75g
Cauliflower	Sp	1 2 4 4 1	12	-	75	30	80g (P) 100g (J)	175g
Coffee	Sp-Su	1 2 2 3 2	10	2 Days	-	-	2,500g (C)	15g
Corn	Su-Fa	2 3 3 3 3	14	4 Days	25	10	150g (P) 187g (J)	50g
Cranberries	Fa	1 2 1 2	7	5 Days	38	15	240g (P) 300g (J)	75g
Eggplant	Fa	1 1 1 1	5	5 Days	20	8	20g (P) 25g (J)	60g
Fairy Rose	Fa	1 4 4 3	12	-	45	18	200g (P) 250g (J)	290g
Fiber	Any	1 2 2 2	7	-	-	-	-	1g
Garlic	Sp	1 1 1	4	-	20	8	40g (P)	60g
Grape	Fa	1 1 2 3 3	10	3 Days	38	15	60g (P) 75g (J)	80g
Green Bean	Sp	1 1 1 3 4	10	3 Days	25	10	60g (P) 75g (J)	40g
Hops	Su	1 1 1 2 4	11	1 Day	45	18	60g (P) 75g (J)	25g
Hot Pepper	Su	1 1 1 1	5	3 Days	13	5	40g (P) 50g (J)	40g
Kale	Sp	1 2 2	6	-	50	20	70g (P) 87g (J)	110g
Melon	Su	1 2 3 3	12	-	113	45	80g (P) 100g (J)	250g
Parsnip	Sp	1 1 1	4	-	25	10	20g (P) 25g (J)	35g
Pineapple	Su	1 3 4 3	14	7 Days	138	62	-	300g
Poppy	Su	1 2 2 2	7	-	45	18	100g (P) 125g (J)	140g
Potato	Sp	1 1 2 1	6	-	25	10	50g (P) 62g (J)	80g
Pumpkin	Fa	2 3 4 3	13	-	-	-	100g (P) 125g (J)	320g
Qi Fruit	Any	1	4	-	-	-	-	1g
Radish	Su	2 1 1	6	-	45	18	40g (P) 50g (J)	90g
Red Cabbage	Su	2 1 2 2	9	-	75	30	100g (P)	260g
Rhubarb	Sp	2 2 3 4	13	-	-	-	100g (O)	220g
Rice**	Sp	1 2 3	8	-	3	1	40g (P)	30g
Starfruit	Su	2 3 2 3	13	-	125	50	400g (O)	750g
Strawberry	Sp	1 2 2 2	8	4 Days	50	20	100g (E)	120g
Summer Spangle	Su	2 3 3	8	-	45	18	50g (P) 62g (J)	90g
Sunflower	Su-Fa	1 2 3 2	8	-	45	18	200g (P) 125g (J)	80g
Sweet Gem Berry	Fa	2 4 6 6 6	24	-	-	-	1,000g (C)	3,000g
Taro Tuber***	Su	1 2 3 4	10	-	38	17	-	100g
Tomato	Su	2 2 2 2 3	11	4 Days	20	8	50g (P) 62g (J)	60g
Tulip	Sp	1 1 2 2	6	-	45	18	20g (P) 25g (J)	30g
Wheat	Su-Fa	1 1 1 1	4	-	-	-	10g (P) 12g (J)	25g
Yam	Fa	1 3 3 3	10	-	45	18	60g (P) 75g (J)	160g

Seed Prices: P: Pierre's J: JojaMart C: Travelling Cart O: Oasis E: Egg Festival
*Cactus Seeds can only be grown indoors in a Garden Pot.
**Rice grows more quickly than shown when planted near water. Produces Unmilled Rice.
***Taro Root grows more quickly than shown when planted near water. Produces Taro Tuber.

Fruit Trees

	Name	Season	Growth Phases (All Trees Fully Grow in 28 Days)	Energy	Health	Sapling Price	Sell Price
	Apple	Fa		38	17	4,000g	100g
	Apricot	Sp		38	17	2,000g	50g
	Banana	Su		75	33	5 Dragon Teeth	150g
	Cherry	Sp		38	17	3,400g	80g
	Mango	Su		100	45	75 Mussels	130g
	Orange	Su		38	17	4,000g	100g
	Peach	Su		38	17	6,000g	140g
	Pomegranate	Fa		38	17	6,000g	140g

Other

	Name	Season	Growth Phases (in Days)	Total	Reharvest	Energy	Health	Seed Price	Sell Price
	Tea Leaves	Sp-Fa	10 10 -	20	1 Day*	-	-	-	55g

* Can be harvested during the last week of each season, Spring through Fall (and Winter in the Greenhouse).

Forageables

	Name	Season	Location	Energy	Health	Sell Price
	Blackberry	Fa	Pelican Town, bushes while in season (Fall 8th-11th)	25	11	20g
	Cactus Fruit	Any	Calico Desert	75	33	75g
	Cave Carrot	Any	The Mines	30	13	25g
	Chanterelle	Fa	Secret Woods	75	33	160g
	Clam	Any	The Beach	-	-	50g
	Coconut	Any	Calico Desert, Ginger Island Palm Trees	-	-	100g
	Common Mushroom	Sp, Fa	Pelican Town, Secret Woods, Big Mushroom Trees	38	17	40g
	Coral	Any	The Beach	-	-	80g
	Crocus	Wi	Pelican Town	0	0	60g
	Crystal Fruit	Wi	Pelican Town, The Mines (Floors 40-80)	63	28	150g
	Daffodil	Sp	Pelican Town	0	0	30g
	Dandelion	Sp	Pelican Town	25	11	40g
	Fiddlehead Fern	Su	Secret Woods	25	11	90g
	Ginger	Any	Ginger Island	25	11	60g
	Grape	Su	Pelican Town	38	17	80g
	Hazelnut	Fa	Pelican Town	30	13	90g
	Holly	Wi	Pelican Town, Secret Woods	-37	0	80g
	Leek	Sp	Pelican Town	40	18	60g
	Magma Cap	Any	Volcano Dungeon	175	78	400g
	Morel	Sp	Secret Woods	20	9	150g
	Mussel	Any	The Beach, Ginger Island Mussel Nodes	-	-	30g
	Nautilus Shell	Wi	The Beach	-	-	120g
	Oyster	Any	The Beach	-	-	40g
	Purple Mushroom	Any	The Mines, Big Mushroom Trees	125	56	250g
	Rainbow Shell	Su	The Beach	-	-	300g
	Red Mushroom	Any	The Mines, Secret Woods (Summer), Big Mushroom Trees	-50	0	75g
	Salmonberry	Sp	Bushes while in season (Spring 15th-18th)	25	11	5g
	Sea Urchin	Any	The Beach	-	-	160g
	Snow Yam	Wi	Pelican Town	30	13	100g
	Spice Berry	Su	Pelican Town	25	11	80g
	Spring Onion	Sp	Cindersap Forest	13	5	8g
	Sweet Pea	Su	Pelican Town	0	0	50g
	Wild Horseradish	Sp	Pelican Town	13	5	50g
	Wild Plum	Fa	Pelican Town	25	11	80g
	Winter Root	Wi	Pelican Town, The Mines (Floors 40-80)	25	10	70g

Star Quality Factors: Price: 1.25x 1.5x 2x Health & Energy: 1.4x ⭐ 1.8x ✦ 2.6x

Mayonnaise Machine

Name	Ingredients			Time	Energy	Health	Sell Price
Dinosaur Mayonnaise	Dinosaur Egg			3 Hours	-	-	800g
Duck Mayonnaise	Duck Egg			3 Hours	-	-	375g
Mayonnaise	Egg (White/Brown/Large)	Ostrich Egg	Golden Egg	3 Hours	-	-	190g
Void Mayonnaise	Void Egg			3 Hours	-75	-	275g

Bee House

Name	Ingredients			Time	Energy	Health	Sell Price
Blue Jazz Honey	Blue Jazz Nearby			3-4 Days	-	-	200g
Fairy Rose Honey	Fairy Rose Nearby			3-4 Days	-	-	680g
Poppy Honey	Poppy Nearby			3-4 Days	-	-	380g
Summer Spangle Honey	Summer Spangle Nearby			3-4 Days	-	-	280g
Sunflower Honey	Sunflower Nearby			3-4 Days	-	-	260g
Tulip Honey	Tulip Nearby			3-4 Days	-	-	160g
Wild Honey	-			3-4 Days	-	-	100g

Tapper & Heavy Tapper

Name	Ingredients			Time	Energy	Health	Sell Price
Common Mushroom	Big Mushroom Tree			Varies	38	17	40g
Maple Syrup	Maple Tree			9 Days*	50	22	200g
Oak Resin	Oak Tree			7-8 Days*	-	-	150g
Pine Tar	Pine Tree			5-6 Days*	-	-	100g
Purple Mushroom	Big Mushroom Tree			Varies	125	56	250g
Red Mushroom	Big Mushroom Tree			Varies	-50	-	75g
Sap	Mahogany Tree			1 Day	-	-	2g

*The Heavy Tapper reduces these harvest times roughly by half.

Preserves Jar

Name	Ingredients			Time	Energy	Health	Sell Price
Aged Fish Roe	Any Fish Roe			~3 Days	100	45	2x Base Val.
Caviar	Sturgeon Roe			~4 Days	175	78	500g
Jelly	Any Fruit			~2 Days	-	-	50g + 2x Base Val.
Pickles	Any Vegetable			~2 Days	-	-	50g + 2x Base Val.

Cheese Press

Name	Ingredients			Time	Energy	Health	Sell Price
Cheese	Milk	Large Milk		~3 Hours	125	56	230g
Goat Cheese	Goat Milk	L. Goat Milk		~3 Hours	125	56	400g

Loom

Name	Ingredients			Time	Energy	Health	Sell Price
Cloth	Wool			4 Hours	-	-	470g

Keg

Name	Ingredients			Time	Energy	Health	Sell Price
Beer	Wheat			1-2 Days	50	22	200g
Coffee	Coffee Bean (5)			2 Hours	3	1	150g
Green Tea	Tea Leaves			3 Hours	13	5	100g
Juice	Any Vegetable			~4 Days	75	33	2.25x Base Val.
Mead	Any Honey			~1 Day	75	33	200g
Pale Ale	Hops			1-2 Days	50	20	300g
Wine	Any Fruit			~7 Days	50	20	3x Base Val.

Oil Maker

Name	Ingredients			Time	Energy	Health	Sell Price
Oil	Corn	Sunflower	Sunflower Seeds	2 Days	13	5	100g
Truffle Oil	Truffle			5-6 Hours	38	17	1,065g

Chickens
Price: 800g
Sell Price (5 Hearts): 1,040g

Name	Energy	Health	Sell Price
Egg / Brown Egg	25	11	50g
Large Egg / Large Brown Egg	38	17	95g

Golden Chickens
Price: N/A
Sell Price (5 Hearts): 1,040g

	Energy	Health	Sell Price
Golden Egg	25	11	500g

Void Chickens
Price: N/A
Sell Price (5 Hearts): 1,040g

	Energy	Health	Sell Price
Void Egg	38	17	65g

Ducks
Price: 1,200g
Sell Price (5 Hearts): 1,560g

	Energy	Health	Sell Price
Duck Egg	38	17	95g
Duck Feather	-	-	250g

Rabbits
Price: 8,000g
Sell Price (5 Hearts): 10,400g

	Energy	Health	Sell Price
Wool	-	-	340g
Rabbit's Foot	-	-	565g

Dinosaurs
Price: N/A
Sell Price (5 Hearts): 1,300g

	Energy	Health	Sell Price
Dinosaur Egg	-	-	350g

Cows
Price: 1,500g
Sell Price (5 Hearts): 1,950g

	Energy	Health	Sell Price
Milk	38	17	125g
Large Milk	50	22	190g

Goats
Price: 4,000g
Sell Price (5 Hearts): 5,200g

	Energy	Health	Sell Price
Goat Milk	63	25	225g
Large Goat Milk	88	35	345g

Sheep
Price: 8,000g
Sell Price (5 Hearts): 10,400g

	Energy	Health	Sell Price
Wool	-	-	340g

Pigs
Price: 16,000g
Sell Price (5 Hearts): 20,528g

	Energy	Health	Sell Price
Truffle	13	5	625g

Ostriches
Price: N/A
Sell Price (5 Hearts): 20,800g

	Energy	Health	Sell Price
Ostrich Egg	38	17	600g

Slimes
Price: N/A
Sell Price (5 Hearts): N/A

	Energy	Health	Sell Price
Blue Slime Egg	-	-	1,750g
Green Slime Egg	-	-	1,000g
Red Slime Egg	-	-	2,500g
Purple Slime Egg	-	-	5,000g
Tiger Slime Egg	-	-	8,000g

	Name	Quest (1)	Quest (3)	Quest (5)	Quest (7)	Spawn Rate	Roe Value
	Albacore	-	Driftwood (3), Frozen Geode, Seaweed (1-2)	Clam (2), Coral (2)	Aquamarine (2), Mussel, Sea Urchin (2)	2 Days	67g
	Anchovy	-	Driftwood (3), Frozen Geode, Seaweed (1-2)	Clam (2), Coral (2)	Aquamarine (2), Mussel, Sea Urchin (2)	1 Day	45g
	Blobfish	Coral (3), Frozen Tear (2), Sea Urchin (2)	Coffee Bean (5), Mayonnaise, Pizza	Cookie, Green Tea, Wine	Rainbow Shell, Rice Pudding	4 Days	280g
	Blue Discus	-	Taro Root (3)	Taro Root (10)		3 Days	90g
	Bream	-	Acorn (3), Bug Meat (10), Maple Seed (3), Pine Cone (3)	Gold Ore (3), Maple Syrup, Mixed Seeds (5)	Crayfish, Honey, Jade (2), Periwinkle	2 Days	52g
	Bullhead	-	Bug Meat (10), Clay (2-3), Green Algae (2-3), Slime (5)	Common Mushroom (2-3), Earth Crystal (1-2), Limestone	Mudstone, Snail, Wild Bait (5)	2 Days	67g
	Carp	-	Green Algae (2)	Cave Carrot (2)	-	1 Day	45g
	Catfish	-	Amethyst (2), Copper Bar (3), Red Mushroom (3), Topaz (2)	Bat Wing (10), Earth Crystal (2), Mixed Seeds (5), Purple Mushroom (2-3)	Diamond, Iron Bar (3), Mayonnaise, Pickles	4 Days	130g
	Chub	-	Acorn (3), Bug Meat (10), Maple Seed (3), Pine Cone (3)	Gold Ore (3), Maple Syrup, Mixed Seeds (5)	Crayfish, Honey, Jade (2), Periwinkle	2 Days	55g
	Cockle	-	Clay (5)	Bug Meat (10), Quartz (5)	Sea Urchin, Solar Essence (5), Wild Bait	2 Days	55g
	Coral	-		-		2 Days	-
	Crab	-	Clay (5)	Bug Meat (10), Quartz (5)	Sea Urchin, Solar Essence (5), Wild Bait	3 Days	80g
	Crayfish	-	Clay (5), Fiber (15)	Bug Meat (10), Cave Carrot, Hardwood (5)	Field Snack, Solar Essence (5), Wild Bait	2 Days	67g
	Dorado	-	Bream (2), Carp (2), Chub (2)	Bullhead (2), Largemouth Bass (2)	Ghostfish (2), Sandfish (2), Woodskip (2)	3 Days	80g
	Eel	-	Driftwood (3), Frozen Geode, Seaweed (1-2)	Clam (2), Coral (2)	Aquamarine (2), Mussel, Sea Urchin (2)	3 Days	72g
	Flounder	-	Driftwood (3), Frozen Geode, Seaweed (1-2)	Clam (2), Coral (2)	Aquamarine (2), Mussel, Sea Urchin (2)	3 Days	80g
	Ghostfish	Quartz (5)	Cave Carrot (5)	White Algae (5)	Dwarf Scroll I, Dwarf Scroll II, Refined Quartz (2)	2 Days	52g
	Halibut	-	Driftwood (3), Frozen Geode, Seaweed (1-2)	Clam (2), Coral (2)	Aquamarine (2), Mussel, Sea Urchin (2)	2 Days	70g
	Herring	-	Driftwood (3)	Coral	-	1 Day	45g
	Ice Pip	Iron Ore (10)	Frozen Tear (5)	Coal (10), Crystal Fruit, Frozen Geode (5)	Iron Bar (4), Refined Quartz (10)	5 Days	280g
	Largemouth Bass	-	Bug Meat (10), Clay (2-3), Green Algae (2-3), Slime (5)	Common Mushroom (2-3), Earth Crystal (1-2), Limestone	Mudstone, Snail, Wild Bait (5)	3 Days	80g
	Lava Eel	Fire Quartz (3)	Basalt, Diamond (2), Dwarf Scroll III	Mega Bomb (2)	Iridium Bar	5 Days	380g
	Lingcod	-	Bream (2), Carp (2), Chub (2)	Bullhead (2), Largemouth Bass (2)	Ghostfish (2), Sandfish (2), Woodskip (2)	3 Days	90g
	Lionfish	-	Ginger (3), Pineapple	Mango	-	3 Days	80g
	Lobster	-	Clay (5)	Bug Meat (10), Quartz (5)	Sea Urchin, Solar Essence (5), Wild Bait	3 Days	90g
	Midnight Carp	-	Bug Meat (10), Clay (2-3), Green Algae (2-3), Slime (5)	Common Mushroom (2-3), Earth Crystal (1-2), Limestone	Mudstone, Snail, Wild Bait (5)	4 Days	105g
	Midnight Squid	-	Coral (3), Sea Urchin	Sardine (2)	Ocean Stone (at population 8)	3 Days	110g*
	Mussel	-	Clay (5)	Bug Meat (10), Quartz (5)	Sea Urchin, Solar Essence (5), Wild Bait	1 Day	45g
	Octopus	-	Coral (3), Honey, Oyster, Refined Quartz (3)	Dried Starfish, Emerald (2), Omni Geode (2-3), Purple Mushroom (2-3)	Green Tea	4 Days	105g
	Oyster	-	Clay (5)	Bug Meat (10), Quartz (5)	Sea Urchin, Solar Essence (5), Wild Bait	2 Days	50g

Name	Quest (1)	Quest (3)	Quest (5)	Quest (7)	Spawn Rate	Roe Value
Perch	-	Acorn (3), Bug Meat (10), Maple Seed (3), Pine Cone (3)	Gold Ore (3), Maple Syrup, Mixed Seeds (5)	Crayfish, Honey, Jade (2), Periwinkle	2 Days	57g
Periwinkle	-	Clay (5), Fiber (15)	Bug Meat (10), Cave Carrot, Hardwood (5)	Field Snack, Solar Essence (5), Wild Bait	1 Day	40g
Pike	-	Bream (2), Carp (2), Chub (2)	Bullhead (2), Largemouth Bass (2)	Ghostfish (2), Sandfish (2), Woodskip (2)	3 Days	80g
Pufferfish	-	Driftwood (3), Frozen Geode, Seaweed (1-2)	Clam (2), Coral (2)	Aquamarine (2), Mussel, Sea Urchin (2)	4 Days	130g
Rainbow Trout	-	Coral (3), Honey, Oyster, Refined Quartz (3)	Dried Starfish, Emerald (2), Omni Geode (2-3), Purple Mushroom (2-3)	Diamond, Gold Bar (3), Iridium Ore, Jelly, Pickles	2 Days	62g
Red Mullet	-	Driftwood (3), Frozen Geode, Seaweed (1-2)	Clam (2), Coral (2)	Aquamarine (2), Mussel, Sea Urchin (2)	2 Days	67g
Red Snapper	-	Driftwood (3), Frozen Geode, Seaweed (1-2)	Clam (2), Coral (2)	Aquamarine (2), Mussel, Sea Urchin (2)	2 Days	55g
Salmon	-	Acorn (3), Bug Meat (10), Maple Seed (3), Pine Cone (3)	Gold Ore (3), Maple Syrup, Mixed Seeds (5)	Crayfish, Honey, Jade (2), Periwinkle	2 Days	67g
Sandfish	-	Cactus Fruit (3), Coconut (3)	Golden Relic	-	4 Days	67g
Sardine	-	Driftwood (3), Frozen Geode, Seaweed (1-2)	Clam (2), Coral (2)	Aquamarine (2), Mussel, Sea Urchin (2)	2 Days	50g
Scorpion Carp	-	Cactus Fruit (3), Coconut (3)	Golden Relic	-	4 Days	105g
Sea Cucumber	-	Driftwood (3), Frozen Geode, Seaweed (1-2)	Clam (2), Coral (2)	Aquamarine (2), Mussel, Sea Urchin (2)	2 Days	67g
Sea Urchin	-				4 Days	110g
Shad	-	Acorn (3), Bug Meat (10), Maple Seed (3), Pine Cone (3)	Gold Ore (3), Maple Syrup, Mixed Seeds (5)	Crayfish, Honey, Jade (2), Periwinkle	2 Days	60g
Shrimp	-	Clay (5)	Bug Meat (10), Quartz (5)	Sea Urchin, Solar Essence (5), Wild Bait	2 Days	60g
Slimejack	Slime (20)	Bug Meat (10)	Algae Soup, Wild Bait (5)	Petrified Slime	3 Days	80g
Smallmouth Bass	-	Acorn (3), Bug Meat (10), Maple Seed (3), Pine Cone (3)	Gold Ore (3), Maple Syrup, Mixed Seeds (5)	Crayfish, Honey, Jade (2), Periwinkle	2 Days	55g
Snail	-	Clay (5), Fiber (15)	Bug Meat (10), Cave Carrot, Hardwood (5)	Field Snack, Solar Essence (5), Wild Bait	2 Days	62g
Spook Fish	-	Amethyst (3), Coral (3), Iron Bar (3), Oyster, Red Mushroom (3), Refined Quartz (3)	Dried Starfish, Emerald (2), Granite, Omni Geode (2-3), Purple Mushroom (2-3)	Diamond, Gold Bar (3), Iridium Ore, Mayonnaise, Pickles	4 Days	140g
Squid	-	Coral (3), Sea Urchin	Sardine (2)	-	3 Days	110g*
Stingray	-	Cinder Shard (7)	Dragon Tooth	-	4 Days	120g
Stonefish	Copper Ore (10)	Earth Crystal (5)	Coal (10), Geode (5)	Copper Bar (4), Refined Quartz (5)	5 Days	180g
Sturgeon	Diamond	Jelly, Maple Syrup (2), Pickles	Omni Geode (3)	Nautilus Shell	4 Days	130g
Sunfish	-	Acorn (2), Geode (2)	Amethyst, Mixed Seeds (3)	-	1 Day	45g
Super Cucumber	-	Coral (3), Honey, Oyster, Refined Quartz (3)	Dried Starfish, Emerald (2), Omni Geode (2-3), Purple Mushroom (2-3)	Diamond, Gold Bar (3), Iridium Ore, Jelly, Pickles	4 Days	155g
Tiger Trout	-				N/A	105g
Tilapia	-	Driftwood (3), Frozen Geode, Seaweed (1-2)	Clam (2), Coral (2)	Aquamarine (2), Mussel, Sea Urchin (2)	2 Days	67g
Tuna	-	Driftwood (3), Frozen Geode, Seaweed (1-2)	Clam (2), Coral (2)	Aquamarine (2), Mussel, Sea Urchin (2)	3 Days	80g
Void Salmon	Void Essence (5)	Bat Wing (10)	Diamond, Void Egg	Iridium Ore	4 Days	105g
Walleye	-	Acorn (3), Bug Meat (10), Maple Seed (3), Pine Cone (3)	Gold Ore (3), Maple Syrup, Mixed Seeds (5)	Crayfish, Honey, Jade (2), Periwinkle	3 Days	82g
Woodskip	Hardwood (10)	Common Mushroom (2-3), Red Mushroom (3)	Oak Resin, Pine Tar	Jade (2), Tea Leaves	2 Days	67g

*Squids and Midnight Squids do not produce Roe; instead, their main product is Squid Ink.

	Name	Ingredients				Recipe From
	Ancient Seeds	Ancient Seed				Museum
	Bait (5)	Bug Meat				Fishing L2
	Barbed Hook	Copper Bar	Iron Bar	Gold Bar		Fishing L8
	Barrel Brazier	Wood (50)	Solar Essence	Coal		Carpenter
	Basic Fertilizer	Sap (2)				Farming L1
	Basic Retaining Soil	Stone (2)				Farming L4
	Bee House	Wood (40)	Coal (8)	Iron Bar	Maple Syrup	Farming L3
	Bomb	Iron Ore (4)	Coal			Mining L6
	Bone Mill	Bone Fragment (10)	Clay (3)	Stone (20)		Gunther
	Brick Floor	Clay (2)	Stone (5)			Carpenter
	Bug Steak	Bug Meat (10)				Combat L1
	Campfire	Stone (10)	Wood (10)	Fiber (10)		-
	Carved Brazier	Hardwood (10)	Coal			Carpenter
	Cask	Wood (20)	Hardwood			House Upgrade
	Charcoal Kiln	Wood (20)	Copper Bar (2)			Foraging L4
	Cheese Press	Wood (45)	Stone (45)	Hardwood (10)	Copper Bar	Farming L6
	Cherry Bomb	Copper Ore (4)	Coal			Mining L1
	Chest	Wood (50)				-
	Cobblestone Path	Stone				-
	Cookout Kit	Wood (15)	Fiber (10)	Coal (3)		Foraging L9
	Cork Bobber	Wood (10)	Hardwood (5)	Slime (10)		Fishing L7
	Crab Pot	Wood (40)	Iron Bar (3)			Fishing L3
	Crab Pot w/Trapper	*Wood (25)*	*Copper Bar (2)*			
	Crystal Floor	Refined Quartz				Krobus
	Crystal Path	Refined Quartz				Carpenter
	Crystalarium	Stone (99)	Gold Bar (5)	Iridium Bar (2)	Battery Pack	Mining L9
	Dark Sign	Bat Wing (5)	Bone Fragment (5)			Krobus
	Deluxe Fertilizer	Iridium Bar	Sap (40)			Walnut Room
	Deluxe Retaining Soil	Stone (5)	Fiber (3)	Clay		Island Trader
	Deluxe Scarecrow	Wood (50)	Fiber (40)	Iridium Ore		All Rarecrows
	Deluxe Speed-Gro	Oak Resin	Coral			Farming L8
	Dressed Spinner	Iron Bar (2)	Cloth			Fishing L8
	Drum Block	Stone (10)	Copper Ore (2)	Fiber (20)		Robin
	Explosive Ammo	Iron Bar	Coal (2)			Combat L8
	Fairy Dust	Diamond	Fairy Rose			Birdie
	Farm Computer	Dwarf Gadget	Battery Pack	Refined Quartz (10)		Demetrius
	Fiber Seeds	Mixed Seeds	Sap (5)	Clay		Linus
	Field Snack	Acorn	Maple Seed	Pine Cone		Foraging L1
	Flute Block	Wood (10)	Copper Ore (2)	Fiber (20)		Robin
	Furnace	Copper Ore (20)	Stone (25)			Clint
	Garden Pot	Clay	Stone (10)	Refined Quartz		Evelyn
	Gate	Wood (10)				-
	Geode Crusher	Gold Bar (2)	Stone (50)	Diamond		Clint
	Glowstone Ring	Solar Essence (5)	Iron Bar (5)			Mining L4
	Gold Brazier	Gold Bar	Coal	Fiber (5)		Carpenter
	Grass Starter	Fiber (10)				Pierre
	Gravel Path	Stone				-
	Hardwood Fence	Hardwood				Farming L6
	Heavy Tapper	Hardwood (30)	Radioactive Bar			Walnut Room
	Hopper	Hardwood (10)	Iridium Bar	Radioactive Bar		Walnut Room
	Hyper Speed-Gro	Radioactive Ore	Bone Fragment (3)	Solar Essence		Walnut Room
	Iridium Band	Iridium Bar (5)	Solar Essence (50)	Void Essence (50)		Combat L9
	Iridium Sprinkler	Gold Bar	Iridium Bar	Battery Pack		Farming L9
	Iron Fence (10)	Iron Bar				Farming L4
	Iron Lamp-post	Iron Bar	Battery Pack			Carpenter
	Jack-O-Lantern	Pumpkin	Torch			Spirit's Eve
	Keg	Wood (30)	Copper Bar	Iron Bar	Oak Resin	Farming L8
	Life Elixir	Red Mushroom	Purple Mushroom	Morel	Chanterelle	Combat L2
	Lightning Rod	Iron Bar	Refined Quartz	Bat Wing (5)		Foraging L6
	Loom	Wood (60)	Fiber (30)	Pine Tar		Farming L7
	Magic Bait	Radioactive Ore	Bug Meat (3)			Walnut Room
	Magnet	Iron Bar				Fishing L9
	Marble Brazier	Marble	Aquamarine	Stone (100)		Carpenter
	Mayonnaise Machine	Wood (15)	Stone (15)	Earth Crystal	Copper Bar	Farming L2
	Mega Bomb	Gold Ore (4)	Solar Essence	Void Essence		Mining L8

	Name	Ingredients						Recipe From
	Mini-Obelisk	Hardwood (30)	Solar Essence (20)	Gold Bar (3)				Wizard
	Monster Musk	Slime (30)	Bat Wing (30)					Wizard
	Oil Maker	Slime (50)	Hardwood (20)	Gold Bar				Farming L8
	Oil of Garlic	Garlic (10)	Oil					Combat L6
	Ostrich Incubator	Bone Fragment (50)	Hardwood (50)	Cinder Shard (20)				Field Office
	Preserves Jar	Wood (50)	Stone (40)	Coal (8)				Farming L4
	Quality Bobber	Copper Bar	Sap (20)	Solar Essence (5)				Willy
	Quality Fertilizer	Sap (2)	Fish					Farming L9
	Quality Retaining Soil	Stone (3)	Clay					Farming L7
	Quality Sprinkler	Iron Bar	Gold Bar	Refined Quartz				Farming L6
	Rain Totem	Hardwood	Truffle Oil	Pine Tar (5)				Foraging L9
	Recycling Machine	Wood (25)	Stone (25)	Iron Bar				Fishing L4
	Ring of Yoba	Gold Bar (5)	Iron Bar (5)	Diamond				Combat L7
	Rustic Plank Floor	Wood						Carpenter
	Scarecrow	Wood (50)	Coal	Fiber (20)				Farming L1
	Seed Maker	Wood (25)	Coal (10)	Gold Bar				Farming L9
	Skull Brazier	Bone Fragment (10)						Carpenter
	Slime Egg-Press	Coal (25)	Fire Quartz	Battery Pack				Combat L6
	Slime Incubator	Iridium Bar (2)	Slime (100)					Combat L8
	Solar Panel	Refined Quartz (10)	Iron Bar (5)	Gold Bar (5)				Caroline
	Speed-Gro	Pine Tar	Clam					Farming L3
	Spinner	Iron Bar (2)						Fishing L6
	Sprinkler	Copper Bar	Iron Bar					Farming L2
	Staircase	Stone (99)						Mining L2
	Stepping Stone Path	Stone						Carpenter
	Stone Brazier	Stone (10)	Coal	Fiber (5)				Carpenter
	Stone Chest	Stone (50)						Robin
	Stone Fence	Stone (2)						Farming L2
	Stone Floor	Stone						Carpenter
	Stone Sign	Stone (25)						-
	Stone Walkway Floor	Stone						Carpenter
	Straw Floor	Wood	Fiber					Carpenter
	Stump Brazier	Hardwood (5)	Coal					Carpenter
	Sturdy Ring	Copper Bar (2)	Bug Meat (25)	Slime (25)				Combat L1
	Tapper	Wood (40)	Copper Bar (2)					Foraging L3
	Tea Sapling	Wild Seeds (2)	Fiber (5)	Wood (5)				Caroline
	Thorns Ring	Bone Fragment (50)	Stone (50)	Gold Bar				Combat L7
	Torch	Wood	Sap (2)					-
	Transmute (Au)	Iron Bar (2)						Mining L7
	Transmute (Fe)	Copper Bar (3)						Mining L4
	Trap Bobber	Copper Bar	Sap (10)					Fishing L6
	Treasure Hunter	Gold Bar (2)						Fishing L7
	Tree Fertilizer	Fiber (5)	Stone (5)					Foraging L7
	Tub o' Flowers	Wood (15)	Tulip Seeds	Blue Jazz Seeds	Poppy Seeds	Spangle Seeds		Flower Dance
	Warp Totem: Beach	Hardwood	Coral (2)	Fiber (10)				Foraging L6
	Warp Totem: Desert	Hardwood (2)	Coconut	Iridium Ore (4)				Desert Trader
	Warp Totem: Farm	Hardwood	Honey	Fiber (20)				Foraging L8
	Warp Totem: Island	Hardwood (5)	Dragon Tooth	Ginger				Island Trader
	Warp Totem: Mountains	Hardwood	Iron Bar	Stone (25)				Foraging L7
	Warrior Ring	Iron Bar (10)	Coal (25)	Frozen Tear (10)				Combat L4
	Weathered Floor	Wood						Dwarf
	Wedding Ring*	Iridium Bar (5)	Prismatic Shard					Travelling Cart
	Wicked Statue	Stone (25)	Coal (5)					Krobus
	Wild Bait (5)	Fiber (10)	Bug Meat (5)	Slime (5)				Linus
	Wild Seeds (Fa) (10)	C. Mushroom	Wild Plum	Hazelnut	Blackberry			Foraging L6
	Wild Seeds (Sp) (10)	Wild Horseradish	Daffodil	Leek	Dandelion			Foraging L1
	Wild Seeds (Su) (10)	Spice Berry	Grape	Sweet Pea				Foraging L4
	Wild Seeds (Wi) (10)	Winter Root	Crystal Fruit	Snow Yam	Crocus			Foraging L7
	Wood Fence	Wood (2)						-
	Wood Floor	Wood						Carpenter
	Wood Lamp-post	Wood (50)	Battery Pack					Carpenter
	Wood Path	Wood						-
	Wood Sign	Wood (25)						-
	Wooden Brazier	Wood (10)	Coal	Fiber (5)				Carpenter
	Worm Bin	Hardwood (25)	Gold Bar	Iron Bar	Fiber (50)			Fishing L8

*Available only in multiplayer.

259

COOKING

	Name	Ingredients				Energy	Health	Stat Bonus	Sell Price	Source
	Algae Soup	Green Algae (4)	-	-	-	75	33		100g	Clint
	Artichoke Dip	Artichoke	Milk	-	-	100	44		210g	TV
	Autumn's Bounty	Yam	Pumpkin	-	-	220	98	+2 +2	350g	Demetrius
	Baked Fish	Sunfish	Bream	Wheat Flour	-	75	33		100g	TV
	Banana Pudding	Banana	Milk	Sugar	-	125	56	+1 +1 +1	260g	Island Trader
	Bean Hotpot	Green Bean (2)	-	-	-	125	56	+30 +32	100g	Clint
	Blackberry Cobbler	Blackberry (2)	Sugar	Wheat Flour	-	175	78		260g	TV
	Blueberry Tart	Blueberry	Wheat Flour	Sugar	Egg	125	56		150g	Pierre
	Bread	Wheat Flour	-	-	-	50	22		60g	TV, Saloon
	Bruschetta	Bread	Oil	Tomato	-	113	50		210g	TV
	Carp Surprise	Carp (4)	-	-	-	90	40		150g	TV
	Cheese Cauliflower	Cauliflower	Cheese	-	-	138	62		300g	Pam
	Chocolate Cake	Wheat Flour	Sugar	Egg	-	150	67		200g	TV
	Chowder	Clam	Milk	-	-	225	101	+1	135g	Willy
	Coleslaw	Red Cabbage	Vinegar	Mayonnaise	-	213	95		345g	TV
	Complete Breakfast	Fried Egg	Pancakes	Hashbrowns	Milk	200	89	+2 +50	350g	TV
	Cookies	Wheat Flour	Sugar	Egg	-	90	40		140g	Evelyn
	Crab Cakes	Crab	Wheat Flour	Egg	Oil	225	101	+1 +1	275g	TV
	Cranberry Candy	Cranberries	Apple	Sugar	-	125	56		175g	TV
	Cranberry Sauce	Cranberries	Sugar	-	-	125	56	+2	120g	Gus
	Crispy Bass	Largemouth Bass	Wheat Flour	Oil	-	90	40	+64	150g	Kent
	Dish O' The Sea	Sardine (2)	Hashbrowns	-	-	150	67	+3	220g	Fishing L3
	Eggplant Parmesan	Eggplant	Tomato	-	-	175	78	+1 +3	200g	Lewis
	Escargot	Snail	Garlic	-	-	225	101	+2	125g	Willy
	Farmer's Lunch	Omelet	Parsnip	-	-	200	89	+3	150g	Farming L3
	Fiddlehead Risotto	Oil	Fid. Fern	Garlic	-	225	101		350g	TV
	Fish Stew	Crayfish	Mussel	Periwinkle	Tomato	225	101	+3	175g	Willy
	Fish Taco	Mayonnaise	Tortilla	Red Cabbage	Tuna	165	74	+2	500g	Linus
	Fried Calamari	Squid	Wheat Flour	Oil	-	80	35		150g	Jodi
	Fried Eel	Eel	Oil	-	-	75	33	+1	120g	George
	Fried Egg	Egg	-	-	-	50	22		35g	-
	Fried Mushroom	C. Mushroom	Morel	Oil	-	135	60	+2	200g	Demetrius
	Fruit Salad	Blueberry	Melon	Apricot	-	263	118		450g	TV
	Ginger Ale	Ginger (3)	Sugar	-	-	63	28	+1	200g	Volcano Dwarf
	Glazed Yams	Yam	Sugar	-	-	200	89		200g	TV
	Hashbrowns	Potato	Oil	-	-	90	40	+1	120g	TV, Saloon
	Ice Cream	Milk	Sugar	-	-	100	44		120g	Jodi
	Lobster Bisque	Lobster	Milk	-	-	225	101	+3 +50	205g	TV, Willy
	Lucky Lunch	Sea Cucumber	Tortilla	Blue Jazz	-	100	44	+3	250g	TV
	Maki Roll	Fish (Any)	Seaweed	Rice	-	100	44		220g	TV, Saloon

	Name	Ingredients				Energy	Health	Stat Bonus	Sell Price	Source
	Mango Sticky Rice	Mango	Coconut	Rice	-	113	50	+3	250g	Leo
	Maple Bar	Maple Syrup	Sugar	Wheat Flour	-	225	101	+1 +1 +1	300g	TV
	Miner's Treat	Cave Carrot (2)	Sugar	Milk	-	125	56	+3 +32	350g	Mining L3
	Omelet	Egg	Milk	-	-	100	44		125g	TV, Saloon
	Pale Broth	White Algae (2)	-	-	-	125	56		150g	Marnie
	Pancakes	Wheat Flour	Egg	-	-	90	40	+2	80g	TV, Saloon
	Parsnip Soup	Parsnip	Milk	Vinegar	-	85	38		120g	Caroline
	Pepper Poppers	Hot Pepper	Cheese	-	-	130	58	+2 +1	200g	Shane
	Pink Cake	Melon	Wheat Flour	Sugar	Egg	250	112		480g	TV
	Pizza	Wheat Flour	Tomato	Cheese	-	150	67		300g	TV, Saloon
	Plum Pudding	Wild Plum (2)	Wheat Flour	Sugar	-	175	78		260g	TV
	Poi	Taro Root (4)	-	-	-	75	33		400g	Leo
	Poppyseed Muffin	Poppy	Wheat Flour	Sugar	-	150	67		250g	TV
	Pumpkin Pie	Pumpkin	Wheat Flour	Milk	Sugar	225	101		385g	TV
	Pumpkin Soup	Pumpkin	Milk	-	-	200	89	+2 +2	300g	Robin
	Radish Salad	Oil	Vinegar	Radish	-	200	89		300g	TV
	Red Plate	Red Cabbage	Radish	-	-	240	107	+50	400g	Emily
	Rhubarb Pie	Rhubarb	Wheat Flour	Sugar	-	215	96		400g	Marnie
	Rice Pudding	Milk	Sugar	Rice	-	115	51		260g	Evelyn
	Roasted Hazelnuts	Hazelnut (3)	-	-	-	175	78		270g	TV
	Roots Platter	Cave Carrot	Winter Root	-	-	125	56	+3	100g	Combat L3
	Salad	Leek	Dandelion	Vinegar	-	113	50		110g	Emily
	Salmon Dinner	Salmon	Amaranth	Kale	-	125	56		300g	Gus
	Sashimi	Fish (Any)	-	-	-	75	33		75g	Linus
	Seafoam Pudding	Flounder	Midnight Carp	Squid Ink	-	175	78	+4	300g	Fishing L9
	Shrimp Cocktail	Wild Horseradish	Shrimp	Tomato	-	225	101	+1 +1	160g	TV
	Spaghetti	Wheat Flour	Tomato	-	-	75	33		120g	Lewis
	Spicy Eel	Eel	Hot Pepper	-	-	115	51	+1 +1	175g	George
	Squid Ink Ravioli	Squid Ink	Wheat Flour	Tomato	-	125	56	+1*	150g	Combat L9
	Stir Fry	Cave Carrot	C. Mushroom	Kale	Oil	200	89		335g	TV
	Strange Bun	Wheat Flour	Periwinkle	Void Mayo	-	100	44		225g	Shane
	Stuffing	Bread	Cranberries	Hazelnut	-	170	76	+2	165g	Pam
	Super Meal	Bok Choy	Cranberries	Artichoke	-	160	71	+40 +1	220g	Kent
	Survival Burger	Bread	Cave Carrot	Eggplant	-	125	56	+3	180g	Foraging L3
	Tom Kha Soup	Coconut	Shrimp	C. Mushroom	-	175	78	+2 +30	250g	Sandy
	Tortilla	Corn	-	-	-	50	22		50g	TV, Saloon
	Triple Shot Espresso	Coffee (3)	-	-	-	8	3	+1	450g	Saloon
	Tropical Curry	Coconut	Pineapple	Hot Pepper	-	150	67	+4	500	Resort
	Trout Soup	Rainbow Trout	Green Algae	-	-	100	44	+1	100g	TV
	Vegetable Medley	Tomato	Beet	-	-	165	74		120g	Caroline

: Attack : Defense : Farming : Fishing : Foraging : Luck : Magnetism : Max Energy : Mining : Speed

*Squid Ink Ravioli also provides temporary immunity against all status debuffs.

Shirts and Tops

Left Table

	Name	Recipe (Cloth + ___)	🧵
	80's Shirt	Cactus Fruit	•
	Antiquity Shirt	Chipped Amphora	
	Aquamarine Shirt	Duck Mayonnaise	
	Arcane Shirt	Void Essence	
	Backpack Shirt	Sandstone	•
	Banana Shirt	Banana Pudding	
	Bandana Shirt	Jasper	
	Bandana Shirt	Kyanite	
	Bandana Shirt	Fluorapatite	
	Basic Pullover	Fiber Wood	•
	Belted Coat	Autumn's Bounty	
	Bikini Top	Rainbow Shell	•
	Black Leather Jacket	Any Alcohol Item	
	Blacksmith Apron	Fiddlehead Risotto	
	Blue Buttoned Vest	Octopus	•
	Blue Hoodie	Frozen Geode	
	Blue Long Vest	Bone Flute	
	Bobo Shirt	Strange Doll (yellow)	
	Bomber Jacket	Any Bomb Item	
	Bridal Shirt	Ornamental Fan	
	Brown Jacket	Mudstone	
	Brown Overalls	Hazelnut	
	Brown Suit	Ancient Seed	
	Burger Shirt	Survival Burger	
	Button Down Shirt	Eggplant Artichoke Pumpkin Bok Choy Yam Beet	•
	Camo Shirt	Stir Fry	
	Canvas Jacket	Chewing Stick	
	Captain's Uniform	Anchor	
	Cardigan	Large Egg	•
	Carp Shirt	Carp Surprise	
	Caveman Shirt	Prehistoric Tool Prehistoric Handaxe	
	Chef Coat	Escargot	
	Circuitboard Shirt	Rusty Cog	
	Classic Overalls	Complete Breakfast	
	Classy Top	Helvite	
	Collared Shirt	Green Algae White Algae	•
	Copper Breastplate	Copper Bar	
	Cowboy Poncho	Rusty Spur	•
	Crab Cake Shirt	Crab Cakes	
	Crop Tank Top	Wheat	•
	Crop Top Shirt	Amaranth	•
	Dark Bandana Shirt	Truffle Truffle Oil	
	Dark Highlight Shirt	Oil of Garlic Life Elixir	
	Dark Jacket	Frozen Tear	
	Dark Shirt	Bat Wing	
	Dark Striped Shirt	Tigerseye	•
	Darkness Suit	Wilted Bouquet	

Right Table

	Name	Recipe (Cloth + ___)	🧵
	Denim Jacket	Field Snack	
	Dirt Shirt	Maple Bar	
	Doll Shirt	Ancient Doll	
	Excavator Shirt	Nautilus Fossil Amphibian Fossil Palm Fossil Trilobite	
	Faded Denim Shirt	Salmon	
	Fake Muscles Shirt	Muscle Remedy	•
	Fancy Red Blouse	Holly	
	Fish Shirt	Ghostfish Sandfish Bream Rainbow Trout Salmon Catfish Sunfish Tiger Trout Dorado Shad	•
	Fishing Vest	Largemouth Bass Walleye Perch Carp Sturgeon Bullhead Chub Lingcod Smallmouth Bass Pike Woodskip	
	Flames Shirt	Spicy Eel	
	Flannel Shirt	Coffee Bean	•
	Fluffy Shirt	Chicken Statue	
	Fried Egg Shirt	Fried Egg	
	Fringed Vest	Chowder	•
	Gaudy Shirt	Soapstone	
	Ginger Overalls	Ginger Ale	
	Globby Shirt	Aged Roe	•
	Gold Breastplate	Gold Bar	
	Gold Trimmed Shirt	Any Dwarf Scroll	•
	Golden Shirt	Dried Starfish	
	"Good Grief" Shirt	Wild Horseradish	
	Goodnight Shirt	Lunarite	
	Gray Hoodie	Geode	
	Gray Suit	Esperite	
	Gray Vest	Quartz	
	Green Belted Shirt	Cave Carrot	
	Green Belted Shirt	Malachite	
	Green Buttoned Vest	Rhubarb Spice Berry	•
	Green Flannel Shirt	Super Meal	
	Green Jacket Shirt	Duck Egg	•
	Green Overalls	Fiddlehead Fern	
	Green Thumb Shirt	Jamborite	
	Green Tunic	Ancient Sword	
	Green Vest	Bean Hotpot	
	Happy Shirt	Lemon Stone	
	Heart Shirt	Strange Bun	•
	High Heat Shirt	Torch	
	High-Waisted Shirt	Tree Fertilizer Any Basic Fertilizer Item	
	High-Waisted Shirt	Any Quality Fertilizer Item	•

	Name	Recipe (Cloth + ____)	🧵
	Holiday Shirt	Pumpkin Pie	
	Hot Pink Shirt	Poi	
	Iridium Breastplate	Iridium Bar	
	Iridium Energy Shirt	Iridium Ore	
	Island Bikini	Golden Coconut	•
	Jester Shirt	Pyrite	
	Jewelry Shirt	Elvish Jewelry	
	Kelp Shirt	Seaweed	
	Leafy Top	Jagoite	
	Letterman Jacket	Energy Tonic	•
	Light Blue Shirt	Mayonnaise	
	Light Blue Striped Shirt	Rice Pudding	
	Lime Green Striped Shirt	Duck Feather	
	Lime Green Tunic	Leek	
	Magenta Shirt	Magma Cap	
	Magic Sprinkle Shirt	Magic Rock Candy	
	Mayoral Suspenders	Vegetable Medley	
	Midnight Dog Jacket	Squid Ink	
	Mineral Dog Jacket	Seafoam Pudding	
	Mint Blouse	Dandelion	
	Morel Shirt	Morel	
	Navy Tuxedo	Rare Disc	
	Necklace Shirt	Refined Quartz	•
	Night Sky Shirt	Blueberry Tart	
	Oasis Gown	Tom Kha Soup	
	Ocean Shirt	Ocean Stone	
	Officer Uniform	Glass Shards	
	Oil Stained Shirt	Oil	
	Omni Shirt	Omni Geode	
	Orange Bow Shirt	Winter Root	
	Orange Gi	Vinegar	•
	Orange Shirt	Chanterelle	
	Pendant Shirt	Diamond	•
	Pink Striped Shirt	Bug Meat	
	Plain Overalls	Egg	•
	Plain Shirt	Wool	
	Polka Dot Shirt	Roe / Void Mayonnaise	•
	Pour-Over Shirt	Coffee / Triple Shot Espresso	
	Prismatic Shirt	Prismatic Shard	
	Prismatic Shirt	Prismatic Shard	
	Prismatic Shirt	Prismatic Shard	
	Purple Blouse	Fire Opal	
	Rain Coat	Crayfish / Snail / Periwinkle	
	Ranger Uniform	Trout Soup	
	Red Flannel Shirt	Hashbrowns	
	Red Hoodie	Magma Geode	
	Red Striped Shirt	Cranberry Candy	
	Red Tuxedo	Red Plate	
	Regal Mantle	Ancient Drum	

	Name	Recipe (Cloth + ____)	🧵
	Relic Shirt	Golden Relic	
	Retro Rainbow Shirt	Ice Cream	
	Rusty Shirt	Rusty Spoon	
	Sailor Shirt	Tilapia / Albacore / Halibut / Pufferfish / Anchovy / Tuna / Sardine / Red Mullet / Herring / Eel / Octopus / Red Snapper / Squid	•
	Sailor Shirt	Clam / Lobster / Crab / Cockle / Mussel / Shrimp / Oyster	•
	Sauce-Stained Shirt	Spaghetti	
	Shirt	Clay	
	Shirt	Goat Milk	
	Shirt	Large Goat Milk	
	Shirt	Baked Fish	
	Shirt	Salmonberry	
	Shirt	Salad	
	Shirt	Sashimi	
	Shirt	Maki Roll	
	Shirt	Snow Yam	
	Shirt	Hardwood	
	Shirt	Coal	
	Shirt	Sweet Pea	
	Shirt	Pink Cake	
	Shirt	Lucky Lunch	
	Shirt	Roasted Hazelnuts	
	Shirt	Fried Eel	
	Shirt	Fire Quartz	
	Shirt	Blackberry Cobbler	
	Shirt	Pumpkin Soup	
	Shirt	Bread	
	Shirt	Opal	
	Shirt	Rhubarb Pie	
	Shirt	Crystal Fruit	
	Shirt	Artichoke Dip	
	Shirt	Cheese	
	Shirt	Daffodil	
	Shirt	Farmer's Lunch	
	Shirt	Algae Soup	
	Shirt	Fairy Stone	
	Shirt	Fruit Salad	
	Shirt	Thunder Egg	
	Shirt	Common Mushroom	
	Shirt	Wild Bait	
	Shirt	Cookie	
	Shirt	Crocus	

	Name	Recipe (Cloth + ____)	🎨
	Shirt	Blackberry	
	Shirt	Alamite	
	Shirt	Void Egg	
	Shirt	Ruby	
	Shirt	Slate	
	Shirt	Parsnip Soup	
	Shirt	Amethyst	
	Shirt	Pickles	
	Shirt	Jelly	
	Shirt	Goat Cheese	
	Shirt	Earth Crystal	
	Shirt	Rabbit's Foot	
	Shirt	Slime	
	Shirt	Basalt	
	Shirt	Neptunite	
	Shirt	Purple Mushroom	
	Shirt	Celestine	
	Shirt	Bixite	
	Shirt	Limestone	
	Shirt	Ghost Crystal	
	Shirt	Geminite	
	Shirt	Joja Cola	
	Shirt	Battery Pack	
	Shirt	Nekoite	
	Shirt	Crispy Bass	
	Shirt	Fried Mushroom	
	Shirt	Dolomite	
	Shirt	Eggplant Parmesan	
	Shirt	Aerinite	
	Shirt	Salmon Dinner	
	Shirt	Roots Platter	
	Shirt	Granite	
	Shirt	Fish Stew	
	Shirt	Lobster Bisque	
	Shirt	Coleslaw	
	Shirt	Emerald	
	Shirt	Aquamarine	
	Shirt	Topaz	
	Shirt	Jade	
	Shirt	Baryte	
	Shirt	Calcite	
	Shirt And Belt	Cauliflower Garlic Green Bean Hops Kale Parsnip Potato Unmilled Rice	•
	Shirt And Tie	Bruschetta	•
	Shirt O' The Sea	Dish o' The Sea	
	Shirt with Bow	Orpiment	•
	Short Jacket	Plum Pudding	•

	Name	Recipe (Cloth + ____)	🎨
	Shrimp Enthusiast Shirt	Shrimp Cocktail	
	Silky Shirt	Radish Salad	•
	Skeleton Shirt	Prehistoric Scapula Skeletal Hand Prehistoric Rib Prehistoric Vertebra Skeletal Tail	
	Skull Shirt	Prehistoric Skull	
	Sleeveless Overalls	Large Milk	•
	Slime Shirt	Petrified Slime	
	Soft Arrow Shirt	Arrowhead	
	Sports Shirt	Juice	•
	Spring Shirt	Spring Onion	
	Star Shirt	Star Shards	•
	Steel Breastplate	Iron Bar	
	Store Owner's Jacket	Fried Calamari	
	Strapped Top	Nautilus Shell Coral Sea Urchin	•
	Striped Shirt	Corn	•
	Studded Vest	Obsidian	
	Sugar Shirt	Sugar	
	Suit Top	Bouquet	
	Sunset Shirt	Glazed Yams	
	Tan Striped Shirt	Sap	
	Tank Top	Radish Red Cabbage	•
	Tea Shirt	Green Tea	
	Toasted Shirt	Cheese Cauliflower	
	Toga Shirt	Marble	
	Tomato Shirt	Tomato	
	Tortilla Shirt	Tortilla	
	Track Jacket	Pancakes	
	Trash Can Shirt	Trash Driftwood Broken Glasses Broken CD Soggy Newspaper	
	Trinket Shirt	Artifact Trove	
	Tropical Sunrise Shirt	Tropical Curry	
	Tube Top	Sea Cucumber Super Cucumber	•
	Tunnelers Jersey	Pepper Poppers	
	Turtleneck Sweater	Copper Ore Iron Ore Gold Ore	•
	Vacation Shirt	Coconut	
	Vintage Polo	Hematite	
	Warm Flannel Shirt	Wheat Flour	
	White Dot Shirt	Poppyseed Muffin	•
	White Gi	Pale Broth	
	White Overalls	Rice	
	White Overalls Shirt	Milk	
	Work Shirt	Stone	
	Wumbus Shirt	Strange Doll (green)	
	Yellow and Green Shirt	Omelet	
	Yellow Suit	Mango Sticky Rice	
	Yoba Shirt	Solar Essence	

Pants, Skirts and Bottoms

	Name	Recipe (Cloth + _____)	🧴
	Baggy Pants	Slime Egg (any color)	•
	Dinosaur Pants	Dinosaur Mayonnaise	
	Farmer Pants	Cranberries Strawberry Wild Plum	•
	Genie Pants	Starfruit Ancient Fruit	•
	Grass Skirt	Hay	
	Long Dress	Fairy Rose Sunflower	•
	Pleated Skirt	Poppy Summer Spangle	•
	Prismatic Genie Pants	Prismatic Shard	
	Prismatic Pants	Prismatic Shard	
	Relaxed Fit Pants	Apple Apricot Cherry Pomegranate	•
	Relaxed Fit Shorts	Orange Peach	•
	Shorts	Melon Blueberry Hot Pepper Grape	
	Simple Dress	Honey (any)	•
	Skirt	Blue Jazz Tulip	•
	Trimmed Lucky Purple Shorts	Lucky Purple Shorts + Gold Bar (No Cloth Needed)	

Hats

	Name	Recipe (Cloth + _____)	🧴
	Beanie	Acorn Maple Seed Pine Cone	
	Blobfish Mask	Blobfish	
	Bridal Veil	Pearl	
	Dinosaur Hat	Dinosaur Egg	
	Fashion Hat	Caviar	
	Fishing Hat	Stonefish Ice Pip Scorpion Carp Spook Fish Midnight Squid Void Salmon Slimejack	
	Flat Topped Hat	Cranberry Sauce Stuffing	
	Floppy Beanie	Maple Syrup Oak Resin Pine Tar	
	Forager's Hat	Ginger	
	Goggles	Bug Steak	
	Golden Mask	Golden Mask	
	Hair Bone	Prehistoric Tibia	
	Logo Cap	Lava Eel	
	Party Hat	Pizza	
	Party Hat	Chocolate Cake	
	Party Hat	Fish Taco	
	Pirate Hat	Treasure Chest	
	Propeller Hat	Miner's Treat	
	Pumpkin Mask	Jack-O-Lantern	
	Qi Mask	Qi Fruit	
	Radioactive Goggles	Radioactive Bar	
	Spotted Headscarf	Red Mushroom	
	Star Helmet	Mushroom Tree Seed	
	Sunglasses	Cinder Shard	
	Swashbuckler Hat	Dragon Tooth	
	Totem Mask	Rain Totem Any Warp Totem	
	Warrior Helmet	Ostrich Egg	
	Wearable Dwarf Helm	Dwarvish Helm Dwarf Gadget	
	White Turban	Sweet Gem Berry	
	Witch Hat	Golden Pumpkin	

FISH, BAIT & TACKLE

Name	Location	Time	Season	Weather	Size	Difficulty	Sell Price
Albacore	Ocean	6am - 11am 6pm - 2am	Fall - Winter	Sunny, Rainy	20-41 in.	60 mixed	75g
Anchovy	Ocean	Any	Spring, Fall	Any	1-17 in.	30 dart	30g
Blobfish	Submarine	5pm - 11pm	Winter 15-17	Any	8-26 in.	75 floater	500g
Blue Discus	Ginger Island Rivers	6am - 2am	Any	Any	2-10 in.	60 dart	120g
Bream	Rivers	6pm - 2am	Any	Any	12-31 in.	35 smooth	45g
Bullhead	Mountain Lake	Any	Any	Any	12-31 in.	46 smooth	75g
Carp	Mountain Lake Sewers, Secret Woods	Any	Spring - Fall Any	Any	15-51 in.	15 mixed	30g
Catfish	Rivers Secret Woods	Any	Spring, Fall Summer	Rainy	12-73 in.	75 mixed	200g
Chub	Forest Rivers, Mountain Lake	Any	Any	Any	12-25 in.	35 dart	50g
Dorado	Forest Rivers	6am - 7pm	Summer	Any	24-33 in.	78 mixed	100g
Eel	Ocean	4pm - 2am	Spring, Fall	Rainy	12-81 in.	70 smooth	85g
Flounder	Ocean	6am - 8 pm	Spring - Summer	Any	4-17 in.	50 sinker	100g
Ghostfish	Mines, dropped by Ghosts	Any	Any	Any	10-36 in.	50 mixed	45g
Halibut	Ocean	6am - 11am 7pm - 2am	Any but Fall	Any	10-34 in.	50 sinker	80g
Herring	Ocean	Any	Spring, Winter	Any	8-21 in.	25 dart	30g
Ice Pip	Mines 60F	Any	Any	Any	7-8 in.	85 dart	500g
Largemouth Bass	Mountain Lake	6am - 7pm	Any	Any	11-31 in.	50 mixed	100g
Lava Eel	Mines 100F	Any	Any	Any	31-33 in.	90 mixed	700g
Lingcod	Rivers, Mountain Lake	Any	Winter	Any	30-51 in.	85 mixed	120g
Lionfish	Ginger Island Ocean	6am - 2am	Any	Any	3-13 in.	50 smooth	100g
Midnight Carp	Mountain Lake	10pm-2am	Fall - Winter	Any	12-53 in.	55 mixed	150g
Midnight Squid	Submarine	5pm - 11pm	Winter 15-17	Any	8-26 in.	55 sinker	100g
Octopus	Ocean	6am - 1pm	Summer	Any	12-48 in.	95 sinker	150g
Perch	Rivers, Forest Pond, Mountain Lake	Any	Winter	Any	10-25 in.	35 mixed	55g
Pike	Rivers, Forest Pond	Any	Summer, Winter	Any	15-61 in.	60 dart	100g
Pufferfish	Ocean	12pm - 4pm	Summer	Sunny	1-37 in.	80 floater	200g
Rainbow Trout	Rivers, Mountain Lake	6am - 7pm	Summer	Sunny	10-26 in.	45 mixed	65g
Red Mullet	Ocean	6am - 7pm	Summer, Winter	Any	8-23 in.	55 smooth	75g
Red Snapper	Ocean	6am - 7pm	Summer - Fall	Rainy	8-26 in.	40 mixed	50g
Salmon	Rivers	6am - 7pm	Fall	Any	24-66 in.	50 mixed	75g
Sandfish	Desert	6am - 10pm	Any	Any	8-24 in.	65 mixed	75g
Sardine	Ocean	6am - 7pm	Any but Summer	Any	1-13 in.	30 dart	40g
Scorpion Carp	Desert	6am - 10pm	Any	Any	12-32 in.	90 dart	150g
Sea Cucumber	Ocean	6am - 7pm	Fall - Winter	Any	3-21 in.	40 sinker	75g
Shad	Rivers	9am - 2am	Spring - Fall	Rainy	20-49 in.	45 smooth	60g
Slimejack	Mutant Bug Lair	Any	Any	Any	8-24 in.	55 dart	100g
Smallmouth Bass	Town Rivers, Forest Pond	Any	Spring, Fall	Any	12-25 in.	28 mixed	50g
Spook Fish	Submarine	5pm - 11pm	Winter 15-17	Any	8-26 in.	60 dart	220g
Squid	Ocean	6pm - 2am	Winter	Any	12-49 in.	75 sinker	80g
Stingray	Pirate Cove	6am - 2am	Any	Any	18-61 in.	80 sinker	180g
Stonefish	Mines 20F	Any	Any	Any	14-16 in.	65 sinker	300g
Sturgeon	Mountain Lake	6am - 7pm	Summer, Winter	Any	12-61 in.	78 mixed	200g
Sunfish	Rivers	6am - 7pm	Spring - Summer	Sunny	5-16 in.	30 mixed	30g
Super Cucumber	Ocean	6pm - 2am	Summer - Fall	Any	12-37 in.	80 sinker	250g
Tiger Trout	Rivers	6am - 7pm	Fall - Winter	Any	10-21 in.	60 dart	150g
Tilapia	Ocean	6am - 2pm	Summer - Fall	Any	11-31 in.	50 mixed	75g
Tuna	Ocean	6am - 7pm	Summer, Winter	Any	23-61 in.	70 smooth	100g
Void Salmon	Witch's Swamp	Any	Any	Any	24-64 in.	80 mixed	150g
Walleye	Rivers, Forest Pond, Mountain Lake	12pm - 2am	Fall	Rainy	10-41 in.	45 smooth	105g
Woodskip	Secret Woods	Any	Any	Any	11-30 in.	50 mixed	75g

Miscellaneous Catches

	Name	Location	Time	Season	Weather	Size	Difficulty	Sell Price
	Green Algae	Mines, Rivers	Anytime	Any	Any	-	-	15g
	Seaweed	Ocean	Anytime	Any	Any	-	-	20g
	White Algae	Mines, Sewers	Anytime	Any	Any	-	-	25g

The Legendary Five

	Name	Location	Time	Season	Weather	Size	Difficulty	Sell Price
	Angler	Cast into the mouth of the River north of JojaMart. Requires level 3 Fishing Skill.	Any	Fall	Any	17-19 in.	85 smooth	900g
	Crimsonfish	Cast from the eastern Beach or Tidal Pool piers. Requires level 5 Fishing Skill.	Any	Summer	Any	19-21 in.	95 mixed	1,500g
	Glacierfish	Cast from the south tip of Arrowhead Island in Cindersap Forest. Requires level 6 Fishing Skill.	Any	Winter	Any	26-28 in.	100 mixed	1,000g
	Legend	Cast near the submerged log in the Mountain Lake. Requires level 10 Fishing Skill.	Any	Spring	Rainy	49-51 in.	110 mixed	5,000g
	Mutant Carp	The Sewers	Any	Any	Any	35-37 in.	80 dart	1,000g

Crab Pot

	Name	Location	Trap Chance	Season	Weather	Size	Difficulty	Sell Price
	Clam	Ocean	15%	Any	Any	-	-	50g
	Cockle	Ocean	30%	Any	Any	-	-	50g
	Crab	Ocean	10%	Any	Any	-	-	100g
	Crayfish	Freshwater	35%	Any	Any	-	-	75g
	Lobster	Ocean	5%	Any	Any	-	-	120g
	Mussel	Ocean	35%	Any	Any	-	-	30g
	Oyster	Ocean	15%	Any	Any	-	-	40g
	Periwinkle	Freshwater	55%	Any	Any	-	-	20g
	Shrimp	Ocean	20%	Any	Any	-	-	60g
	Snail	Freshwater	25%	Any	Any	-	-	65g

Bait, Tackle & Other Equipment

	Name	Ingredients			Buy Price	Sell Price	Recipe From
	Bait (5)	Bug Meat	-	-	5g	1g	Fishing L2
	Barbed Hook	Copper Bar	Iron Bar	Gold Bar	1,000g	-	Fishing L8
	Cork Bobber	Wood (10)	Hardwood (5)	Slime (10)	750g	-	Fishing L7
	Crab Pot With Trapper	Wood (40) Wood (25)	Iron Bar (3) Copper Bar (2)	-	1,500g	-	Fishing L3
	Curiosity Lure	-	-	-	-	500g	-
	Dressed Spinner	Iron Bar (2)	Cloth	-	1,000g	-	Fishing L8
	Lead Bobber	-	-	-	200g	-	-
	Magic Bait (5)	Radioactive Ore	Bug Meat (3)	-	5 Qi Gems	1g	Walnut Room
	Magnet (3)	Iron Bar	-	-	1,000g	15g	Fishing L9
	Quality Bobber	Copper Bar	Sap (20)	Solar Essence (5)	-	300g	Special Order
	Spinner	Iron Bar (2)	-	-	500g	-	Fishing L6
	Trap Bobber	Copper Bar	Sap (10)	-	500g	-	Fishing L6
	Treasure Hunter	Gold Bar (2)	-	-	750g	-	Fishing L7
	Wild Bait (5)	Fiber (10)	Slime (5)	Bug Meat (5)	-	15g	Linus

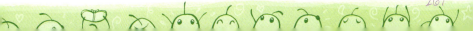

Ores & Resources

	Name	Location	Sell Price
	Coal	The Mines (All Levels), Charcoal Kiln. Also dropped by some enemies.	15g
	Copper Ore	The Mines (All Levels)	5g
	Gold Ore	The Mines (Levels 80+)	25g
	Iridium Ore	Meteorites, Quarry, Skull Cavern, Magma Geode, Omni Geode, Statue of Perfection	100g
	Iron Ore	The Mines (Levels 40+)	10g
	Radioactive Ore	The Mines (Danger in the Deep quest), Skull Cavern (Skull Cavern Invasion quest)	300g

Bars & Refinements

	Name	Location	Sell Price
	Copper Bar	Furnace (5 Copper Ore, 1 Coal, 30 Minutes)	60g
	Gold Bar	Furnace (5 Gold Ore, 1 Coal, 5 Hours)	250g
	Iridium Bar	Furnace (5 Iridium Ore, 1 Coal, 8 Hours), Skull Cavern	1,000g
	Iron Bar	Furnace (5 Iron Ore, 1 Coal, 2 Hours)	120g
	Radioactive Bar	Furnace (5 Radioactive Ore, 1 Coal, 10 Hours)	3,000g
	Refined Quartz	Furnace (1 Quartz / Fire Quartz*, 1 Coal, 1 Hour 30 Minutes), Recycling Machine	50g

*1 Fire Quartz yields 3 Refined Quartz when using a Furnace

Geodes

	Name	Location	Sell Price
	Geode	The Mines (Levels 1-39)	50g
	Frozen Geode	The Mines (Levels 41-79), Fishing Treasure	100g
	Magma Geode	The Mines (Levels 81-120), Fishing Treasure	150g
	Omni Geode	The Mines (All Levels), Skull Cavern, Panning, Oasis (Wed), Krobus (Tues)	-
	Artifact Trove	Desert Trader (5 Omni Geodes)	-
	Golden Coconut	Ginger Island Palm Trees, Island Trader (10 Coconuts)	-

Gems & Minerals

	Name	Location	Sell Price
	Aerinite	Frozen Geode, Omni Geode	125g
	Alamite	Geode, Omni Geode	150g
	Amethyst	Amethyst Node, Gem Node, The Mines (All Levels), Panning	100g
	Aquamarine	Aquamarine Node, Gem Node, The Mines (Levels 40+), Panning, Fishing Treasure	180g
	Baryte	Magma Geode, Omni Geode	50g
	Basalt	Magma Geode, Omni Geode	175g
	Bixite	Magma Geode, Omni Geode	300g
	Calcite	Geode, Omni Geode	75g
	Celestine	Geode, Omni Geode	125g
	Diamond	Diamond Node, Gem Node, The Mines (Levels 50+), Panning	750g
	Dolomite	Magma Geode, Omni Geode	300g
	Earth Crystal	The Mines (Level 1-39), Panning, Geode	50g
	Emerald	Emerald Node, Gem Node, The Mines (Levels 80+), Panning	250g
	Esperite	Frozen Geode, Omni Geode	100g

	Name	Location	Sell Price
	Fairy Stone	Frozen Geode, Omni Geode	250g
	Fire Opal	Magma Geode, Omni Geode	350g
	Fire Quartz	The Mines (Level 80+), Panning	100g
	Fluorapatite	Frozen Geode, Omni Geode	200g
	Frozen Tear	The Mines (Level 40-79), Panning, Fishing Treasure	75g
	Geminite	Frozen Geode, Omni Geode	150g
	Ghost Crystal	Frozen Geode, Omni Geode	200g
	Granite	Geode, Omni Geode	75g
	Helvite	Magma Geode, Omni Geode	450g
	Hematite	Frozen Geode, Omni Geode	150g
	Jade	Jade Node, Gem Node, The Mines (Levels 40+), Panning, Fishing Treasure	200g
	Jagoite	Geode, Omni Geode	115g
	Jamborite	Geode, Omni Geode	150g
	Jasper	Magma Geode, Omni Geode	150g
	Kyanite	Frozen Geode, Omni Geode	250g
	Lemon Stone	Magma Geode, Omni Geode	200g
	Limestone	Geode, Omni Geode	15g
	Lunarite	Frozen Geode, Omni Geode	200g
	Malachite	Geode, Omni Geode	100g
	Marble	Frozen Geode, Omni Geode	110g
	Mudstone	Geode, Omni Geode	25g
	Nekoite	Geode, Omni Geode	80g
	Neptunite	Magma Geode, Omni Geode	400g
	Obsidian	Magma Geode, Omni Geode	200g
	Ocean Stone	Frozen Geode, Omni Geode	220g
	Opal	Frozen Geode, Omni Geode	150g
	Orpiment	Geode, Omni Geode	80g
	Petrified Slime	Geode, Omni Geode	120g
	Prismatic Shard	Iridium Node, Mystic Stone, Omni Geode, Statue of True Perfection. Also a very rare drop from strong monsters.	2,000g
	Pyrite	Frozen Geode, Omni Geode	120g
	Quartz	The Mines (All Levels)	25g
	Ruby	Ruby Node, Gem Node, The Mines (Levels 80+), Panning	250g
	Sandstone	Geode, Omni Geode	60g
	Slate	Geode, Omni Geode	85g
	Soapstone	Frozen Geode, Omni Geode	120g
	Star Shards	Magma Geode, Omni Geode	500g
	Thunder Egg	Geode, Omni Geode	100g
	Tigerseye	Magma Geode, Omni Geode	275g
	Topaz	Topaz Node, Gem Node, The Mines (All Levels), Panning	80g

	Name	Location	HP	Damage	Defense	Speed	EXP	Notes
	Armored Bug	Skull Cavern	150	16	Extreme	2	1	Their super-hard shells make them nigh-indestructible.
	Bat	The Mines (Lv. 31-39)	24	6	1	3	3	Your ordinary cave Bat.
	Big Slime	The Mines Skull Cavern	Varies	Varies	Varies	Varies	Varies	Can split into many smaller Slimes upon defeat.
	Bug	The Mines (Lv. 1-29)	1	8	0	2	1	Flies around aimlessly.
	Carbon Ghost	Skull Cavern	190	25	3	4	20	Watch out! Where there's Mummies, there's Carbon Ghosts.
	Cave Fly	The Mines (Lv. 1-29)	22	6	1	2	10	Quickly buzzes in to attack.
	Duggy	The Mines (Lv. 6-29)	40	6	0	2	10	Tunnels through soft soil, ambushing from below.
	Dust Sprite	The Mines (Lv. 40-79)	40	6	2	3	2	Attacks in groups.
	Dwarvish Sentry	Volcano Dungeon	300	18	5	3	15	Disguises itself as ancient technology to ambush prey.
	False Magma Cap	Volcano Dungeon	290	15	3	3	14	Disguises itself as a Magma Cap to ambush unsuspecting foragers.
	Frost Bat	The Mines (Lv. 41-79)	36	7	1	3	7	Stronger than a normal Bat, and quite a bit colder.
	Ghost	The Mines (Lv. 51-90)	96	10	3	4	15	It'll pursue you relentlessly.
	Grub	The Mines (Lv. 10-29)	20	4	0	1	2	Mostly harmless, but can turn into a pesky Cave Fly.
	Haunted Skull	Quarry Mine	80	15	1	3	15	Often gathers in groups, so use caution when exploring.
	Hot Head	Volcano Dungeon	215	18	8	2	16	Speeds up greatly when low on health, and explodes on defeat!
	Iridium Bat	Skull Cavern (Lv. 50+)	300	30	1	3	22	The newly-crowned strongest of the Bats.
	Iridium Crab	Skull Cavern (Lv. 25+)	240	15	3	3	20	Hides amongst Iridium Nodes to catch brave miners off-guard.
	Lava Bat	The Mines (Lv. 80-119)	80	15	1	3	15	The strongest and hottest of the Bats in the Mines.
	Lava Crab	The Mines (Lv. 80-119)	120	15	3	3	12	A well-placed swing of the Pickaxe will get it moving.
	Lava Lurk	Volcano Dungeon	220	15	5	2	12	Hides beneath the lava, only surfacing to breathe fire at prey!
	Magma Duggy	Volcano Dungeon	380	16	0	2	18	A stronger, hotter take on your average Duggy.
	Magma Sparker	Volcano Dungeon	380	15	8	21	17	Causes nasty burns, which lower both speed and defense.
	Magma Sprite	Volcano Dungeon	220	15	8	2	15	Charges quickly to attack, and can easily gather in swarms.
	Metal Head	The Mines (Lv. 80-119)	40	15	8	2	6	Its thick metal helmet lets it take a licking.
	Mummy	Skull Cavern	260	30	0	2	20	Must be destroyed with explosives.
	Mutant Grub	Mutant Bug Lair	100	12	0	1	6	Will try to flee and transform into a Mutant Fly when injured.
	Mutant Fly	Mutant Bug Lair	66	12	1	2	10	Can be a real handful when they attack in swarms.
	Pepper Rex	Skull Cavern	300	15	3	2	7	Slow-moving, but they breathe streams of fire!
	Rock Crab	The Mines (Lv. 1-29)	30	5	1	2	4	Disguises itself as an ordinary rock to catch its prey unaware.
	Serpent	Skull Cavern	150	23	0	2	20	They're fast, and bigger than they look; be careful!!
	Shadow Brute	The Mines (Lv. 81-119)	160	18	2	3	15	He's not too quick, but packs a punch.
	Shadow Shaman	The Mines (Lv. 81-119)	80	17	2	3	15	Can heal other monsters, as well as temporarily lower your defense.
	Skeleton	The Mines (Lv. 71-79)	140	10	1	2	8	Can attack from a distance by throwing bones.
	Slime	The Mines Skull Cavern	Varies	Varies	Varies	Varies	Varies	Slimes of all types, colors and stats can be found everywhere.
	Squid Kid	The Mines (Lv. 81-119)	1	18	2	3	15	Attacks by spitting fireballs that can bounce off walls.
	Stone Golem	The Mines (Lv. 30-39)	45	5	5	2	5	They lurk in the shadows, only detectable by their glowing eyes.
	Wilderness Golem	Wilderness Farm	30	5	1	2	5	Its stats scale with your Combat Skill level.

Wild Slime Guide

	Name	Location	HP	Damage	Defense	Speed	EXP	Notes
	Big Frost Jelly	Mines (41-79) Secret Woods	120	5	0	2	14	Often splits into Frost Jellies upon defeat. Very rare.
	Big Green Slime	Mines (1-39) Secret Woods	60	5	0	2	7	Often splits into Green Slimes upon defeat. Very rare.
	Big Purple Sludge	Skull Cavern	240	15	0	2	21	Often splits into Purple Sludges upon defeat.
	Big Red Sludge	Mines (81-119)	180	10	0	2	21	Often splits into Red Sludges upon defeat. Very rare.
	Black Slime	Slime Hutch	Varies	Varies	0	2	Varies	Product of the Witch's curse; a Wicked Statue repels the Witch.
	Copper Slime	Quarry Mine	102	16	0	4	10	Not too tough, but they're faster than your average slime!
	Frost Jelly	Mines (41-79) Secret Woods	106	7	0	2	6	All Slimes in the icy levels of the Mines are Frost Jellies.
	Green Slime	Mines (1-39) Secret Woods	24	5	1	2	3	All Slimes in the upper levels of the Mines are Green Slimes.
	Iron Slime	Quarry Mine	205	16	0	1	10	They're pretty slow, but can take a beating!
	Purple Sludge	Skull Cavern	410	16	0	2	10	All Slimes in the Skull Cavern are Purple Sludges.
	Red Sludge	Mines (81-119)	205	16	0	2	10	All Slimes in the volcanic levels of the Mines are Red Sludges.
	Tiger Slime	Ginger Island	415	23	0	2	20	Found in the Volcano Cavern and a grove on the island's west side.

Monster Loot

	Monster Type	Dropped By	Ingredient For	Sell Price
	Bat Wing	Bat, Frost Bat, Lava Bat	Dark Sign (5), Lightning Rod (5), Monster Musk (30)	15g
	Bone Fragment	Skeleton, Lava Lurk	Bone Mill (10), Dark Sign (5), Hyper Speed-Gro (3), Ostrich Incubator (50), Skull Brazier (10), Thorns Ring (50)	12g
	Bug Meat	Bug, Cave Fly, Grub, Mutant Fly, Mutant Grub	Bait, Bug Steak (10), Magic Bait (3), Sturdy Ring (25), Wild Bait (5)	8g
	Slime	Slimes	Cork Bobber (10), Monster Musk (30), Oil Maker (50), Slime Incubator (100), Sturdy Ring (25), Wild Bait (5)	5g
	Solar Essence	Ghost, Metal Head, Mummy, Squid Kid	Barrel Brazier, Glowstone Ring (5), Hyper Speed-Gro, Iridium Band (50), Mega Bomb, Mini-Obelisk (20), Quality Bobber (5)	40g
	Void Essence	Shadow Brute, Shadow Shaman, Serpent	Iridium Band (50), Mega Bomb	50g

Eradication Goals

Remember to visit Gil at the Adventurer's Guild to claim each reward.

	Monster Type	Quantity		Reward	Notes
	Slimes	1000		Slime Charmer Ring	All regular-sized Slimes count toward the total, regardless of location, color or type.
	Void Spirits	150		Savage Ring	Void Spirits include Shadow Brutes, Shadow Shamans and Shadow Snipers.
	Bats	200		Vampire Ring	All types of Bats count toward the total.
	Skeletons	50		Skeleton Mask	
	Cave Insects	150		Insect Head	All insects count toward the total, including Mutant Flies and Mutant Grubs.
	Duggies	30		Hard Hat	Magma Duggies are included in the count.
	Dust Sprites	500		Burglar's Ring	
	Rock Crabs	60		Crabshell Ring	All crabs count toward the total, including Lava Crabs and Iridium Crabs.
	Magma Sprites	150		Marlon's Phone Number	Magma Sparkers are included in the count.
	Mummies	100		Arcane Hat	
	Pepper Rex	50		Knight's Helmet	
	Serpents	250		Napalm Ring	Royal Serpents are included in the count.

Swords

WEAPONS

: Speed   : Defense   : Weight   : Crit. Chance   : Crit. Power

Name	Level	Damage	Stats	Location	Buy Price	Sell Price
Bone Sword	5	20-30	+4 +2	Purchased from Adventurer's Guild after reaching level 75 in the Mines.	6,000g	250g
Claymore	5	20-32	-4 +2 +3	Purchased from Adventurer's Guild after reaching level 45 in the Mines.	2,000g	250g
Cutlass	3	09-17	+2	Purchased from Adventurer's Guild after reaching level 25 in the Mines.	1,500g	150g
Dark Sword	9	30-45	-5 +2 +5	Rare drop from Haunted Skulls in the Quarry Mine.	-	450g
Dragontooth Cutlass	13	75-90	+50	Chest in the Volcano Dungeon.	-	650g
Dwarf Sword	13	65-75	+2 +4	Chest in the Volcano Dungeon.	-	650g
Forest Sword	3	08-18	+2 +1	Rare drop on levels 20-60 in the Mines.	-	150g
Galaxy Sword	13	60-80	+4	Hold a Prismatic Shard as you step into the center of the three pillars in the Calico Desert.	50,000g	650g
Golden Scythe	0	13		Found on the Reaper Statue in the Quarry Mine.	-	-
Holy Blade	4	18-24	+3	Dropped by monsters after level 60 in the Mines.	-	200g
Infinity Blade	17	80-100	+4 +2	Forged by infusing three Galaxy Souls into a Galaxy Sword.	-	850g
Insect Head	4	10-20	+2 +2	Rare drop from Cave Insects. Reward for eradicating 125 Cave Insects.	10,000g	200g
Iron Edge	3	12-25	-2 +1 +3	Dropped by monsters after level 40 in the Mines.	-	150g
Lava Katana	10	55-64	+3 +25 +3	Purchased from Adventurer's Guild after reaching bottom of the Mines.	25,000g	500g
Neptune's Glaive	5	18-35	-1 +2 +4	Rare treasure obtained while fishing.	-	250g
Obsidian Edge	6	30-45	-1 +10	Chest at level 90 in the Mines.	-	300g
Ossified Blade	6	26-42	-2 +2 +1	Possible reward from chests in the Mines if remixed rewards are set.	-	300g
Pirate's Sword	2	08-14	+2	Dropped by monsters after level 20 in the Mines, and purchased from Adventurer's Guild after reaching level 30.	850g	100g
Rusty Sword	1	02-05	-	Given to you at the entrance of the Mines.	-	50g
Scythe	0	01-03	-	One of your starting farm tools.	-	-
Silver Saber	2	08-15	+1	Purchased from Adventurer's Guild after reaching level 20 in the Mines.	750g	100g
Steel Falchion	8	28-46	+4 +20	Purchased from Adventurer's Guild after reaching level 90 in the Mines.	9,000g	400g
Steel Smallsword	1	04-08	+2	Chest at level 20 in the Mines.	-	50g
Templar's Blade	5	22-29	+1	Purchased from Adventurer's Guild after reaching level 55 in the Mines.	4,000g	250g
Wooden Blade	1	03-07	-	Purchased from Adventurer's Guild.	250g	50g
Yeti Tooth	7	26-42	+4 +10	Found inside crates in levels 60-120 of the Mines.	-	350g

Daggers

	Name	Level	Damage	Stats	Location	Buy Price	Sell Price
	Broken Trident	5	15-26	+1	Rare treasure obtained while fishing.	-	250g
	Burglar's Shank	4	07-12	+2 +25	Rare drop from Serpents, and found inside crates in the Skull Cavern.	-	200g
	Carving Knife	1	01-03	+2	Found before level 20 in the Mines.	-	500g
	Crystal Dagger	4	04-10	+2 +50 +5	Chest at level 60 in the Mines.	-	200g
	Dragontooth Shiv	12	40-50	+3 +100 +5	Chest in the Volcano Dungeon.	-	600g
	Dwarf Dagger	11	32-38	+1 +6 +2 +5	Chest in the Volcano Dungeon.	-	550g
	Elf Blade	2	3-5	+2	Possible reward in the chest on level 20 of the Mines with remixed rewards set.	-	100g
	Galaxy Dagger	8	30-40	+1 +1 +5	Purchased from Adventurer's Guild after obtaining the Galaxy Sword.	35,000g	400g
	Infinity Dagger	16	50-70	+1 +3 +4 +5	Forged by infusing three Galaxy Souls into a Galaxy Dagger.	-	800g
	Iron Dirk	1	02-04	+2	Purchased from Adventurer's Guild after reaching level 15 of the Mines.	500g	50g
	Iridium Needle	12	20-35	+6 +200	Rare drop from special slimes in the Mines when the Shrine of Challenge is active.	-	600g
	Shadow Dagger	4	10-20	+2	Found inside crates in levels 60-79 and below 100 in the Mines, and as a possible reward from the level 80 chest with remixed rewards set.	-	200g
	Wicked Kris	8	24-30	+4	Found inside crates in the Skull Cavern.	-	400g
	Wind Spire	1	01-05	+1 +10 +5	Found before level 40 in the Mines.	-	50g

Clubs

	Name	Level	Damage	Stats	Location	Buy Price	Sell Price
	Dragontooth Club	14	80-100	+50 +3	Chest in the Volcano Dungeon.	-	700g
	Dwarf Hammer	13	75-85	+2 +5	Chest in the Volcano Dungeon.	-	650g
	Femur	2	06-11	+2	Possible reward in the chest on level 10 of the Mines with remixed rewards set.	-	100g
	Galaxy Hammer	12	70-90	+2 +5	Purchased from Adventurer's Guild after obtaining the Galaxy Sword.	75,000g	600g
	Infinity Gavel	17	100-120	+2 +1 +5	Forged by infusing three Galaxy Souls into a Galaxy Hammer.	-	850g
	Kudgel	5	27-40	-1 +4 +2	Found inside crates in levels below 100 in the Mines, and as a possible reward from the level 80 chest with remixed rewards set.	-	250g
	Lead Rod	4	18-27	-4	Found after level 60 in the Mines. Also a random drop in the Skull Cavern.	-	200g
	The Slammer	7	40-55	-2	Dropped by monsters after Level 40 in Skull Cavern.	-	350g
	Wood Club	2	09-16	-	Dropped by monsters before level 40 in the Mines.	-	100g
	Wood Mallet	3	15-24	+2 +3	Purchased from Adventurer's Guild after reaching level 40 in the Mines. Also a random drop after level 40 in the Mines.	2,000g	150g

Slingshots

	Name	Level	Damage	Stats	Location	Buy Price	Sell Price
	Master Slingshot	-	02-06	-	Chest at level 70 in the Mines.	1,000g	-
	Slingshot	-	01-03	-	Chest at level 40 in the Mines.	500g	-

	Name	How to Obtain	Buy Price
	Arcane Hat	Adventurer's Guild (Defeat 100 Mummies)	20,000g
	Archer's Cap	Achievement: Gourmet Chef (Cook Every Recipe)	1,000g
	Beanie	Tailoring (Cloth + Acorn, Maple Seed or Pine Cone)	-
	Blobfish Mask	Tailoring (Cloth + Blobfish)	-
	Bluebird Mask	Island Trader	30 Taro Root
	Blue Bonnet	Achievement: Treasure Trove (Donate 40 Different Items)	1,000g
	Blue Cowboy Hat	Find a Treasure Floor in the Skull Cavern	-
	Bowler Hat	Achievement: Millionaire (1,000,000g Earned)	1,000g
	Bridal Veil	Tailoring (Cloth + Pearl)	-
	Butterfly Bow	Achievement: A New Friend (5-heart Friendship with Someone)	1,000g
	Cat Ears	Achievement: The Beloved Farmer (10-heart Friendship w/8 People)	1,000g
	Chef Hat	Achievement: Gourmet Chef (Cook Every Recipe)	1,000g
	Chicken Mask	Achievement: A Big Help (Complete 40 Quests)	1,000g
	Cone Hat	Purchase at the Night Market	Varies
	Cool Cap	Achievement: Homesteader (250,000 Earned)	1,000g
	Copper Pan	Complete all Fish Tank Bundles (any Copper Pan can be worn as a hat)	2,500g
	Cowboy Hat	Achievement: A Complete Collection (Complete the Museum)	1,000g
	Cowgal Hat	Achievement: Monoculture (Ship 300 of One Crop)	1,000g
	Cowpoke Hat	Achievement: Polyculture (Ship 15 of Each Crop)	1,000g
	Daisy	Achievement: D.I.Y. (Craft 15 Items)	1,000g
	Dark Cowboy Hat	Find a Treasure Floor in the Skull Cavern	-
	Delicate Bow	Achievement: Cook (Cook 10 Different Recipes)	1,000g
	Deluxe Cowboy Hat	Island Trader	30 Taro Root
	Deluxe Pirate Hat	Volcano Dungeon Treasure Chest	-
	Dinosaur Hat	Tailoring (Cloth + Dinosaur Egg)	-
	Earmuffs	Achievement: Popular (5-heart Friendship w/20 People)	1,000g
	Elegant Turban	Earn every achievement	1,000g
	Emily's Magic Hat	Reward for Emily's 14-heart event	-
	Eye Patch	Achievement: Master Angler (Catch Every Fish)	1,000g
	Fashion Hat	Tailoring (Cloth + Caviar)	-
	Fedora	Win 500 Star Tokens at the Stardew Valley Fair	1,000g
	Fishing Hat	Tailoring (Cloth + Ice Pip, Midnight Squid, Scorpion Carp, Slimejack, Spook Fish, Stonefish or Void Salmon)	-
	Flat Topped Hat	Tailoring (Cloth + Cranberry Sauce or Stuffing)	-
	Floppy Beanie	Tailoring (Cloth + Maple Syrup, Oak Resin or Pine Tar)	-
	Forager's Hat	Tailoring (Cloth + Ginger)	-
	Frog Hat	Fishing in Gourmand's Cave	-
	Garbage Hat	Rare drop when checking trash cans	-
	Gnome's Cap	Achievement: Craft Master (Craft Every Item)	1,000g
	Goblin Mask	Achievement: Full Shipment (Ship Every Item)	1,000g
	Goggles	Tailoring (Cloth + Bug Steak)	-
	Golden Helmet	Tailoring (Cloth + Golden Coconut)	-
	Golden Mask	Tailoring (Cloth + Golden Mask Artifact)	-
	Good Ol' Cap	Achievement: Greenhorn (15,000g Earned)	1,000g
	Green Turban	Desert Trader (50 Omni Geodes)	-
	Hair Bone	Tailoring (Cloth + Prehistoric Tibia)	-
	Hard Hat	Adventurer's Guild (Defeat 30 Duggies)	20,000g

	Name	How to Obtain	Buy Price
	Hunter's Cap	Achievement: Living Large (Upgrade Your House a Second Time)	1,000g
	Knight's Helmet	Adventurer's Guild (Defeat 50 Pepper Rex)	-
	Living Hat	Rare drop from Wilderness Golem, or when cutting Weeds	-
	Logo Cap	Tailoring (Cloth + Lava Eel)	-
	Lucky Bow	Achievement: Cowpoke (50,000g Earned)	1,000g
	Magic Cowboy Hat	Desert Trader (odd-numbered days, 333 Omni Geodes)	-
	Magic Turban	Desert Trader (even-numbered days, 333 Omni Geodes)	-
	Mouse Ears	Achievement: Best Friends (10-heart Friendship with Someone)	1,000g
	Mr. Qi's Hat	Walnut Room Vending Machine	5 Gems
	Mushroom Cap	Rare drop when chopping down a Mushroom Tree	-
	Official Cap	Achievement: Ol' Mariner (Catch 20 Different Fish)	1,000g
	Party Hat	Tailoring (Cloth + Pizza)	-
	Party Hat	Tailoring (Cloth + Chocolate Cake)	-
	Party Hat	Tailoring (Cloth + Fish Taco)	-
	Pink Bow	Volcano Dwarf	10,000g
	Pirate Hat	Tailoring (Cloth + Treasure Chest)	-
	Plum Chapeau	Achievement: Sous Chef (Cook 25 Different Recipes)	1,000g
	Polka Bow	Achievement: Gofer (Complete 10 Quests)	1,000g
	Propeller Hat	Tailoring (Cloth + Miner's Treat)	-
	Pumpkin Mask	Tailoring (Cloth + Jack-O-Lantern)	-
	Qi Mask	Tailoring (Cloth + Qi Fruit)	-
	Radioactive Goggles	Tailoring (Cloth + Radioactive Bar)	-
	Red Cowboy Hat	Find a Treasure Floor in the Skull Cavern	-
	Sailor's Cap	Winter Festival (Win the Fishing Competition)	-
	Santa Hat	Achievement: Networking (5-heart Friendship w/10 People)	1,000g
	Skeleton Mask	Adventurer's Guild (Defeat 50 Skeletons)	20,000g
	Small Cap	Island Trader	30 Taro Root
	Sombrero	Achievement: Legend (10,000,000g Earned)	1,000g
	Sou'wester	Achievement: Fisherman (Catch 10 Different Fish)	1,000g
	Spotted Headscarf	Tailoring (Cloth + Red Mushroom)	-
	Squire's Helmet	Rare drop from Metal Head	-
	Star Helmet	Tailoring (Cloth + Mushroom Tree Seed)	-
	Straw Hat	Spring Festival (Win the Egg Hunt)	-
	Sunglasses	Tailoring (Cloth + Cinder Shard)	-
	Swashbuckler Hat	Tailoring (Cloth + Dragon Tooth)	-
	Tiara	Achievement: Cliques (5-heart Friendship w/5 People)	1,000g
	Tiger Hat	Tiger Slime Drop	-
	Top Hat	8,000 Qi Coins in Qi's Casino	8,000Q
	Totem Mask	Tailoring (Cloth + Any Totem)	-
	Tropiclip	Achievement: Moving Up (Upgrade Your House)	1,000g
	Trucker Hat	Achievement: Artisan (Craft 30 Different Items)	1,000g
	Warrior Helmet	Tailoring (Cloth + Ostrich Egg)	-
	Watermelon Band	Achievement: Mother Catch (Catch 100 Fish)	1,000g
	Wearable Dwarf Helm	Tailoring (Cloth + Dwarvish Helm or Dwarf Gadget)	-
	White Turban	Tailoring (Cloth + Sweet Gem Berry)	-
	Witch Hat	Tailoring (Cloth + Golden Pumpkin)	-
	???	Volcano Caldera Monkey (100% Perfection)	-

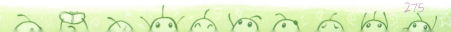

Footwear

	Name	Stats	Location	Buy Price	Sell Price
👟	Cinderclown Shoes	🛡+6 🔵+5	Purchased from the Dwarf in the Volcano Dungeon.	Cinder Shard (100)	550g
👟	Combat Boots	🛡+3	Purchased from Adventurer's Guild.	1,250g	150g
👟	Crystal Shoes	🛡+3 🔵+5	Chest at level 100 of the "dangerous" Mines, as well as a possible chest reward on level 110 of the Remixed Mines. Also a random drop from monsters in the Skull Cavern.	-	400g
👟	Dark Boots	🛡+4 🔵+2	Purchased from Adventurer's Guild after reaching level 80 in the Mines.	2,500g	300g
👟	Dragonscale Boots	🛡+7	Chest in the Volcano Dungeon.	-	350g
👟	Emily's Magic Boots	🛡+4 🔵+4	Gift received at the end of Emily's 14-heart event.	-	400g
👟	Firewalker Boots	🛡+3 🔵+3	Chest at level 80 of the Mines.	2,000g	300g
👟	Genie Shoes	🛡+1 🔵+6	Rare treasure obtained while fishing. Also a random drop from monsters in the Skull Cavern.	-	350g
👟	Leather Boots	🛡+1 🔵+1	Chest at level 10 of the Mines.	500g	100g
👟	Leprechaun Shoes	🛡+2 🔵+1	Rare drop from the train north of the Carpenter's Shop.	-	150g
👟	Mermaid Boots	🛡+5 🔵+8	Found by breaking metal boxes in the Volcano Dungeon.	-	-
👟	Rubber Boots	🔵+1	Rare drop from Green Slimes in the Mines.	-	50g
👟	Sneakers	🛡+1	Purchased from Adventurer's Guild after completing "Initiation". Also a random drop from monsters in the early levels of the Mines.	500g	50g
👟	Space Boots	🛡+4 🔵+4	Chest at level 110 of the Mines.	5,000g	400g
👟	Thermal Boots	🛡+1 🔵+2	Random drop from monsters in the Mines.	-	150g
👟	Tundra Boots	🛡+2 🔵+1	Chest at level 50 of the Mines.	750g	150g

Rings

	Name	Ingredients	Effect	Location	Buy Price	Sell Price
	Amethyst Ring	-	Increases knockback by 10%.	Purchased from Adventurer's Guild after completing "Initiation".	1,000g	100g
	Aquamarine Ring	-	Increases critical strike chance by 10%.	Purchased from Adventurer's Guild after reaching level 40 in the Mines.	2,500g	200g
	Burglar's Ring	-	Monsters have a greater chance of dropping loot.	Reward for eradicating 500 Dust Sprites at the Adventurer's Guild.	-	750g
	Crabshell Ring	-	Increases defense by 5.	Reward for eradicating 60 Rock, Lava and Iridium Crabs at the Adventurer's Guild.	15,000g	1,000g
	Emerald Ring	-	Increases weapon speed by 10%.	Purchased from Adventurer's Guild after reaching level 40 in the Mines.	5,000g	300g
	Glow Ring	-	Emits a constant light.	Random drop from Slimes and Skeletons in the Mines. Also found inside barrels and boxes.	-	100g
	Glowstone Ring	Iron Bar (5) Solar Essence (5)	Emits a constant light, and also increases your radius for collecting items.	Crafting (Mining Level 4) Stardew Valley Fair booth	1,000★	100g
	Hot Java Ring	-	Greatly increases your chance to find coffee drinks when slaying monsters.	Treasure chest in the Volcano Dungeon.		200g
	Immunity Band	-	Increases Immunity by 4, lessening the chance of status ailments.	Random drop from enemies in the Mines beyond level 100, and in the Skull Cavern.	-	500g
	Iridium Band	Iridium Bar (5) Solar Essence (50) Void Essence (50)	Glows, attracts items, and increases attack damage by 10%.	Crafting (Combat Level 9) Also a rare treasure obtained while fishing.	-	2,000g
	Jade Ring	-	Increases critical strike power by 10%.	Purchased from Adventurer's Guild after reaching level 40 in the Mines.	2,500g	200g
	Lucky Ring	-	Increases Luck by 1.	Random drop from enemies in the Skull Cavern. Also rarely found when panning.	-	200g
	Magnet Ring	-	Increases your radius for collecting items.	Random drop from enemies in the Mines between levels 40-80. Also found inside barrels and boxes.	-	100g
	Napalm Ring	-	Causes monsters to explode upon defeat.	Reward for eradicating 100 Serpents at the Adventurer's Guild.	30,000g	1,000g
	Phoenix Ring	-	Once per day, revive with 50% of your max health when defeated by monsters.	Treasure chest in the Volcano Dungeon.		200g
	Protection Ring	-	Stay invincible for a little while longer after taking damage.	Treasure chest in the Volcano Dungeon.		200g
	Ring of Yoba	Iron Bar (5) Gold Bar (5) Diamond	Occasionally shields the wearer from damage.	Crafting (Combat Level 7)	-	750g
	Ruby Ring	-	Increases attack by 10%.	Purchased from Adventurer's Guild after reaching level 80 in the Mines.	5,000g	300g
	Savage Ring	-	Gain a short speed boost whenever you slay a monster.	Reward for eradicating 150 Void Spirits at the Adventurer's Guild.	-	750g
	Slime Charmer Ring	-	Prevents damage from slimes.	Reward for eradicating 1,000 Slimes at the Adventurer's Guild.	-	350g
	Small Glow Ring	-	Emits a small, constant light.	Reward for completing the Night Fishing Bundle. Also a random drop in the early levels of the Mines.	-	50g
	Small Magnet Ring	-	Slightly increases your radius for collecting items.	Reward for completing the Adventurer's Bundle. Also a rare treasure while fishing.	-	50g
	Soul Sapper Ring	-	Gain a little bit of energy every time you slay a monster.	Treasure chest in the Volcano Dungeon.		200g
	Sturdy Ring	Copper Bar (2) Bug Meat (25) Slime (25)	Cuts the duration of negative status effects in half.	Crafting (Combat Level 1)	-	750g
	Thorns Ring	Bone Fragment (50) Stone (50) Gold Bar	When enemies damage you, they will take damage themselves.	Crafting (Combat Level 7)		200g
	Topaz Ring	-	Increases weapon precision by 10%.	Purchased from Adventurer's Guild after completing "Initiation".	1,000g	100g
	Vampire Ring	-	Gain a little health every time you slay a monster.	Reward for eradicating 200 Bats at the Adventurer's Guild.	-	750g
	Warrior Ring	Iron Bar (10) Coal (25) Frozen Tear (10)	Occasionally infuses the wearer with "Warrior Energy" after slaying a monster.	Crafting (Combat Level 4)		750g
	Wedding Ring	Iridium Bar (5) Prismatic Shard	An old Zuzu City tradition... It's used to ask for another farmer's hand in marriage.	Crafting (Recipe purchased from Travelling Cart for 500g)		2,000g

Egg Festival

Spring 13
9am-2pm

Item	Price
Colorful Set	500g
Decorative Pitchfork	2,000g
Lawn Flamingo	400g
Pastel Banner	1,000g
Plush Bunny	2,000g
Seasonal Plant	350g
Seasonal Plant	350g
Strawberry Seeds	100g

Flower Dance

Spring 24
9am-2pm

Item	Price
Ceiling Leaves	400g
Ceiling Leaves	400g
Daffodil	50g
Dandelion	50g
Rarecrow #5	2,500g
S. Wall Flower	800g
Seasonal Decor	350g
Seasonal Plant	350g
Seasonal Plant	350g
Tub o' Flowers	250g
Tub o' Flowers Recipe	1,000g
Wall Flower	800g

Luau

Summer 11
9am-2pm

Item	Price
Ceiling Leaves	400g
Ceiling Leaves	400g
Ceiling Leaves	400g
Jungle Decal	800g
Jungle Decal	800g
Jungle Decal	800g
Jungle Decal	800g
Plain Torch	700g
Starfruit	3,000g
Totem Pole	1,000g
Wall Palm	1,000g

Dance of the Moonlight Jellies

Summer 28
10pm-11:50pm

Item	Price
Cloud Decal	1,200g
Cloud Decal	1,200g
Modern Rug	4,000g
Moonlight Jellies Banner	800g
Seafoam Pudding	5,000g
Starport Decal	1,000g

Stardew Valley Fair

Fall 16
9am-3pm

Permanent Stock	Price
Dried Sunflowers	100 Star Tokens
Fedora	500 Star Tokens
Light Green Rug	500 Star Tokens
Rarecrow #1	800 Star Tokens
Stardrop (One-time Purchase)	2,000 Star Tokens

Random Stock	Price
Glowstone Ring	1,000 Star Tokens
Hay x100	500 Star Tokens
Mixed Seeds x25	1,000 Star Tokens
Pepper Poppers	250 Star Tokens
Triple Shot Espresso	400 Star Tokens

Spirit's Eve

Fall 27
10pm-11:50pm

Item	Price
Funky Rug	4,000g
Grave Stone	350g
Jack-O-Lantern	750g
Jack-O-Lantern Recipe	2,000g
Rarecrow #2	5,000g

Festival of Ice

Item	Winter 8 9am-2pm
	Price
Cranberry Sauce	200g
'Frozen Dreams'	2,000g
Icy Banner	800g
Icy Rug	4,000g
Pumpkin Soup	250g
Rarecrow #4	5,000g
Stuffing	200g
Tree of the Winter Star	5,000g
Wall Sconce	1,000g
Winter Dining Table	3,000g
Winter End Table	1,000g

Winter Night Market

	Winter 15-17 5pm-2am
Seasonal Decoration Vendor's Items	**Price**
Big Green Cane	200g
Big Red Cane	200g
Clouds Banner	1,000g
Green Canes	200g
Mixed Canes	200g
Plain Torch	800g
Red Canes	200g
Seasonal Decor	500g
Seasonal Plant	500g
Seasonal Plant	500g
Seasonal Plant	500g
Seasonal Plant	500g
Seasonal Plant	500g
Seasonal Plant	500g
Stump Torch	800g
Lupini's Paintings	
'Red Eagle'	1,200g
'Portrait of a Mermaid'	1,200g
'Solar Kingdom'	1,200g
'Clouds'	1,200g
'1000 Years From Now'	1,200g
'Three Trees'	1,200g
'The Serpent'	1,200g
'Tropical Fish #173'	1,200g
'Land Of Clay'	1,200g
Mysterious Vendor's Items	
Grave Stone	200g
Stone Frog	500g
Suit of Armor	200g
Stone Parrot	500g
Log Section	200g
Stone Owl	500g
Cone Hat	2,500-10,000g
Iridium Fireplace	15,000g
Rarecrow #7 (Once first is obtained via the Museum)	5,000g
Rarecrow #8 (Once first is obtained via the Museum)	5,000g
Seeds & Starters (15th: Spring, 16th: Summer, 17th: Fall)	Varies

Feast of the Winter Star

Item	Winter 25 9am-2pm
	Price
Decorative Axe	1,000g
Festive Dining Table	3,000g
House Plant	700g
L. Light String	800g
Large Red Rug	1,000g
Log Panel	500g
Log Panel	700g
Manicured Pine	800g
Ornate Window	1,000g
S. Pine	500g
Tree of the Winter Star	5,000g
Winter Banner	1,000g
Wood Panel	500g

Valley Artifacts

	Name	Location	Sell Price
	Amphibian Fossil	Forest, Mountain, Fishing Chest	150g
	Anchor	Beach, Fishing Chest	100g
	Ancient Doll	Mountain, Forest, Bus Stop, Town, Fishing Chest, Mines, Feast of the Winter Star	60g
	Ancient Drum	Mines, Bus Stop, Forest, Town, Omni Geode	100g
	Ancient Seed	Forest, Mountain, Fishing Chest, Omni Geode, Random drop in Mines	5g
	Ancient Sword	Forest, Mountain, Fishing Chest	100g
	Arrowhead	Mountain, Forest, Bus Stop	40g
	Bone Flute	Mines, Mountain, Forest, Town, Fishing Chest	100g
	Chewing Stick	Mountain, Forest, Town, Fishing Chest	50g
	Chicken Statue	Fishing Chest	50g
	Chipped Amphora	Town	40g
	Dinosaur Egg	Mines, Mountain, Fishing Chest	350g
	Dried Starfish	Beach, Fishing Chest	40g
	Dwarf Gadget	Mines, Omni Geode	200g
	Dwarf Scroll I	Mines, Secret Woods	1g
	Dwarf Scroll II	Mines, Secret Woods	1g
	Dwarf Scroll III	Mines, Skull Cavern	1g
	Dwarf Scroll IV	Mines	1g
	Dwarvish Helm	Mines, Omni Geode	100g
	Elvish Jewelry	Forest, Fishing Chest	200g
	Glass Shards	Beach, Fishing Chest	20g
	Golden Mask	Desert	500g
	Golden Relic	Desert	250g
	Nautilus Fossil	Beach, Fishing Chest	80g
	Ornamental Fan	Beach, Forest, Town, Fishing Chest	300g
	Palm Fossil	Forest, Beach, Desert	100g
	Prehistoric Handaxe	Mountain, Forest, Bus Stop	50g
	Prehistoric Rib	Town	100g
	Prehistoric Scapula	Town, Forest	100g
	Prehistoric Skull	Mountain	100g
	Prehistoric Tibia	Forest, Railroad	100g
	Prehistoric Tool	Bus Stop, Mountain, Forest, Fishing Chest	50g
	Prehistoric Vertebra	Bus Stop	100g
	Rare Disc	Mines, Fishing Chest	300g
	Rusty Cog	Mountain, Mines, Fishing Chest	25g
	Rusty Spoon	Town, Fishing Chest, Mines	25g
	Rusty Spur	Fishing Chest	25g
	Skeletal Hand	Beach, Backwoods	100g
	Skeletal Tail	Mines, Fishing Chest	100g
	Strange Doll	Everywhere, Skull Cavern, Mines, Fishing Chest	1,000g
	Strange Doll	Everywhere, Skull Cavern, Mines, Fishing Chest	1,000g
	Trilobite	Forest, Beach, Mountain	50g

Island Artifacts

	Name	Location	Sell Price
	Fossilized Leg	Dig Site	100g
	Fossilized Ribs	Dig Site, Southern Beach	100g
	Fossilized Skull	Golden Coconuts	100g
	Fossilized Spine	Dig Site, Southern Beach	100g
	Fossilized Tail	Dig Site	100g
	Mummified Bat	Eastern Island region	100g
	Mummified Frog	Volcano Dungeon	100g
	Snake Skull	Dig Site, Western Island region	100g
	Snake Vertebrae	Western Island region	100g

Museum Rewards

	Name	Location	Sell Price
	'A Night On Eco-Hill'	Donate 20 items.	-
	Ancient Seeds (+Recipe)	Donate Ancient Seed.	30g
	Bear Statue	Donate 50 items.	-
	'Burnt Offering'	Donate 11 artifacts, including the Rare Disc and Dwarf Gadget.	-
	Cauliflower Seeds (9)	Donate 5 items.	40g each
	Chicken Statue	Donate Chicken Statue.	-
	Crystal Chair	Donate 41 minerals.	-
	Crystalarium	Donate 50 minerals.	-
	Drum Block	Donate Ancient Drum.	100g
	Dwarvish Translation Guide	Donate Dwarf Scrolls I-IV.	-
	Flute Block	Donate Bone Flute.	100g
	'Jade Hills'	Donate 25 items.	-
	Lg. Futan Bear	Donate 30 items.	-
	Magic Rock Candy	Donate 90 items.	5,000g
	Melon Seeds (9)	Donate 10 items.	40g each
	Obsidian Vase	Donate 31 minerals.	-
	Pumpkin Seeds (9)	Donate 35 items.	50g each
	Rarecrow #7	Donate 20 artifacts.	-
	Rarecrow #8	Donate 40 items.	-
	Rusty Key	Donate 60 items.	-
	Singing Stone	Donate 21 minerals.	-
	Skeleton Statue	Donate 15 artifacts.	-
	Sloth Skeleton L	Donate Prehistoric Skull, Skeletal Hand and Prehistoric Scapula.	-
	Sloth Skeleton M	Donate Prehistoric Rib and Prehistoric Vertebra.	-
	Sloth Skeleton R	Donate Prehistoric Tibia and Skeletal Tail.	-
	Standing Geode	Donate 11 minerals.	-
	Stardrop	Donate all 95 items.	-
	Starfruit Seeds	Donate 15 items.	200g
	Triple Shot Espresso (3)	Donate 70 items.	450g each
	Warp Totem: Farm (5)	Donate 80 items.	20g each

Field Office Rewards

	Name	Location	Sell Price
	Banana Sapling	Complete the large animal skeleton. (Also awards 6 Golden Walnuts)	500g
	Golden Walnut	Complete the Purple Flower survey.	-
	Golden Walnut	Complete the Purple Starfish survey.	-
	Golden Walnut	Donate a Fossilized Bat.	-
	Golden Walnut	Donate a Fossilized Frog.	-
	Mango Sapling	Complete the snake skeleton. (Also awards 3 Golden Walnuts)	500g
	Ostrich Incubator Recipe	Donate every fossil and complete both surveys.	-

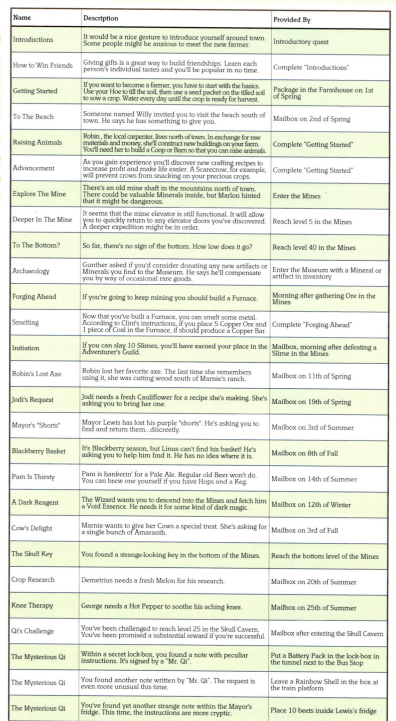

QUESTS

Name	Description	Provided By
Introductions	It would be a nice gesture to introduce yourself around town. Some people might be anxious to meet the new farmer.	Introductory quest
How to Win Friends	Giving gifts is a great way to build friendships. Learn each person's individual tastes and you'll be popular in no time.	Complete "Introductions"
Getting Started	If you want to become a farmer, you have to start with the basics. Use your Hoe to till the soil, then use a seed packet on the tilled soil to sow a crop. Water every day until the crop is ready for harvest.	Package in the Farmhouse on 1st of Spring
To The Beach	Someone named Willy invited you to visit the beach south of town. He says he has something to give you.	Mailbox on 2nd of Spring
Raising Animals	Robin , the local carpenter, lives north of town. In exchange for raw materials and money, she'll construct new buildings on your farm. You'll need her to build a Coop or Barn so that you can raise animals.	Complete "Getting Started"
Advancement	As you gain experience you'll discover new crafting recipes to increase profit and make life easier. A Scarecrow, for example, will prevent crows from snacking on your precious crops.	Complete "Getting Started"
Explore The Mine	There's an old mine shaft in the mountains north of town. There could be valuable Minerals inside, but Marlon hinted that it might be dangerous.	Enter the Mines
Deeper In The Mine	It seems that the mine elevator is still functional. It will allow you to quickly return to any elevator doors you've discovered. A deeper expedition might be in order.	Reach level 5 in the Mines
To The Bottom?	So far, there's no sign of the bottom. How low does it go?	Reach level 40 in the Mines
Archaeology	Gunther asked if you'd consider donating any new artifacts or Minerals you find to the Museum. He says he'll compensate you by way of occasional rare goods.	Enter the Museum with a Mineral or artifact in inventory
Forging Ahead	If you're going to keep mining you should build a Furnace.	Morning after gathering Ore in the Mines
Smelting	Now that you've built a Furnace, you can smelt some metal. According to Clint's instructions, if you place 5 Copper Ore and 1 piece of Coal in the Furnace, if should produce a Copper Bar.	Complete "Forging Ahead"
Initiation	If you can slay 10 Slimes, you'll have earned your place in the Adventurer's Guild.	Mailbox, morning after defeating a Slime in the Mines
Robin's Lost Axe	Robin lost her favorite axe. The last time she remembers using it, she was cutting wood south of Marnie's ranch.	Mailbox on 11th of Spring
Jodi's Request	Jodi needs a fresh Cauliflower for a recipe she's making. She's asking you to bring her one.	Mailbox on 19th of Spring
Mayor's "Shorts"	Mayor Lewis has lost his purple "shorts". He's asking you to find and return them...discreetly.	Mailbox on 3rd of Summer
Blackberry Basket	It's Blackberry season, but Linus can't find his basket! He's asking you to help him find it. He has no idea where it is.	Mailbox on 8th of Fall
Pam Is Thirsty	Pam is hankerin' for a Pale Ale. Regular old Beer won't do. You can brew one yourself if you have Hops and a Keg.	Mailbox on 14th of Summer
A Dark Reagent	The Wizard wants you to descend into the Mines and fetch him a Void Essence. He needs it for some kind of dark magic.	Mailbox on 12th of Winter
Cow's Delight	Marnie wants to give her Cows a special treat. She's asking for a single bunch of Amaranth.	Mailbox on 3rd of Fall
The Skull Key	You found a strange-looking key in the bottom of the Mines.	Reach the bottom level of the Mines
Crop Research	Demetrius needs a fresh Melon for his research.	Mailbox on 20th of Summer
Knee Therapy	George needs a Hot Pepper to soothe his aching knee.	Mailbox on 25th of Summer
Qi's Challenge	You've been challenged to reach level 25 in the Skull Cavern. You've been promised a substantial reward if you're successful.	Mailbox after entering the Skull Cavern
The Mysterious Qi	Within a secret lock-box, you found a note with peculiar instructions. It's signed by a "Mr. Qi".	Put a Battery Pack in the lock-box in the tunnel next to the Bus Stop
The Mysterious Qi	You found another note written by "Mr. Qi". The request is even more unusual this time.	Leave a Rainbow Shell in the box at the train platform
The Mysterious Qi	You've found yet another strange note within the Mayor's fridge. This time, the instructions are more cryptic.	Place 10 beets inside Lewis's fridge

282

Name	Description	Provided By
The Mysterious Qi	You found another note in the sand dragon's eye. It seems Mr. Qi's strange scavenger hunt has come to an end.	Place a Solar Essence in the sand dragon's mouth
Carving Pumpkins	Caroline wants to carve a Pumpkin with her daughter. She asked you to bring her one from the farm.	Mailbox on 19th of Fall
Fresh Fruit	Emily wants a taste of spring. She's asking for a fresh Apricot.	Mailbox on 6th of Spring, Year 2
Aquatic Research	Demetrius is studying the toxin levels of the local Pufferfish. He'd like you to bring him one.	Mailbox on 6th of Summer, Year 2
A Soldier's Star	Kent wants to give his wife a Starfruit for their anniversary.	Mailbox on 15th of Summer, Year 2
Mayor's Need	Lewis wants Truffle Oil. He won't explain what it's for. Maybe it's none of your business.	Mailbox on 21st of Summer, Year 2
Wanted: Lobster	Gus put out a notice requesting a fresh Lobster.	Mailbox on 6th of Fall, Year 2
Pam Needs Juice	Pam 's TV remote is dead. She's having a tough time going back and forth between the couch and the TV dial.	Mailbox on 19th of Fall, Year 2
Fish Casserole	Jodi swung by the farm to ask you to dinner at 7:00pm. Her only request was that you bring a Largemouth Bass for her fish casserole.	Jodi's 4-Heart Event
Catch a Squid	Willy is challenging you to catch a Squid. He says you can fish them from the ocean on winter nights.	Mailbox on 2nd of Winter
Pierre's Notice	Pierre will pay "top coin" to whoever brings him a plate of Sashimi. Apparently he's really craving the stuff.	Mailbox on 21st of Spring, Year 2
Clint's Attempt	Clint wants you to give Emily an Amethyst. He wants you to tell her it's from him.	Mailbox on 6th of Winter
A Favor For Clint	Clint got a new hammer and he wants to test it out on a variety of metals.	Mailbox on 17th of Winter
Staff of Power	The Wizard is creating a staff of phenomenal power. Who knows what it's for. He needs an Iridium Bar to finish it.	Mailbox on 5th of Winter, Year 2
Granny's Gift	Evelyn wants to surprise her husband with a gift.	Mailbox on 15th of Spring, Year 2
Exotic Spirits	Gus wants to make a Coco-no-no, but he's missing the main ingredient.	Mailbox on 19th of Winter, Year 2
Catch a Lingcod	Willy is challenging you to catch a Lingcod.	Mailbox on 13th of Winter, Year 2
Dark Talisman	The Wizard asked me to retrieve the Magic Ink from his ex-wife's house... but to gain access I'll need a Dark Talisman. Enter the Sewers and ask Krobus about the Dark Talisman.	Railroad cutscene (after completing the Community Center Bundles or Joja Warehouse tasks)
Goblin Problem	There's a goblin blocking the path to the Witch's hut. There must be some way to get him to move... Perhaps I should seek out more information on Goblins.	Through the cave by the Railroad after completing the Dark Talisman quest
Strange Note	You found a note, barely legible, asking you to bring "may-pal serrup" to the "seecrit wuds".	Secret Note
Cryptic Note	You found a note that reads, "Someone is waiting for you on level 100 in the Skull Cavern"	Secret Note
A Winter Mystery	You encountered a suspicious looking figure by the bus stop. When it saw you, it fled toward town. Could there be a clue to its whereabouts?	Bus Stop, Winter morning
Errand for Your Wife	Your wife asked you to bring her 200 pieces of fiber for a secret project.	Emily's 14-Heart Event
Haley's Cake-Walk	Your wife is organizing a charity cake-walk in the town square. She asked you to bring a chocolate cake.	Haley's 14-Heart Event
Missing Necklace	I 'borrowed' a necklace from Mom, but lost it somewhere near the bath house.. She's going to freak out if she notices it's missing.	Secret Note
The Pirate's Wife	An old lady living on Ginger Island is asking you to find a keepsake of her husband's. She gave you an old photograph of a soldier that washed up on shore, hoping it would help in some way.	Birdie, on the western shore of Ginger Island

SPECIAL ORDERS & MISC.

Pelican Town

Name	Description	Client	Reward
Aquatic Overpopulation	For unknown reasons, the local population of [Fish] has grown to an unsustainable level. I need a local angler to help reduce their numbers. *Catch 10 of the requested Fish. 7 Days.*	Demetrius	Farm Computer Recipe Selling price of the Fish
Biome Balance	For unknown reasons, the local population of [Fish] has grown to an unsustainable level. I need a local angler to help reduce their numbers. *Catch 10 Fish of the requested type (Lake, Ocean, River). 7 Days.*	Demetrius	Farm Computer Recipe 1,500g
Cave Patrol	The number of [Monster] in the local caves have made mining dangerous... for other people, not me! There's good money for anyone willing to slay 50 of them. -Clint *Slay 50 of the requested Monster. 7 Days.*	Clint	Geode Crusher Recipe 6,000g
Community Cleanup	I have an idea. There's a lot of trash in the water. Why don't we fish some out to make the valley more beautiful? -Linus *Fish 20 Trash items from the valley's waters. 7 Days.*	Linus	Fiber Seeds Recipe 500g, Friendship
Crop Order	[Crop] are in high demand this year. Anyone who ships 100 [Crop] by the end of the season will earn a substantial reward from the Pelican Town Agricultural Fund. *Harvest and ship 100 of the requested Crop. 28 Days.*	Lewis	Mini-Shipping Bin 50% of Crop selling price
A Curious Substance	I seek an extremely rare and powerful goop, known as 'ectoplasm'. It can be found in the remains of slain ghosts. -M. Rasmodius *Retrieve an Ectoplasm from a Ghost and give it to Wizard. 7 Days.*	Wizard	Mini-Obelisk Recipe 2,500g
Fragments of the Past	Calling all amateur paleontologists! I need 100 pieces of bone for my studies. Please drop them off at the museum counter! -Gunther *Deposit 100 Bone Fragments into the Museum counter slot. 7 Days.*	Gunther	Bone Mill Recipe 3,500g
Gifts for George	George thinks no one in town cares about him. I'd like to prove him wrong! A dozen leeks should do the trick... they're his favorite. -Evelyn *Collect 12 Leeks and give them to Evelyn. 28 Days.*	Evelyn	Coffee Maker 2,000g
Gus' Giant Omelet	I've got the urge to make my famous giant omelet... but I'll need two dozen eggs. Any takers? *Collect 12 Eggs and give them to Gus. 14 Days.*	Gus	Mini-Fridge 3,000g
Island Ingredients	I want to experiment with tropical cooking, but it's hard to find any ingredients. If someone could ship 100 [Crop], it might help! *Ship 100 of the requested Island Crop (Ginger, Pineapple, Taro Root). 28 Days.*	Caroline	Solar Panel Recipe 50% of Crop selling price
Juicy Bugs Wanted!	Hey there, I'm looking for a big wad o' bug guts. The juicier the better... at least that's what the crabs seem to like... 100 pieces should do the trick. *Gather 100 pieces of Bug Meat and give them to Willy. 7 Days.*	Willy	Quality Bobber Recipe 3,000g
Pierre's Prime Produce	Hello there. For an upcoming promotion, I'm thinking of offering some high-quality vegetables at a slight premium... Know where a thrifty shopkeep might find 25 gold-star vegetables? *Harvest 25 Gold-star Vegetables and deposit them in Pierre's bin. 28 Days.*	Pierre	Mini-Shipping Bin 2,500g
Prismatic Jelly	I require assistance in tracking down the rare and dangerous prismatic slime, within the local caves. Bring me a jar of its prismatic jelly and you will be duly rewarded. -M. Rasmodius *Retrieve a Prismatic Jelly and give it to Wizard. 7 Days.*	Wizard	Monster Musk Recipe 5,000g
Robin's Project	Hey! I have an idea for a new style of bed, but I'll need 80 hardwood to make it happen. Can anyone help? -Robin *Collect 80 pieces of Hardwood and give them to Robin. 7 Days.*	Robin	Deluxe Red Double Bed available to purchase 2,000g, Friendship
Robin's Resource Rush	I'm putting on a little promotion, just for fun. If anyone can collect 1000 pieces of [Resource] in a week, they'll earn a reward. And you can keep the [Resource]! -Robin *Collect 1,000 pieces of the requested Resource (Stone, Wood). 7 Days.*	Robin	Stone Chest Recipe 2,500g
Rock Rejuvenation	Hey! I'm going to invite some friends over to do a "rock rejuvenation" ceremony, but I'll need some crystals to channel the right energies. Do you think you could lend me a hand? *Give Emily an Amethyst, Emerald, Jade, Ruby, and Topaz. 7 Days.*	Emily	Sewing Machine 1,000g, Friendship
The Strong Stuff	Heard there's a spirit made out of potatoes that really packs a wallop, if you know what I mean. Mind dropping a few taters into a keg and bringing me a batch or two? *Brew 12 bottles of Potato Juice in Kegs, and give them to Pam. 14 Days.*	Pam	F.I.B.S. TV Channel 3,000g, Friendship
Tropical Fish	There's nothin' like tropical fishing... To keep the art alive, I'm offering a reward for whoever can bring in a good island haul. *Catch 5 of each Island Fish (Blue Discus, Lionfish, Stingray). 7 Days.*	Willy	Deluxe Fish Tank 2,500g

Walnut Room

Name	Description	Reward
Qi's Crop	I've hidden Qi Beans throughout the world. Find them, grow them, propagate them, and ship 500 Qi Fruit within the time limit. *28 Days.*	100
Let's Play A Game	Think you can score 50,000 points in Jumino Kart endless mode? Prove it. *7 Days.*	10
Four Precious Stones	Find 4 prismatic shards. Place them in my collection box. *28 Days.*	40
Qi's Hungry Challenge	Your task is to make it to level 100 in the Skull Cavern. However, you can't eat or drink anything while there. *7 Days.*	25
Qi's Cuisine	Ship 100,000g worth of freshly cooked items. *14 Days.*	25
Qi's Kindness	Give 50 loved gifts in one week. *7 Days.*	40
Extended Family	Family members of the legendary fish have returned to the valley. You have three days to catch Ms. Angler, Glacierfish Jr., Son of Crimsonfish, Radioactive Carp, and Legend II. *3 Days*	20
Danger in the Deep	The mine elevator system has been reset, and new dangers have emerged from deep underground. Make it to the bottom of the mines in one week. *7 Days.*	50
Skull Cavern Invasion	The Skull Cavern has been invaded by powerful monsters. Make it to level 100 in one piece. *7 Days.*	40
Qi's Prismatic Grange	Find 100 each of red, orange, yellow, green, blue, and purple items. Place them in my collection box. *14 Days.*	35

Dangerous Invaders*

	Name	Location	HP	Notes
	Armored Bug	Invaded Skull Cavern	250	As nearly-impossible to kill as ever!
	Bat	Dangerous Mines (Lv. 31-39)	268	Faster and more aggressive than the usual cave bat.
	Blue Squid	Dangerous Mines (Lv. 11-29)	310	Can be a real handful when they attack in swarms.
	Bug	Dangerous Mines (Lv. 1-29)	250	Still slow, still non-aggressive, but much hardier.
	Cave Fly	Dangerous Mines (Lv. 41-69)	266	These flying pests can withstand lesser weapons now.
	Duggy	Dangerous Mines (Lv. 6-29)	280	Much stronger than your everyday Duggy.
	Dust Sprite	Dangerous Mines (Lv. 41-69)	280	These bounders have taken a forest-appropriate fungal form.
	Frost Bat	Dangerous Mines (Lv. 41-79)	277	More vicious, and better suited to its forest environment.
	Grub	Dangerous Mines (Lv. 41-69)	265	Can take more of a beating before trying to retreat.
	Haunted Skull	Dangerous Mines (Lv. 71-79)	310	These fiends have found their way into the Mines!
	Lava Crab	Dangerous Mines (Lv. 81-119)	340	Disguises itself as a Gold Ore Node to catch miners unaware.
	Metal Head	Dangerous Mines (Lv. 81-119)	280	Shrugs off blows better than ever.
	Mummy	Invaded Skull Cavern	445	Can take a lot of damage before falling, and still gets back up!
	Putrid Ghost	Dangerous Mines (Lv. 51-69)	1000	Its belch causes nausea, which can only be cured with Ginger.
	Rock Crab	Dangerous Mines (Lv. 1-29)	272	Stronger than typical Rock Crabs.
	Royal Serpent	Invaded Skull Cavern	362+	The longer they are, the more health they have!
	Shadow Brute	Dangerous Mines (Lv. 81-119)	370	Bigger and tougher than a normal Shadow Brute.
	Shadow Shaman	Dangerous Mines (Lv. 81-119)	310	Their spells are far more potent than any seen before.
	Shadow Sniper	Dangerous Mines (Lv. 81-119)	500	Their crossbow attacks can cause temporary blindness!
	Skeleton	Dangerous Mines (Lv. 71-79)	655	Their bone-throwing attacks are relentless and precise.
	Skeleton Mage	Dangerous Mines (Lv. 71-79)	355	Fires bolts of ice magic that can stop you in your tracks!
	Slime	Dangerous Mines, Skull Cavern	Varies	Cooler than your average slime, and capable of stacking.
	Spider	Dangerous Mines (Lv. 51-69)	325	Hops around erratically, often attacking in groups.
	Squid Kid	Dangerous Mines, Skull Cavern	250	Much more resilient than its common counterpart.
	Stick Bug	Dangerous Mines (Lv. 41-69)	1050	Disguises itself as a simple stick to ambush adventurers.
	Stone Golem	Dangerous Mines (Lv. 31-39)	283	They're fast, and blend in better than ever with the darkness.

*These invaders are even more powerful if the Shrine of Challenge is active.
Some HP values are approximate.

The Forge

Weapon Enhancement	Cost*	Effect
Critical Chance		Increases critical chance by 1.
Critical Damage		Increases damage by 10%
Damage		Increases damage by 10%.
Defense		Increases defense by 1.
Knockback		Increases weight by 1.
Speed		Increases speed by 2-3.
Artful		50% faster cooldown for special moves.
Bug Killer		Double damage to bugs, allows killing armored bugs.
Crusader		50% more damage to undead and void spirits. Kills mummies.
Haymaker		Collect extra Fiber, and possibly Hay when cutting weeds.
Vampiric		Chance to regain some health when destroying monsters.

Tool Enhancement	Tool(s)	Cost*	Effect
Auto-Hook			Automatically hooks fish/junk when they bite.
Archaeologist			Double chance of finding artifacts in artifact spots.
Bottomless			Infinite water.
Efficient	All Tools		Uses no energy.
Generous			50% chance of digging up double items.
Master			Adds an extra fishing level to the player while held.
Powerful			Add 1 extra power level for Pickaxe, 2 for Axe.
Preserving			50% chance that bait and tackle aren't consumed.
Reaching			Adds 5x5 tile charging range.
Shaving			Extra Wood, Hardwood or Crops from chopping.
Swift			Tool use is faster.

*Prismatic Shard enchantments cost 20 Cinder Shards, and are applied *at random*.
Each weapon can be forged with up to 3 Gems, at a cost of 10, 15 and then 20 Cinder Shards.
A Diamond can be used instead to fill all remaining forging slots randomly for 10 Cinder Shards.

Additional Forge Abilities	Effect
Combining Rings	Any two different rings can be forged together at a cost of 20 Cinder Shards, resulting in a single Combined Ring with all the abilities of both of the original rings.
Infinity Weapons	Forging three Galaxy Souls into a Galaxy weapon (at a total cost of 60 Cinder Shards) results in an Infinity weapon, the most powerful weapon of its type!
Weapon Appearance	Any two melee weapons of the same kind can be combined at a cost of 10 Cinder Shards, creating a new weapon with the stats of one and the appearance of the other.

MOVIES & CONCESSIONS

Legend: 🟨 : Liked Movie/Snack   🟥 : Loved Movie/Snack

	Abigail	Alex	Caroline	Clint	Demetrius	Dwarf	Elliott	Emily	Evelyn	George	Gus	Haley	Harvey	Jas	Jodi	Kent	Krobus	Leah	Leo	Lewis	Linus	Marnie	Maru	Pam	Penny	Pierre	Robin	Sam	Sandy	Sebastian	Shane	Vincent	Willy	Wizard
Movies																																		
The Brave Little Sapling	♥	L	L	L	L		L	L	L	L	L	L	L	♥	L	L	L	L	L	L	L	L	L	L	♥	L	L	L	L	L	L	♥	♥	L
Journey of the Prairie King	L		L		L	L	L		L					L	L	L		L	L			L	L		L	L	L	♥		L		L	L	
Mysterium	♥	L		L	L	L					L	L	L		L	L	♥	L		L	L	L	L	L	L	L	L		L	L	L			♥
The Miracle at Coldstar Ranch	L	L	L	L	L		♥	♥	♥	L	L	L	L	L	L	L		L	L	L		♥	L	L	♥	L	L		L	L	L		L	
Natural Wonders	L	L	L	♥	♥		L	L	L	L	L	L	L	♥	L			L	L	L	♥	L	L	L	L	L	L		L	L	L	L	L	
Wumbus	♥	L	L	L		♥			L	L	L		L	L	L					L	L	L	L	L		L	L	L	L		L	♥	L	
It Howls in the Rain	L	L		L	L	L					L			L	L	L	♥	L	♥				L	L		L		L		♥	L			
The Zuzu City Express	L		L	L	L		L		L	L	L	L	♥	L	L	L		L		L		L	L	L	L	L	L		L	L	L		L	
Concessions:																																		
Apple Slices	L	L	L	L	L		L	L	L	L	L	L	♥	L	L	L		L		L	L	L	L	L	L	L	L	L	L	L	L	L	L	L
Black Licorice	L		L	L		L	L			L			L		L		♥							L	L						L			♥
Cappuccino Mousse Cake	L	L	L	♥	L	♥	L	L	L	L	L	L	L	L	L	L		L		L		L	L	L	L	L	L	L	L	L	L		L	
Chocolate Popcorn	L	L	L	L	L		L	L	L	L	L	L	L	♥	L	L		L	L	L		L	L	L	L	L	L	L	L	L	L	L	L	
Cotton Candy	L	L	L	L	L	L	L	L		L	L	L	L	L	L			L	♥	L		L	L	L	L	♥	L	L	♥	L	L	L	L	
Fries	L		L	♥	L		L	L		L	L	L		L	L	L		L		L	L	L	L	L	L	L	L	L	L	L	L	L	L	
Hummus Snack Pack	L	L	L	L	L	L	L	L	L	L	L	L	L	L	L	L		L		L	L	L	L	L	L	L	L	♥	L	L	L		L	
Ice Cream Sandwich	L	L	L	L	L		L	L	L	L	L	L	L	L	L	L		L	♥	L		L	L	L	L	L	L	L	L	L	L	L	L	
Jasmine Tea	L	L	L	L	L		L	L		L	L	L	L	♥	L			L		L		L	L	L	L	L	L	L	L	L	L		L	
Jawbreaker	L	L	L	L	L	L	L	L		L	L	L		L	L			L	♥	L		L	L	L	L	L	L	L	L	L	L	L	L	
Joja Cola																																		
JojaCorn																																		
Kale Smoothie	L	L		L	♥		L	L	L		L		L	L				L		L	L	L	L		L	L	L	L	L	L			L	
Nachos	L	L	L	L	L	L	L	L	L	L	L	L	L	♥	L	L		L	L	L		L	L	L	L	L	L	L	L	L	L	L	L	
Panzanella Salad	L	L	L	L	L		L	L	L	L	L	♥	L	L	L	L		L		L	L	L	L	L	L	L	L	L	L	L	L		L	
Personal Pizza	L	L	L	L	L		L	L	L	L	L	L	L	L	L	♥		L		L	L	L	L	♥	L	L	♥	L	L	L	L	L	L	
Popcorn	L	L	L	♥	L		L	L	L	L	L	L	L	L	♥	L		L	L	L		L	L	L	L	L	L	L	L	L	L	L	L	
Rock Candy	♥		L	L	♥		L	L		L	L	L		L	L			L		L		L	L	L	L	L	L	L	L	L	L		L	
Salmon Burger	♥	L	L	L	L		L	L	L	L	L	L	L	L	L			♥		L	L	L	L	L	L	L	L	L	L	L	L		♥	
Salted Peanuts	L	L	L	L	L		L	L	L	L	L	L	L	L	L	L		L		L	L	L	L	L	L	♥	L	L	L	L	L	L	L	
Sour Slimes	L	L	L	L	L	L	L	L		L	L	L	L	♥	L		L	L		L		L	L	L	L	L	L	L	L	L	L	L	L	
Star Cookie	L	L	L	L	L		L	L	L	L	L	L	L	L	L			L	♥	L		L	L	L	L	L	L	L	L	L	L	L	♥	
Stardrop Sorbet	♥	♥	♥	♥	♥	♥	♥	♥	♥	♥	♥	♥	♥	♥	♥	♥	L	♥	♥	♥	♥	♥	♥	♥	♥	♥	♥	♥	♥	♥	♥	♥	♥	♥
Truffle Popcorn	L	L	L	L	L	L	L	L	L	L	L	L	L	L	L	L		L		L	L	L	L	L	L	L	L	L	L	L	L	L	L	

Key Items

	Name	Location
	Bear's Knowledge	Follow the clues from a certain Secret Note.
	Club Card	Complete all of Mr. Qi's challenges.
	Dark Talisman	Search for it in the Mutant Bug Lair.
	Dwarvish Translation Guide	Donate all four Dwarf Scrolls to the Museum.
	Key to the Town	Purchase from Mr. Qi's Walnut Room for 20 Qi Gems.
	Magic Ink	Gain access to the Witch's hut.
	Magnifying Glass	Follow the Shadow Guy to his hiding place in Winter.
	Rusty Key	Donate 60 items to the Museum.
	Skull Key	Reach the bottom of the Mines.
	Special Charm	Follow the clues from a certain Secret Note.
	Spring Onion Mastery	View Jas & Vincent's 8-Heart Event.

Perfection

Progress can be tracked via the terminal in Mr. Qi's Walnut Room.

Category	Requirement	Percentage
Produce & Forage Shipped	Ship one of every Crop and Forage item.	15%
Obelisks on Farm	Build one of each Obelisk (Earth, Water, Desert & Island) on your Farm.	4%
Gold Clock on Farm	Build a Gold Clock on your Farm.	10%
Monster Slayer Hero	Complete all Adventurer's Guild Monster Eradication Goals.	10%
Great Friends	Reach the maximum number of Hearts with every villager.	11%
Farmer Level	Reach the maximum level in all Skills for a total Farmer level of 25.	5%
Found All Stardrops	Collect all 7 Stardrops.	10%
Cooking Recipes Made	Cook every food item.	10%
Crafting Recipes Made	Craft every item.	10%
Fish Caught	Catch one of every Fish, including the Legendary Five.	10%
Golden Walnuts Found	Find all 130 Golden Walnuts scattered around Ginger Island.	5%

Stardrops

Each Stardrop can only be obtained once.

	How to Obtain
	Purchase at the Stardew Valley Fair for 2,000 Star Tokens.
	Reach level 100 in the Mines.
	Catch every fish.
	Reach 13 hearts with your spouse.
	Feed a Sweet Gem Berry to the statue of Old Master Cannoli in the Secret Woods.
	Purchase from Krobus for 20,000g.
	Donate all 95 items to the Museum.

The Junimo Alphabet

A	B	C	D	E	F	G	H	I	J	K	L	M
N	O	P	Q	R	S	T	U	V	W	X	Y	Z
0	1	2	3	4	5	6	7	8	9	0	?	!